MW01038290

The Global Oracle

A Spiritual Blueprint

by Edward Tarabilda
and Douglas Grimes

Sunstar
PUBLISHING LTD.

The Global Oracle
A Spiritual Blueprint
By Edward Tarabilda and Douglas Grimes

United States Copyright, 1997
Sunstar Publishing, Ltd.
116 North Court Street
Fairfield, Iowa 52556

First Edition 1997
Printed in the United States of America

Library of Congress Catalog Card Number: 97-065710

ISBN: 1-887472-22-3

Cover Design: Therese Cross
Graphics: Sharon Dunn

Readers interested in obtaining further information on the subject matter of this book are invited to correspond with The Secretary, Sunstar Publishing, Ltd.
116 North Court Street, Fairfield, Iowa 52556
More Sunstar books at: http://www.newagepage.com

Table of Contents

Introduction

1. Why a Global Oracle?
Personal Statements by the Authors

By Douglas Grimes:

I knew Edward Tarabilda for years before I realized that his insights were far more than another set of bright ideas that would fall by the wayside of intellectual history. When we met in 1980, he struck me as a modern Abe Lincoln in appearance and demeanor. He was a simple, amiable fellow who avoided philosophical speculation not wedded to real-life questions of health and happiness. We kept in touch for several years, then lost contact as we pursued our separate careers.

I followed a computer career, but my deep interests were spiritual development and holistic living. I was charmed by the archetypal images of astrology, but disturbed by the conflicting claims and the huge gap between theory and practice. It was clear that modern science and technology had transformed the outer shell of human life without beginning to understand the inner essence. Was it possible to find a systematic order to our inner as well as our outer existence, a Rosetta stone for understanding all aspects of life as a perfectly integrated whole?

By the time Edward and I reconnected in the late 1980s I was impressed by his unshakable new confidence and penetrating insights. I saw a vast difference between his approach to spiritual, emotional, and physical development and other approaches to these subjects. The central focus of his work was the eight archetypal spiritual paths, a historic discovery of incalculable value for any spiritual aspirant. (Please see The Eight Great Paths to God, Part II Chapter 1.) He showed me how all fields of living fit together in a seamless whole, united by a common set of archetypal principles which underlie our subjective and objective universe. Moreover, his theory blended smoothly into practice. His personal advice had inestimable value for me and many of my friends.

This book sets forth those basic archetypal principles in their most fundamental order. Although we primarily use the language of astrology to describe this order, the languages of other disciplines, from mythology and psychology to biology and physics, might also be used. Edward's unique contribution to the understanding of archetypes is to show how major ancient oracles (divinatory tools), such as astrology, the I-Ching and the Tarot, all express the same fundamental principles in the same order. They are not isolated divinatory tools, but different creative expressions of the same archetypal patterns of creation, which we have tried to express as a truly global oracle.

All of the essential knowledge in this book (the archetypes, their order, and their application to daily life) is from Edward. My contribution was only assistance in writing. We coauthored all sections except those which carry my name.

By Edward Tarabilda:

The first half of my life was rather conventional. I was raised in a traditional Catholic home and attended Catholic schools, including four years of seminary. Eventually I became an attorney in Springfield, Illinois, and a professor of law and government.

My first exposure to archetypal principles was my study of the Science of Creative Intelligence, developed by Maharishi Mahesh Yogi, the founder of Transcendental Meditation. Maharishi uses this science as a basis for interdisciplinary studies at his schools world wide, from kindergarten through Ph.D. I also studied archetypes through the works of Carl Jung and Joseph Campbell. Although impressed by all these approaches to archetypal knowledge, I felt they lacked a certain scientific rigor in practical application.

I began to explore various divinatory tools in search of patterns of intelligence and creativity which might integrate the archetypes and show their practical use in daily life. In the mid-1980s I began to have spiritual cognitions of the various oracles and their interrelationships. These cognitions were not intellectual ideas, but inner knowledge structured in pure awareness. The archetypes arose spontaneously from pure awareness in a sequential manner. It took years to decipher their sequence through a combination of intuition and logical reasoning. It became apparent that all the major systems of divination use exactly the same archetypal principles in the same order. Too often, the oracles are treated as isolated developments, rather than different cultural representations of the same cosmological blueprint. A global oracle transcends the varied forms of expression and illuminates the underlying significations and patterns.

If you put your attention on these principles in a loving way, they have the capacity to take on a life of their own. This is why the ancient Vedic sages referred to these principles as "devas," which can be translated as aspects of God or beings of light. These divinatory principles, which permeate our inner and outer life, have an aspect of pattern or intelligence, and an aspect of creativity. It is this creative aspect which makes their study so joyful. I hope you can share this joy as you put your attention on these living, light-filled archetypes.

2. How to Use and Enjoy this Book

There are three ways of using this book: First, as a global oracle— for meditation, play, or an aid in decision-making. Second, as a guidebook for the study of archetypes. Third, as an introduction to holistic living.

Whatever your purpose, we recommend a meditative or contemplative approach. If you rush through this book trying to stuff your brain with maximum information in minimum time, you will gain nothing except mental clutter. No wonder students who take that approach to their studies are so frustrated! Memorizing facts without relating them to inner experience or daily life leaves you feeling alienated from the world and shut off from yourself. It is totally contrary to holistic development, which requires more attention to the inner experience of learning than to any information gained from outside.

Please contemplate these archetypes as vibrant, living realities, completely invisible yet manifesting everywhere. Spend a whole day on each one, infusing it into your thinking, feeling and willing. Let them permeate your whole being so that you enliven the creative aspect, the feeling and flow of each archetype, as well as the intelligence aspect. The common response of those who really apply their full energy into each archetype is, "I had no idea how deeply each one affects my life!"

For further guidance in using this book as a global oracle, please see Appendix B.

Part I

A Spiritual Blueprint
—The Archetypes—

Introduction to the Archetypes

1. The Cosmic DNA

Our goal in this book is to reveal the spiritual blueprint of the cosmos and its relationship to daily living. This blueprint is a set of universal archetypes which combine in myriad ways, like the simple genetic alphabet of a cosmic DNA, to express the infinite diversity of creation. Cognized by ancient seers, it can still be seen in the common order which underlies the major oracles of antiquity. We have chosen three of the best-known ancient oracles—astrology, the I-Ching, and the Tarot—to represent the divinatory tools of different ancient mystery schools. We have also added a modern oracle with ancient roots, The Secret Dakini Oracle, as an example of a creative contemporary approach. This book is the first publication in history to reveal the underlying order of creation.

Without a commonly held understanding of the underlying archetypal patterns, the proper use of all these oracles was lost at least one or two thousand years ago. Their commentaries became vague and confused, but enough of the original insights remain that we can see general patterns, like the verdant mounds covering long-buried Mayan pyramids that guide archeologists to new discoveries in the dense jungle. For example, the sixth hexagram of the I-Ching, "Conflict," suggests that conflicts can be harmonized through love, peace, and positivity. The corresponding principles in the other oracles—the Tarot card called "The Lovers" and the planet Venus in astrology—express the same core message. Similar close correspondences can be found for every single archetype if you look beyond the often confused commentaries to the underlying principle in each of the ancient oracles.

This ordering of the archetypes transcends the limitations of time and culture. It is too systematic and precise to be called only an art or a subjective belief system. When different oracles from vastly diverse cultures express the same detailed blueprint of creation, it is no more an accident than the fact that gravity behaves the same in China as India, Egypt or the U.S. Thus we call it a subjective science, distinguishing it from objective science, but giving it equal or greater stature in its potential to transform our lives. (Please see Appendix C, Preliminary Thoughts on Creating a Subjective Science of Archetypes.)

Any new discovery takes time for widespread verification and public acceptance. Chastisement and ridicule often greet the pioneer. Church authorities silenced Galileo for propagating the Copernican concept that the earth revolves around the Sun. Scientific authority can be equally obtuse. In the 1840s the Hungarian obstetrician Philipp Ignaz Semmelweis, was fired by two hospitals and discredited by medical authorities because he insisted that doctors assisting in childbirth wash their hands, even though careful research had demonstrated that this simple measure dramatically reduced puerperal (childbirth) fever.

2. *From Abstract Archetypes to Practical Living*

The archetypes express both creativity and intelligence. The creative aspect is seen in movement, flow, and dynamism; intelligence aspect is expressed in the orderly patterns in which they unfold. Jung, Campbell, and other western innovators in this field have delved deeply into the creative aspect, but not the intelligence aspect, the underlying order of the archetypes. They have also underestimated their importance outside of psychology and mythology. Archetypes have been thought of as merely subjective, psychological constructs, lurking deep in the individual and collective subconscious, hiding from the light of reason and systematic investigation.[1] We hold that the archetypes pervade all aspects of life, inner and outer.

This book attempts to restore the missing links between creativity and intelligence, between spontaneous self-expression and perfect order. Since these archetypes and their inherent order are common to all fields of knowledge, both subjective and objective, they provide a solid bedrock for the long-sought ideal of interdisciplinary learning. Educators and researchers in all fields will enjoy elaborating on these fundamental principles in their own disciplines and unveiling the hidden links with other disciplines. Such work is essential if we are to heal our fragmented, impersonal educational system and enliven the innate creativity and intelligence in every student.

The development of interdisciplinary studies has faltered because there has been no subjective science to complement objective science. Scholars missed the link between the archetypal principles (the creative aspect) and their order (the intelligence aspect), so there was no union of creativity and intelligence. A true subjective science is possible only when both develop together.

The Art of Multidimensional Living™ has four branches:

1. Interdisciplinary knowledge—The archetypal principles common to all disciplines, both subjective and objective (Part I).

2. Transdisciplinary knowledge—The different spiritual paths, which correspond to the first eight archetypes. (The Eight Great Paths to God, Part II Chapter 1)

3. Multidisciplinary knowledge—How different disciplines relate to each other. All fields of knowledge, subjective and objective, are viewed in a three-by-eight matrix. The three columns relate to heart (spiritual disciplines), mind (intellectual life), and will (applied disciplines, which receive the most attention today). The eight rows express the first eight archetypes. (Multidisciplinary Knowledge, Part II Chapter 2)

4. Holistic Living—a practical framework for applying these abstract principles to daily life. (The Eight Fields of Living™, Part II Chapter 3)

3. How the Archetypes Are Organized

The most prominent oracles of antiquity are the I-Ching from China, the Tarot from Egypt, and astrology, whose birthplace is claimed by several cultures. The inner keys to these tools were probably restricted to a very few priests and sages, while their outer expressions were more commonly known. With the passage of time, the inner knowledge of the oracles was lost and the outer understanding blurred. Different commentators who lacked a clear internal awareness of the underlying archetypes added layer after layer of conflicting opinions. In our view, the widespread modern skepticism of such oracles is merited, but does not diminish the validity of their ancient sources.

All knowledge has three aspects—knower, known, and process of knowing. The sixty-four principles are grouped as one way of seeing these three aspects. The first group consists of nine principles related to the process of knowing. These are represented by the nine "planets" known to the ancients. (Technically, the Sun, Moon, and Nodes of the Moon are not planets, but it is customary in astrological circles to speak of them as such.) From our perspective on earth, the planets are the most dynamic feature of the heavens. They reflect the most changeable aspect of our life, our feelings.

The second group of principles relates to the knower, or subject. These are represented by the twelve signs of the zodiac and the twenty-seven nakshatras, or lunar mansions. The signs and nakshatras are different divisions of the same fixed background of stars, the cosmic stage on which the drama of life occurs.

The third group of principles relates to the object of knowledge or experience. These are represented by the houses of astrology, the twelve divisions of the equatorial circle. The Sun rises in the first house, to the East, and sets in the seventh house, to the West. At noon it is in the tenth house, directly overhead, and at midnight it rests in the fourth house, directly underneath us.

The nine planets, twelve signs, twenty-seven nakshatras, and twelve houses add up to sixty fundamental principles. In addition, four summary principles, marked with asterisks* below, are needed to maintain the numerical correspondence with the ancient oracles. Here is an overview:

1—9 The 9 planets
10* The zodiac as a whole
11—22 The 12 signs of the zodiac
23—31 The 9 tamasic (destructive) lunar mansions (nakshatras)
32* Pure tamas (destructive tendency)
33—41 The 9 rajasic (creative) lunar mansions
42* Pure rajas (creative tendency)
43—51 The 9 sattwic (preservative or balancing) lunar mansions
52* Pure sattwa (preservative tendency)
53—64 The 12 houses

Some oracles, such as the Tarot, also include sixteen additional principles which are covered in advanced works by Edward Tarabilda.

Each of the sixty-four chapters in Part I contains five sections:

1. Creative Principle—summary of the principle. The first eight principles have three sub-principles—"Heart," "Mind," and "Will"

2. Favorite Fantasies: a few examples of common fantasies related to each archetype

3. Key Idea for Education—How to apply this principle to education

4. Divinatory Message—How to interpret this card for decision-making

5. Relationship to Other Oracles[2]—How this principle is explained in the I-Ching, the Tarot and the Secret Dakini Oracle.[3] If, like most readers, you are not familiar with these oracles, this section may be difficult to understand, and can be skipped on first reading. However, for the serious student

of archetypes, it may be the most important section, because it shows how all the ancient oracles use the same universal archetypes in the same order. Wherever we refer to a particular principle in one of the other oracles, it is the corresponding principle which we explain. In the above example of Venus, it is the seventh principle in all three oracles. The numbers vary slightly once we go beyond the first nine principles (the planets). The tenth principle of the Secret Dakini Oracle, the I-Ching and the Tarot has no corresponding number in the astrological sequence. It corresponds to the zodiac as a whole. So the tenth principle in astrology (Aries) corresponds to the eleventh principle in the other oracles.

Additional brief sections are added as needed.

This sequence of archetypes may be thought of as a master script of creation because it reveals a pattern which can be observed repeatedly in any field of life. It is certainly not the only valid order, but we feel it is the most fundamental.

We recommend that you first read the introductions to the four sections (planets, signs, lunar mansions, and houses) to gain an overview. Then read the first nine principles (the planets), which lay the foundation of the later archetypes. The remaining principles can be read in any order.

Since the conflict between opposites is a major theme of Western culture, it is commonplace to expect every archetype to have a polar opposite—villain vs. hero, sage vs. fool, etc. Indeed, there are some classic polarities in our ordering of the archetypes, such as Sun and Moon, or Venus and Mars. However, these pairings reflect no value judgments. The essential polarity of good vs. evil is inherent in every archetype. Thus, the Sun contains both the supremely benevolent self-sacrificing leader and the absolute despot, Christ and anti-Christ, or in Indian mythology, Rama and Ravana. Similarly, the Moon contains both unbounded compassion and cruel, possessive insensitivity. In astrological terms, these qualitative values depend on the relative strength and placement of each planet, sign, etc.[4]

Introduction to the Planets

The seven planets visible to the naked eye represent the most fundamental archetypes of creation. They are the primordial energies whose infinite combinations give rise to the whole subjective-objective universe. An understanding of the other archetypes—signs, nakshatras (lunar mansions) and houses—comes only on the basis of an understanding of the planets.

It is curious that various cultures throughout the world name the days of the week after the same seven planets, and use the very same ordering of these planets:

Sunday	Sun
Monday	Moon
Tuesday	Mars
Wednesday	Mercury
Thursday	Jupiter
Friday	Venus
Saturday	Saturn

This is the spiritual order of the planets. Other sequences apply to physical and emotional matters.

Strictly speaking, the Sun and Moon are luminaries, not planets. However, it is appropriate to group them with the planets for this discussion. Likewise, the North and South Nodes of the Moon (Rahu and Ketu), are abstract points in space, not physical planets. But for many purposes it is meaningful to discuss them with the other planets. Western astrology has incorporated the outer planets visible only with telescopes—Neptune, Pluto, and Uranus. We believe these outermost planets have archetypal significance, but are beyond the scope of this book.

1

Sun: The King — Leading, Uniting and Inspiring All

Creative Principle: Fullness of life from which life springs, and to which life returns. This fullness of life is the fullness of spirit.

The solar principle is represented by the highest in all fields—trees among plants, gold among metals, kings among people. The tree gives fruit and shade to all, good and bad, rich and poor, happy and sad. Gold represents the Sun's generosity, liberality, and benevolence, ever free of rust. The king integrates and balances the various factions in his kingdom.

In religious terms, Christ is the supreme solar figure of Christianity, integrating heaven and earth, spirit and matter, divinity and humanity. Rama and Krishna, the avatars of the Indian epics *Ramayana* and *Mahabharata*, respectively, are both solar figures, although Krishna also has a strong lunar quality.

In modern works on mythology, the Sun is Joseph Campbell's *Hero with a Thousand Faces* and Robert Bly's *Iron John*. The Sun can temporarily play the roles of all the other planets, but he always returns to leadership status in the end. This is not to say that all heroes are solar; the other planetary archetypes can also play heroic roles, both male and female. However, they will not have the Sun's grandeur and ability to unify diverse roles.

Heart: Those who follow the path of the sun follow the integral path to God, uniting heart, mind, and will in service to the Supreme. This is all paths and no path, for the king supports all and listens to all, but follows his own inner guide rather than another person's path.

Mind: The Sun is the pivot of the solar system. He integrates all the various philosophies and points of view without being pulled into any of them, just as the Sun remains firm relative to all the planets that revolve around Him.

Will: The Sun integrates all areas of applied knowledge. He consults the specialists but is more concerned with the whole than the parts. He shines best as the prime mover of a community, sometimes as a visible leader, and sometimes as a silent catalyst.

Favorite Fantasies: The Sun represents fantasies of power and authority. Almost any dream of fame and fortune fits this archetype. Every aspiring politician, actor, or CEO is playing out the solar fantasy. A strong sun tends toward benevolent power. A weak sun tends toward tyrannical dictatorship.

Key Idea for Education: The Sun is the principle of self-sufficiency. He shines from within and does not conform to fragmented or overly specialized concepts of education.

Divinatory Message: Apply the solar principle to the question at hand. For example, if the choice is between two jobs, give preference to the one that has more solar qualities—universality, integration, leadership, and shining in front of others.

Relationship to Other Oracles: The Sun is the very first principle in the other three oracles. He is the "The Creative" in the I-Ching, where one learns about leadership. He is "The Magician" of the Tarot and "The Mercury" of the Secret Dakini Oracle, symbols of the magical transformations which produce gold (spiritual awakening), a symbol of the Sun.

2
Moon: The Mother and Queen — Devoted, Compassionate, and Intuitive

Creative Principle: The moon expresses the fullness of life which overflows in love for all creation. It is the vibrant beginning of life, the seed germinating under a protective and nourishing covering of soil. The lunar principle is the power of love to surmount all obstacles, the infinite power of the Divine Mother to nourish and uplift all creation.

As queen of the celestial court, the Moon is coequal with her husband, the king. Together they are the paired principles of yin and yang, the primal duality in Chinese philosophy and health-care—feminine, receptive, and cool (yin), and masculine, directive, and hot (yang).

Like all the fundamental principles of Creative Intelligence, the queen has both an active and a passive phase. In her passive phase she is the principle of receptivity, ever sensitive to the wishes of the king and his subjects. In her active phase she is the executrix of Divine Will. In this role she is the moving, manifest side of creation, and the solar principle is the silent stillness sustaining change.

The Moon represents pure intuition, the wisdom of the heart. She is both the High Priestess and the loving mother who senses her children's needs before they do. Her light is the reflection of the pure consciousness of the Sun. As the Moon brings light to the darkness of the night, the lunar principle reveals hidden truths in the collective subconscious. She rules the seas and controls the body's fluids and the great tides of emotion expressed in dreams.

Heart: The path of devotion, such as bhakti yoga, spontaneous surrender to Christ, or genuine heartfelt devotion in any religion.

Mind: Philosophies and thought-styles based on a deep intuitive sense of truth and recognition of the oneness which underlies duality.

Will: Myth and archetype, such as expressed by the great Swiss psychologist Carl Jung or the American mythologist Joseph Campbell.

Favorite Fantasies: Benign lunar fantasies are expressed in over-mothering: doting on children, indiscriminate trying to nurture, or lavishing affection on strangers. The Moon as high priestess also fantasizes instant intuitional knowledge of anything. A strong Moon sees herself nourishing and healing the whole world, and sees everyone as her children. A weak Moon has cruel and possessive fantasies, craves affection, and clings to relationships in a controlling way.

This important archetype is often suppressed in patriarchal western society. Modern women often postpone motherhood in favor of a career, in effect favoring aggressive, male roles instead of nurturing, female roles. From the fifteenth through the early nineteenth centuries, both protestants and catholics killed many intuitive women for witchcraft or heresy. Fear of the moon's intuitive skills is still expressed as aversion to esoterica in mainstream academia, news media, and politics. The conventional medical industry likewise shuns intuitive and psychic healing, in spite of enormous evidence of their potential.

Key Idea for Education: Reverence for all life and reverence for knowledge: As the great sage Rudolph Steiner pointed out, without reverence there is no real learning, just accumulation of surface information. Reverence inspires receptivity to knowledge, especially knowledge of the fundamental principles of life.

Reverence is almost totally absent from schools today. Students revolt and rebel. Why? Because the educational system ignores their inner needs. For students to have reverence for their teachers and studies, the teachers must respect the students' emotional and spiritual needs as much as their intellectual needs. This can be done in a nondenominational way when the curriculum connects the subject and object of study, both in theory and practice.

Divinatory Message: Listen to your heart to resolve the issue at hand, or choose the option that uplifts and nourishes your heart the most. For example, if you have the choice of spending a vacation on the beach or caring for an ailing family member, the indication is to care for the family member first.

Relationship to Other Oracles: The Moon is the second principle in the other three oracles—"The Receptive" hexagram of the I-Ching, the "High Priestess" of the Tarot and the Secret Dakini Oracle. All of these symbolize the higher intuitive wisdom of the feminine archetype.

3

Mars: The Warrior — Adventurous, Courageous, and Energetic

Creative Principle: Mars is the principle of will. Along with the Sun and Moon, he completes the fundamental trinity of creation which can be expressed in many different ways, such as:

thinking, feeling, and willing

experiencer, process of experience, and object of experience

spirit, soul, and matter

In the Christian tradition these are the Father, the source or "prime mover" of creation, the Son which expresses His divine love for creation, and the Holy Ghost, who embodies Divinity in matter. In the Vedic tradition these are the three *gunas*—*rajas*, the active principle of creation (Sun); *sattwa*, the balancing/harmonizing force (Moon); and *tamas*, the force of destruction (Mars). Prior to creation the three *gunas* exist in equilibrium. It is the stirring of Mars, the silent flow of unbounded consciousness within itself, that breaks the perfect symmetry of forces and begins each cycle of evolution.

The Sun and Moon cannot create without the energizing force of Mars. Mars is the principle of primordial activity that activates the silent union of Sun and Moon. Mars is the eternal spinning of the cycle of Yin and Yang, the interplay of opposites that begins the descent of spirit into matter. On the physical plane he is the energy of male sexuality, seeking fulfillment through intimate communion with his feminine counterpart, Venus.

Mars' strengths are vitality, courage and willpower. The potential danger is overaggressiveness and insensitivity to others. Rape, murder and war are classic examples of misdirected Mars energy.

Mars is both the warrior and the primal force of mother nature. These two images are totally compatible when we see three levels of the warrior:

1. The solo soldier of fortune, who fights for another only to further his own end. This is the egotistical exercise of will for selfish desires.
2. The disciplined soldier who serves a higher good in cooperation with others. Their collective strength is greater than the sum of their parts.
3. The invincible power of nature as a whole, and the soldier who spontaneously serves this power (not the religious zealot in a holy war). On a micro level there is always competition between parts within any system. On a macro level there is always perfect cooperation among all elements. The countless predator/prey relationships of different plants and animals in the food chain are examples of microcosmic conflict that contribute to macrocosmic harmony of the biosphere.

Heart: Mars governs Laya or Kundalini yoga, the path of the warrior. The spiritual adventurer uses courage and discipline to conquer his primal drives and surrender to the Supreme Will.

Mind: Mars rules primal ritual through sound, including mantra.

Will: The art and science of sound is expressed publicly in music in harmony with Natural Law. The first defense of an enlightened society is its music, which generates an atmosphere of harmony that turns potential enemies into friends. (Sadly, most modern music has the opposite effect!)

Favorite Fantasies: Do you dream of adventure? Want to climb mighty mountains, snatch victory from defeat, and overcome all obstacles to glory? The warrior/adventurer/defender role of Mars is perhaps the number one theme from ancient epics to modern movies.

For the great mythologist Joseph Campbell, author of *Hero with a Thousand Faces*, all heroes are variations on one universal archetype, whether they be religious saviours, soldiers, or politicians, both male and female. Our intent is to distinguish among the various archetypes. The Sun and Mars archetypes most obviously fit the "hero" label. However, any of the sixty-four archetypes can be a hero.

Mars fantasies pervade our culture like salt in the ocean. We idolize physical strength and power. Arnold Schwarzenegger, Sylvester Stallone, Clint Eastwood, and John Wayne portray semirealistic warriors on screen. Superman and the Incredible Hulk are fantasy characters of the same ilk. Comics and muscle magazines abound in hypermuscled heroes, and sports figures are among the highest paid and most popular public figures. And male sex symbols are too numerous to mention.

Key Ideas for Education: Supplement competition among peers with competition with oneself. Let each student create challenges for himself and measure his successes against his own goals, rather than against others. Competition with others has value, but when the pleasure of play is lost in the obsession with victory, it tends to inflate the winner's ego while humiliating the loser.

Divinatory Message: Exert your will to overcome obstacles. Be bold and adventurous, yet vigilant to dangers.

Relationship to Other Oracles: Mars is the third principle in each of the other oracles. As the third hexagram of the I-Ching, "Difficulty at the Beginning," He shows how to push against any obstacle to achieve fulfillment. Mars is the power and force of the

"Empress," the third Tarot card, and the primal sexual force of "The Scarlet Lady" in the Secret Dakini Oracle.

The key meaning of the third principle in all these oracles is the primal force of nature. It can manifest as either strongly masculine or strongly feminine. In patriarchal societies the masculine warrior image dominates, corresponding to the first two levels above. On the third and highest level the Mars principle is female—the primal executrix of life, the supreme power of Mother Nature.

4

Mercury: The Young Sage— Quick, Articulate, and Adaptable

Creative Principle: Mercury is the power of intellect to organize existence. It is discrimination and the ability to make clear decisions. The strength of Mercury is flexibility and quickness of intellect. The danger is vacillation, indecision, and lack of steadfastness.

Heart: The path of the intellect, which discriminates between truth and illusion, change and nonchange.

Mind: The discipline of self-discovery through the question, "Who am I?"

Will: Application of discrimination in activity, i.e. intelligent organization of our affairs. A true science of the stars is an ideal expression of this principle, as it shows how to organize all eight fields of living in accord with the cosmic blueprint for each individual, nation, and world. (See Part II, Chapter 3, The Eight Fields of Living.™)

Favorite Fantasies: Do you ever wish you had the perfect answer for everything? Do you try to have a quick-witted retort for any verbal challenge? Do you see yourself as a grand master in chess, a best-selling author, a super sleuth, or a master journalist? Do you dream of juggling complex equations, or solving ancient mysteries of the universe? Do you surf the Internet trying to dazzle fellow cyberfans with your cleverness or knowledge? If so, part of you is a modern-day Merlin, a Mercurial magician of logic and language.

Key Idea for Education: Education has to be flexible, adaptable, and varied in theme to keep students' interest lively. A two-way flow of communication is essential. A one-way flow from teachers to students is merely pseudoeducation which denies students the feedback necessary for deep assimilation. Students must express knowledge in their own terms in order to possess it, and they must receive feedback from teachers and peers to refine their understanding.

Divinatory Message: Sharpen your discrimination by observing people's motives, especially your own. The answer will be clear when you see the underlying desires of all the players clearly. This development of discrimination may be assisted by a great teacher with a sharp intellect. If you already have keen discrimination, this teacher may be your own higher Self, which teaches how to avoid getting caught in the trap of desire.

Relationship to Other Oracles: Mercury is the fourth principle in each of the other three oracles. In the I-Ching He is "Youthful Folly," an undeveloped Mercury who needs a teacher to help him develop higher discrimination. He is the "Emperor" of the Tarot. Like the emperor, the intellect has the power to govern the material plane of life. He is also the "Hot Seat" of the Secret Dakini Oracle. Discrimination requires difficult choices. The emperor sits on the hot seat of discrimination!

5

Jupiter: The Priest—
Learned, Proper and Loyal

Creative Principle: Jupiter represents a life of selfless service. His benevolent and expansive nature finds expression in love for family, community, and divinity. Albert Schweitzer's life is a wonderful example of Jupiterian selfless giving.

Jupiter prospers when he performs action without attachment to the fruits, i.e., he serves out of love for duty and desire for others' benefit. He governs ethical behavior—action which helps others and upholds society.

Heart: Karma yoga, the path of selfless service

Mind: Psychology and philosophies which unfold the nature of the mind, the inner faculty that converts the raw data from the senses into coherent perceptions and conceptions.

Will: The science of ritual. The purpose of ritual is to guide us from the mundane to the divine. When ritual becomes deep and habitual, all our thoughts become joyous prayers, and ordinary activities are transformed into a spontaneous sacrifice to the Almighty.

Favorite Fantasies: Do you dream of being The Great Benefactor, giving millions to charity? Are you generous to a fault, or blinded by loyalty to family, alma mater, and religion? Would you like to be the final judge of right and wrong, or the high priest who intercedes with God on behalf of ordinary souls? Do you condemn others for unethical behavior, either out loud or in your private inner dialogues? Do you worship your spiritual teacher as well-nigh infallible?

All these are Jupiterian desires—*sattwic* attachments to philanthropy, tradition, religion, and morality. Jupiter's weak side is most evident as moral condescension toward others or condescension toward ourselves in the form of guilt and remorse. In either case, we are demeaning someone by measuring him or her against our own subjective moral standards.

Key Idea for Education: We must introduce into education a key idea of all religions—the principle of giving rather than receiving. Many highly paid professionals are deeply frustrated because they are not serving society in accord with their own inner gifts or society's needs. When they adjust careers in order to follow their inner bliss and simultaneously serve others, they invariably experience greater satisfaction.

Divinatory Message: Transform self-interest into a genuine humanitarian interest. Find some need in society which will be a joy to satisfy, especially as a teacher or religious leader. But avoid the trap of self-righteousness. The danger of Jupiter is attachment to rigid beliefs and judgmentalism. The Inquisition and countless religious wars are sad examples of the negative potential of the normally benefic Jupiter, imposing his beliefs on others through force.

Relationship to Other Oracles: Jupiter is the fifth principle in the other three oracles. He is "Waiting (Nourishment)" of the I-Ching, which implies confidence and perseverance in pursuing goals that nourish society. He is the "Pope" of the Tarot, a clear Jupiterian signification, as Jupiter governs religious institutions and their leaders. He is "Ganesh (Lord of Obstacles)" of the Secret Dakini Oracle. Ganesh, like Jupiter, traditionally brings abundance and sacred knowledge. Ganesh is also famous for overcoming obstacles. Jupiter's skill in action and selfless service overcome obstacles to success.

6
Venus: The Lover—
Beautiful, Charming and Harmonizing

Creative Principle: Venus governs the senses. The enlightened use of the senses is for discovering the ultimate beauty of life without becoming addicted to sensory pleasures. Venus thrives on sweetness, positivity, and affirmation of all that is good and beautiful.

By pursuing inward beauty in meditation one balances the search for outward beauty through the physical senses. Michelangelo is a perfect example of a Venusian artist who expressed love for the Divine in sensual physical forms. Romeo and Juliet are tragic examples of an idealized Venusian love that transcends death.

Heart: Raj Yoga, the path of positivity, beauty and art.

Mind: Careful observation through the senses, such as bird watching, stargazing, or collecting data for scientific research.

Will: The art and science of sculpture, architecture, and community planning. These studies are variously known as Stapathya Veda in India, Feng Shui in China, and geomancy in the West.

Favorite Fantasies: Do you wish you were the most beautiful woman or most handsome man in the world? Do you dream of being Cinderella or Prince Charming, unsullied by the grubby details of mundane work? Do you fantasize about finding your perfect partner, your true soul mate, or your luscious lover in a problem-free Eden? Such Venusian fantasies abound in fairy tales, popular songs, ads that glorify youth and beauty, and countless romance novels, movies, and TV shows.

As C. G. Jung said, "Every archetype is capable of infinite development and differentiation."[5] Venus can play many roles, especially as peacemaker and harmonizer of differences. In the religious sphere, Venus is an idealist and dreamer, ready to sacrifice today's earthly pleasures for eternal bliss in Paradise.

Venus and Mars are the two most all-pervasive archetypes in our culture. In their lower forms Venus represents sexuality and Mars represents violence. In their higher forms, Venus represents idealized beauty and harmony, and Mars represents power in service of the Divine Will. No archetype is good or bad by itself; each has a huge range of lower and higher manifestations.

Key Idea for Education: Learn to see the positive and valuable aspects of everyone and everything. In the school environment this can mean finding the good qualities in teachers, classmates, and studies. Condemnation creates pain; affirmation creates bliss!

Divinatory Message: Apply sweetness, harmony, and positivity to your problem. This may be an idealized romantic love, as sung by medieval troubadours, or a peacemaking mission, or an ideal friendship with no sexual overtones. Wherever true Venusian love occurs, it is not abstract, but sweet and pleasing to the senses.

Relationship to Other Oracles: Venus corresponds to the sixth principle in the other oracles. Although the I-Ching refers to this principle as "Conflict," the hexagram is really about the resolution of conflict through affirmation, harmonization, positivity, love, and peace. Without these Venusian qualities, the senses lead to irreconcilable conflict.

Venus is also "The Lovers" of the Tarot and "The Wish-Fulfilling

Gem" of the Secret Dakini Oracle. Both describe the positive thinking of Venus, and the resulting fulfillment of desires.

7
Saturn: The Perfectionist—
Disciplined, Methodical, and Cautious

Creative Principle: Saturn gives:

* Patient perseverance in performing humble tasks others might find demeaning.

* Clear, well-defined structure and boundaries. Saturn is the most concrete and physical planetary energy.

* Comfort in solitude, simplicity, and restraint of the senses.

Relative life is bounded in time, space, and causation. As Lord of Time, Saturn sets boundaries in time by delaying fulfillment of desires. Such delays occur only when we fail to live fully in the present; they help us learn to live in the present, the only time frame in which real joy can be experienced. As ruler of the body, Saturn sets boundaries in space by defining our physical structure. Finally, as Lord of Karma, Saturn sets boundaries in causation by determining the exact reaction for every action. In brief, Saturn helps us step off the stimulus-response treadmill and bring spirituality into the physical.

Heart: Hatha yoga, tai chi, and all forms of physical culture which lead to higher awareness.

Mind: Cold, dry logic as a means of finding truth, such as scientific reasoning and courtroom rules of evidence.

Will: The science of health and longevity and its social counterpart, the institution of marriage, which is the basis of the health and longevity of the human race.

Favorite Fantasies: Do you want to go back to the land, find your roots, and feel the earth? Do you yearn for quiet time in nature, away from the hustle and bustle of city life? Do you believe less is more, and shun the commotion and complexity of modern living? Do you prefer precise, logical talk to vague, dreamy speculation?

If so, then Saturn is speaking through you. Saturn is so practical and down-to-earth that it doesn't drift off in the wild flights of fantasy characteristic of some of the more imaginative archetypes, such as Venus. But it has an enormous influence in our materialistic science-infatuated culture.

Key Idea for Education: Give children a period of silence every day for meditation or contemplation. Such silence is not idleness. It is essential training in Self-awareness, Self-sufficiency, and the natural alternation of rest and activity.

Divinatory Message: Draw into silence to make a decision, or persevere in a task already begun. Be simple and focused, avoiding distractions and detours.

Relationship to Other Oracles: Saturn is the seventh principle in each of the other oracles. He is "The Army" of the I-Ching, which thrives in order and discipline. He is "The Chariot" of the Tarot, triumphing over adversity through perseverance, obedience, and orderliness. He is also the "Cremation Ground/Meditation" of the Secret Dakini Oracle. Saturn governs the process of withdrawing the senses from their objects, which happens in both death and meditation.

8

North Node of the Moon (Rahu): The Rebel—Destroyer of Falseness

Creative Principle: The two nodes of the Moon—Rahu and Ketu—are not physical planets. They are called "shadow planets" because they hide the Sun and the Moon during eclipses. They govern shadow activities, such as silent crime and behind-the-scenes plots against authority. Rahu relates to outer rebellion; Ketu to inner rebellion.

The North Node of the Moon signifies the principle of rebelliousness, uniqueness, and diversity. Even outlawish and seemingly anti-social behavior can benefit society in unexpected ways. Knowingly or unknowingly, society's outcastes can contribute to the whole. Robin Hood is an excellent example of a North Nodian character who sought justice outside the law, robbing from the rich to give to the poor in order to redress inequality in the distribution of wealth and power.

The North Node serves to purify society of outdated, rigid, or calcified conventions and institutions. Although he acts contrary to mainstream laws and ethics, he fills an essential role in evolution, just as sharks, vultures, and parasitic insects fill a huge need in biosystems. Honoring scavengers, rebels, and outcastes is essential for a balanced view of social systems, too.

A surface understanding of the Rahu principle can be used to rationalize all kinds of criminal and psychopathic behavior. A deeper understanding empowers one to rebel against all forms of societal inculcation which block one from discovering one's own inner potential. Thus any rebelliousness which harms another rather than achieving higher ends is a perversion of this principle.

Life in society is busy and beset by innumerable and often contradictory do's and don'ts. The North Node revels in silence and solitude, which may be seen as a form of rebellion against social obligations. But silence and occasional solitude are necessary for inner equilibrium.

Inner equilibrium, another signification of Rahu, is represented by the number "8" (eight), which is in perfect equilibrium with itself. The rebelliousness of Rahu frees us from any imbalances in society and lets us experience our own innermost nature without externally imposed preconceptions.

Heart: Tantra, the spiritual path of flowing with desire, rather than resisting it. (See The Eight Great Paths to God, Part II, Chapter 1.)

Mind: Systems of thought which do not fit traditional labels or stereotypes, but which rely on each individual's unique insights. Rahu thinking challenges authority in philosophical systems, affirming "Conventional truth is not my truth."

Will: The North Node stands for those individuals and institutions who revolt against outmoded norms and forms, such as anarchists and revolutionaries, or in perverted forms, such as gangsters and other criminals.

Favorite Fantasies: Do you idolize outlaws and rebels like Elvis, Mick Jagger, or Michael Jackson? Do you dream of exposing government fraud and official misconduct? Do you revel in the downfall of high and mighty public figures? Do you resent outside authority, uniformity, and anything that suppresses your individuality? Then you have a Rahu streak, so characteristic of the modern age.

Key Idea for Education: Learn to support a child's legitimate rebellious tendencies, rather than suppress them. Children are inherently interested in whatever they need to know at each stage in their development. When their natural curiosity is squelched by adults, it is normal and healthy for children to rebel. When adults become attuned to the natural stages of cognitive development and the different interests of each child, they will see their children's anger and frustration turn to enthusiasm for learning. This is the learning environment that children crave.

Children also rebel against hypocrisy, pretension, and any form of shallowness, yet welcome gentle discipline, as they sense a need for boundaries. When adults honor the differences among children and behave with candor and compassion, both sides enjoy the learning experience beyond measure.

Divinatory Message: Find your own unique and even rebellious solution to the problem at hand. Do not count on traditional solutions. Move against convention, but do so in way that helps others or frees you to pursue spiritual goals.

Relationship to Other Oracles: The North Node corresponds to the eighth principle in each of the other oracles. He is "Holding Together" of the I-Ching, which calls for holding the personality together in a manner represented by the figure "8." He is "Justice" (Balance) of the Tarot. The figure "8" is the symbol of infinity turned sideways, infinity in the finite. "8" also represents the snake, a universal symbol of inner transformation connected to the nodes of the Moon. In Vedic mythology, the two nodes, Rahu and Ketu, were a snake which was beheaded by the Sun for stealing the nectar of immortality. Although cut in half, their immortal status is seen when they rebel against the authority of the luminaries, hiding the Sun or Moon in every eclipse.

Rahu is also the "Living Goddess" of the Secret Dakini Oracle, who represents unique virginal essence, untainted by social conditioning. The "Living Goddess" also represents an equilibrium or balance—although the beauty and innocence of the goddess may seem at odds with the sometimes violent Rahu, the North Node's main role is to restore balance when conventional roles have become corrupted and oppressive to individual rights.

9

South Node of the Moon (Ketu): The Hermit—Solo and Silent

Creative Principle: Rahu, the North Node of the Moon, represents the rebelliousness which brings a fundamental balance sometimes called "cosmic consciousness," where one's Self is experienced as separate from activity. Ketu, the South Node of the Moon, gives the capacity to cut through the gross aspects of creation to the intense beauty and bliss of the subtler levels of creation in a state called God consciousness, and eventually to surrender this sublime beauty for the undifferentiated Absolute in unity consciousness. These higher states require an even greater inner silence than cosmic consciousness, plus a more refined awareness of the external world.

Thus Ketu represents an even deeper revolution of the psyche than Rahu. In God consciousness one surrenders one's cosmic Self to the Divine, and thereby unlocks the subtle structure of creation to direct perception. Rahu strips away social conventions and restrictions; Ketu strips away deeper limitations on feeling and perception. The deepest knots in the heart are dissolved in tidal waves of love. One discovers that beauty is truly in the eye of the beholder, and that infinite beauty is everywhere.

Rahu and Ketu, respectively, represent the outer and inner aspects of personal transformation. Both Nodes cut through boundaries with quickness and ferocity. Rahu rebels against outer limitations, especially outmoded social conventions. Ketu strips away limiting belief structures, such as the belief that we need fame or fortune to be happy.

Rahu, the head of the dragon, represents outer rebellion and frees us from social constraints. Ketu, the tail of the dragon, represents inner surrender and frees us from egotistical attachments. At first glance, surrender may seem to contradict the rebel principle of the nodes. A deeper view sees that inner surrender is only possible when we cut ourselves free from the tyranny of social convention, egotistical attachments, and unconscious beliefs. Only when we are truly free can we surrender to the higher states of consciousness beyond cosmic consciousness.

All sixty-four principles of Creative Intelligence have higher and lower meanings as well as dangers and opportunities. Rahu and Ketu are considered malefics and are often feared because they bring loss. This attitude reflects a undeveloped understanding of the Nodes. Any loss they bring is necessary loss on the path to higher consciousness. Any pain associated with such loss is due to attachment to finite values and resistance to the infinite.

Favorite Fantasies: Do you dream of retiring to a simple, almost solitary existence? Does the monastic life appeal to you? Are you happiest when you cut out all the clutter and complexity of living in society and focus on life's essentials by yourself? These are healthy Ketu traits which are often mistaken for neuroses.

Key Idea for Education: Teach children that the universe is not restricted to what is experienced through the external senses. A greater universe lies within. Just as scientists use a solar eclipse to study the physical sun, each of us can discover our inner Sun in times of silence and solitude.

Divinatory Message: Find your answer in a deep and prolonged silence which will make the answer to the question at hand self-evident. You must literally drop the question in order for the answer to arise of its own accord at a later time. In other words, surrender the question to the Divine Will, which will answer only when you are ready.

Relationship to Other Oracles: The South Node of the Moon is traditionally associated with hermits and ascetics. He is the ninth principle in the other three oracles. He is "The Hermit" of the Tarot, a solitary seeker who goes very deep into the silence of his own soul. He is the "Way Through" of the Secret Dakini Oracle, a great key to unlock the secrets of the universe. Finally, He is "The Taming of the Small" of the I-Ching, where more and more refinement and subtlety ("the small") tames the almighty power of the universe as it unfolds its secrets to our awareness.

Introduction to the Signs

As discussed in the Introduction to the Planets, the planets represent the basic energies of creation. The signs of the zodiac represent how those energies develop. They describe the unfoldment of energy throughout the eternal cycle of involution and evolution, from the fullness of spirit, to the emptiness of matter, and back to the fullness of spirit and matter together. They are the cosmic circle of time, twelve divisions of the celestial sphere through which all the planets march at various paces.

In astrology, the signs of the zodiac are the primary determinants of planetary strength. Thus the Sun is strongest in its sign of exaltation, Aries, and weakest in its sign of debilitation, Libra. The planets are like different animals, some at home on land (earth signs), others in the air, others in the water, and others in the heat of transformation, symbolized by fire. The planets also take on different qualities in each sign, like a chameleon whose color adapts to its environment.

The circle of signs (the zodiac) also represents the full cycle of action. Life moves from the fullness of Aries to the fullness of Pisces. Each step of the way demands the integration of the qualities of the preceding signs with the quality of the current one:

Aries represents	the impetus to act
Taurus	purpose
Gemini	beginning of action
Cancer	refinement of action into concrete steps
Leo	leadership of others as we progress ourselves
Virgo	ability to synthesize & organize through discrimination
Libra	integration of stability and adaptability in action
Scorpio	enjoyment from integration
Sagittarius	inspiration to achieve the highest goal in life
Capricorn	testing the thoroughness of one's inspiration
Aquarius	increasing the flow of harmony in diversity
Pisces	completion: fulfillment or frustration of one's purpose

10

The Zodiac as a Whole: Endless Circle of Time

Creative Principle: This archetype tells us that we are leaving the planetary energies and moving into the signs of the zodiac. These signs represent the great ages through which humanity and the universe rise and fall. The individual's horoscopic ascendent marks his place on the wheel. As human beings we must tread this wheel of time without getting stuck on it. We must be "in the world, but not of the world."

Favorite Fantasies: Do you ever envision yourself as Mr. or Ms. Do-Everything —business whiz, superathlete, social charmer, invincible hero, etc.—but you are not caught up in any of the roles, nor are you drained by all the activity? On the contrary, you feel rejuvenated because you see it all as a game with infinite options. One part of you is treading in activity, and another deeper part of you is floating above it all.

Key Idea for Education: A true spirituality does not take us away from worldly duties. It enhances our sense of responsibility because it lets us see that life has two halves—treading the wheel of time and floating above it. All too often, education only emphasizes the relative half (treading), and ignores the absolute (floating). Absolute, pure consciousness must be incorporated into education in both theory and practice. That will increase our love for the world, rather than making us want to escape it.

Divinatory Message: If you feel lost in the whirlwind of daily activities, step back and observe the cycles of nature. In that observation see that some part of you is unchanging in the midst of change. On the other hand, if you feel separate and alienated from worldly affairs, plunge into purposeful activity without losing your center of balance.

Relationship to Other Oracles: The I-Ching calls the tenth principle "Treading (Contact)." Treading represents the idea of marching on the cosmic wheel. The Secret Dakini Oracle similarly refers to the tenth principle as the "Wheel of Great Time." The Tarot calls it the "Wheel of Fortune." One can also think of this principle as representing unity or Brahman consciousness—the zodiac as a whole symbolizes the fullness of all knowledge in Brahman.

11
Aries: Initiative and Enthusiasm
—the Impetus to Act

Creative Principle: Aries is the fullness of energy seeking ways to begin the process of manifestation. People under the influence of this sign are often better at beginning projects than completing them. This is partly because Aries wants to conserve energy while displaying it.

Aries is an energetic self-starter that takes the initiative in new endeavors. Potential dangers include impetuosity, impatience, lack of follow-through, and dissipating energy in too many diverse activities.

Aries is the principle of strength of will which exists in fullness and yearns for expression. Those who are fully aware of this storehouse of forcefulness know how to conserve energy through the law of least action.

Aries is also the field of all possibilities. Unless the energy is directed to a clear purpose (Taurus), it tends to be scattered and wasted. Thus Aries comprehends opposite values. If focused and directed, it conserves energy. If scattered and directionless, it wastes energy.

Favorite Fantasies: Are you bursting with enthusiasm for a new enterprise, even before you have a clear idea of what it will be? Do you fall head over heals for a potential lover before your first date?

Key Idea for Education: In today's society we tend to dissipate our energy through excess sensory attractions and distractions. Aries teaches us how to restore a sense of peace and strength to our whole being, which in turn stimulates self-reliance and self-confidence. In contrast, television and other mass media bombard our minds and senses into a passive state of ever greater dependence on external stimulation. When children have the opportunity to play in nature, they develop self-sufficiency and resourcefulness. However, this can only happen if they are not lured into dependence on radio, TV, movies, etc.

Divinatory Message: Take the initiative! Begin to move in a new direction even if you don't have a long-term plan. Aries indicates a new beginning, an initial exploration, a fresh start. Follow your inner enthusiasm rather than outer dictates.

Relationship to Other Oracles: This archetype corresponds to "Peace," the eleventh hexagram of the I-Ching, which suggests great potential energy which must be harnessed and applied. It is the time of year at the end of winter when the forces of nature are preparing for the new spring, i.e. the time of Aries.

Aries corresponds to "Strength" in the Tarot. (Note: The popular Tarot deck by A. E. Waite mistakenly reverses the eighth and eleventh cards. The "Strength" card is properly understood as the eleventh card of the Tarot, rather than the eighth. Likewise, "Justice" is properly the eighth, not the eleventh.) This archetype also corresponds to the "Self-Created" of the Secret Dakini Oracle, where creativity flowers in the fullness of energy.

12
Taurus: Initial Direction
—Taking a Purpose

Creative Principle: The fullness of energy manifests through desire and purposefulness. This purposefulness is the intelligence aspect of Creative Intelligence.

Proper planning and goal setting are the second step in the movement from fullness to fullness. A clear purpose also gives the ability to manage time efficiently. Time management is a great skill of the practical, determined Taurean.

The fullness of the raw energy of Aries finds concrete purpose in Taurus. The danger of Taurus is becoming so attached to material goals that we lose sight of spiritual ones.

Favorite Fantasies: Do you feel a deep sense of purpose, even if the steps for achieving it are unclear? Can you be overly stubborn and fixed in pursuit of your goals? Taurus does not represent the detailed maps and itineraries of a journey, so much as an overall sense of direction, the final goal of our efforts.

Key Idea for Education: Teach children the art of planning, but also teach them nonattachment to the goal. This is the message Lord Krishna gave to Arjuna on the battlefield in the *Bhagavad Gita*. You have control over action alone, never over its fruits. So don't be attached to the fruits of action (the result or goal), and don't avoid action. Just do your duty to the best of your ability, and let Nature take care of the result.

Divinatory Message: Plan action in precise, concrete steps, setting definite goals with specific time lines for their completion. This card also suggests that you develop the tenacity of a bull in dealing with life's practical problems, without becoming identified or trapped in the process.

Relationship to Other Oracles: Taurus corresponds to the twelfth principle in the other three oracles. It is represented by "The Hanged Man" of the Tarot, a man hanging upside down, with his foot caught in a noose. The noose represents attachment to a purpose, i.e. pursuing a narrow goal to the extent that we are trapped by it.

This principle is also the "Slay the Ego" card of the Secret Dakini Oracle, where we must learn to deal with material things in a practical way without becoming attached to them. The danger of material preoccupation is also the message of the twelfth hexagram of the I-Ching, "Standstill (Stagnation)."

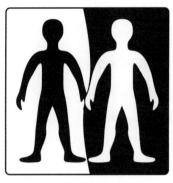

13

Gemini: Lightness and Movement — Diving Into Play

Creative Principle: Once one establishes a purpose for activity (Taurus), that activity begins to manifest spontaneously. This spontaneity is the chief attribute of Gemini. Other attributes are usefulness, flexibility, adaptability, variability, diversity, quickness, and ease of performance, especially intellectual performance. These are also characteristics of Mercury, the ruler of Gemini.

Gemini is symbolized by twins because the intellect functions only in duality. Two or more alternatives are required to make a decision. The concept of twins also implies companionship, i.e., even the most disparate choices complement and strengthen each other in the light of clear discrimination.

The dangers of Gemini are superficiality, vacillation, and over-diversity. The two twins of Gemini have instantaneous communication with each other and can maintain many interests, but they may have so many interests that they lose focus and direction.

Another Gemini image is a juggler. He can keep many balls in the air simultaneously, but if he tries too many, all the balls come crashing down.

Favorite Fantasies: Do you like to juggle many projects at once?

Improvise on a theme, always devising new solutions? Do you dream of being the quick and clever magician, able to blithely dance or talk yourself out of danger's way? Above all, can you turn drudgery into play, and find entertainment in every situation?

Key Idea for Education: In keeping with the dual nature of Gemini, we offer two suggestions here. First, children must learn to manage time well, balancing planning with spontaneity. Planning (Taurus) is not opposed to spontaneity (Gemini). On the contrary, spontaneity thrives when the plan includes free time, the purpose is clear, and one is not attached to the goal.

Second, both children and adults must learn to recognize when they are projecting their own values onto others. Judgmentalism is based on an inability to see how our own emotions color our perception of others. It is a projection of our inner shadows onto others. If we label someone as unintelligent, unattractive, unethical, or otherwise unlovable, it is only because we are afraid of the possibility of the same shortcomings in ourselves. To fully appreciate the divinity in all humanity, we must learn to accept ourselves and others as we are.

Divinatory Message: Use spontaneity, adaptability, and flexibility to resolve the situation at hand. But keep anchored in your purpose to avoid vacillation and becoming scattered.

Relationship to Other Oracles: Gemini corresponds to the thirteenth principle in the other three oracles. The twins represent the intellect's ability to discriminate and honor difference. The thirteenth hexagram of the I-Ching, "Fellowship with Men" conveys both ideas—companionship and discrimination. True discrimination not only divides, but brings the parts into a harmonious whole, i.e., maintaining their friendship!

The intellect (Mercury) abstracts objects into words. To a certain extent this is the death of the object, since words are only verbal symbols, not the objects themselves, just as a shadow is not a man.

This is why the corresponding Tarot card is called "Death" and the Secret Dakini Oracle card is called "Death/Transfiguration." In both cases, death has both positive and negative connotations. In the ancient literature the sign Gemini connotes quarrel, fighting, and even death by treachery.

This destructive principle of Gemini manifests only when one is attached to one's purpose or desire. The higher potential of Gemini is to sever the ego's attachments. The ego dies without attachment, so Gemini is the death of individuality and the birth of universality. Another side of nonattachment is freedom from slavery to desire, so that one can engage in spontaneously life-supporting activity. So Gemini is the fulfillment of Taurus, because without Gemini's clear discrimination between action and desire for the fruit of action, one gets attached to the fruit.

Attachment and desire are commonly misunderstood. Desire is not the enemy, since life is not possible without basic desires to eat, sleep, etc. It is the attachment to desire—believing our happiness comes only from satisfying outer drives—that ties us to a petty ego-bound existence. Gemini clarifies both the need for desire and the means to free ourselves from subservience to desire.

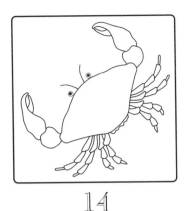

14

Cancer: Deepening Emotions —Concrete Steps of Action

Creative Principle: Spontaneous action must be channeled into specific steps toward a goal. Cancer represents the growing emotional attraction of a goal, along with the tempering of emotions to achieve the goal. When we really want something, we are inspired to find ways to achieve it. We develop internal discipline as we adapt to external obstacles.

Cancer's symbol, a crab, has great sideways agility. Thus Cancer guides us in sometimes tortuous or meandering movements to reach our goal. The power of emotion sustains our motivation through the inevitable ups and downs on the journey.

Action achieves its purpose when motivation is deep and directed. Cancer's gift is fullness of heart. Unless one's heart is fully engaged in action, performance falters and achievement is limited. Cancer's wisdom is from the heart—a deep attunement to the ebb and flow of emotion. Just as land crabs migrate in sync with the lunar tides, Cancer intuitively senses both the individual and collective subconscious. Cancer is ruled by the Moon, the most universal symbol of primal emotion, especially the love and compassion associated with motherhood.

Cancer is not blind emotion. It cultivates the quality the Tarot calls

"Temperance," the tempering of emotions and the channeling of the raw power of emotion toward a purpose. In other words, tempering is moderation and wise management of emotions.

The danger of Cancer is emotional attachment that narrows our vision. This might be staying in a destructive relationship, mad pursuit of a dead-end career, or blind loyalty to an overly zealous religious group.

Favorite Fantasies: In your quiet moments, do your concerns gravitate toward others' feelings? Do you hope to comfort and console, nurture and uplift others? Can you intuitively hear the broken hearts and shattered dreams behind the smiling masks that say "I'm fine"? If you see and hear through your heart and your motive is unselfish compassion, then you know the strong side of Cancer. However, if you feel like a drowning crab helplessly tossed by tidal waves of emotions, grasping to hold onto others with your claws, then you know the weak side of Cancer.

Key Idea for Education: The educational environment must inspire the heart as well as the mind. Here are a few of the many factors to look for:

> Physical environment: Trees and other live plants. Attractive buildings, of mostly natural materials, like wood and stone, rather than concrete, plastic, etc.
>
> Timetables and deadlines appropriate to each student.
>
> Teachers relate to students as friends and mentors.
>
> Respect for religious and spiritual pursuits, even when these seem to violate the prevailing paradigm of scientific materialism.
>
> More emphasis on subjective character traits and moral development than objective scores, such as grades and standardized tests.

Divinatory Message: Look at your primal emotions in the issue at hand and decide if those emotions are freeing and useful, or binding and destructive. For example, if you are pursuing studies because of parental pressure rather than personal interest, the Cancerian approach would be to recognize your emotional motivation and decide whether your emotions are helping or hindering your progress.

Relationship to Other Oracles: Cancer relates to the fourteenth principle in the other three oracles. It is "Temperance" in the Tarot, as mentioned above. It is "Puja Purification" in the Secret Dakini Oracle, whereby we are taught to infuse meaningful emotion into action. It is the fourteenth hexagram of the I-Ching, "Possession in Great Measure," which teaches us how to manage our possessions. This requires awareness of one's emotions so that one is not swept away by them. A deeper meaning of "possessions" is our attachment to our goals. Unless we temper our attachments, they become obstacles to progress.

15
Leo: Leadership Manifests —Individuality Thrives

Creative Principle: This is the principle of progress toward greater specificity and individuality by finding one's own unique approach. Leo represents a personality which transcends all stereotypes and inculcations, one which finds its own solutions. It is the principle of self-actualization, the realization of one's own unique gifts. This implies inner self-reliance, as opposed to dependence on others.

Self-actualization is essential for leadership, signified by the lion and the Sun, ruler of Leo. The natural leader inspires others with his own confidence and poise, and his ability to integrate, like a king who manages the diverse functions of his kingdom with balance, justice, and grace.

The dangers of Leo are pride, domination, egotism, and a love of ostentation. Replace them with nobility, magnanimity, integration, and balance, and you will experience the power and grace of a lion.

Favorite Fantasies: Do you dream of being unique and admired by thousands? Everyone is unique, and everyone is a king in the sense that we must all make tough decisions to reconcile conflicting interests. Leo represents the awareness of one's own unique inner guide to higher purpose. As long as we act from a need for others' approval, we suppress that guide. A weak Leo pursues outer power and status to hide from inner fear and dis-unitedness. A strong Leo naturally attracts others' respect because he radiates confidence, benevolence, and the true leadership that can only come from Self-awareness.

Key Idea for Education: Allow each child to be unique and explore his or her own leadership potential without encouraging vanity, which is merely a symptom of misidentification—believing yourself to be the doer rather than the witness. Great leaders are not swayed by either criticism or adulation. They see through the trap of self-infatuation and act magnanimously toward all.

The mass media foster hero worship of popular entertainers and athletes, feeding their vanity and tacitly devaluing nonheroes. Hero worship stifles self-reliance among the worshippers. It is good to honor achievement, especially unselfish work that benefits others. However, it is questionable to make cult heroes of entertainers, especially the North Nodian outlaws who dominate the film and rock music industries.

Competition for sports, grades, and jobs is healthy as long as it is tempered with the realization that these tangible signs of success are less important than nobler but less visible virtues. Obsession with winning tends to inflate the winners and deflate the losers, to their mutual detriment.

Divinatory Message: Take a leadership role to resolve the problem at hand. It may be through outward leadership of others, or inward leadership—defining the problem more precisely and actively pursuing a solution, rather than passively waiting for outside help. In either case, the solution must honor your personal uniqueness.

Relationship to Other Oracles: Leo relates to the fifteenth principle in the other three oracles. A truly great leader rises above both humility and pride. However, if the different facets of his personality are not integrated (a function of the Sun), he may become the

"Devil" of the Tarot. The devil wreaks havoc through the arrogance and power of an imbalanced Sun.

The "Ally" of the Secret Dakini Oracle represents "help to overcome lower orders of consciousness." His symbol is also a devil, representing the raw power of the subconscious when the ego is not tamed by higher Leonine traits like benevolence and generosity.

The fifteenth hexagram of the I-Ching, "Modesty," is a perfect expression of the ideal Leo, who maintains modesty while dispensing heavenly blessings like a mountain.

16
Virgo: Self-Analysis
—Stepping Back to Transcend

Creative Principle: You can only progress so far without transcending, going to deeper levels of the problem where opposites are reconciled. The ego must become strong before its materialistic limitations can be transcended. Leo represents the maximum power of the ego. In Leo the ego can either be dissolved in infinity, or become infatuated with its individuality and eventually shattered by its self-intoxication.

The entire universe is a field of problems. Nothing finite is ever complete and nothing lasts forever. The greatest people, the greatest achievements, and the greatest civilizations eventually crumble and are forgotten. Yet perfection is possible, even inevitable, not in any physical sense, but in consciousness. The whole cycle of involution and evolution is nothing but the crystallization of spirit (pure consciousness) into thought and matter, and the return to spirit through an infusion of pure consciousness into matter and thought.

In its highest meaning, Virgo represents the virginal essence of infinite silence, truth, and bliss. Virginity is innocence and simplicity— these are the qualities necessary for transcendence. More manifest levels of Virgo are attention to detail, necessary for increasing the specificity of action, and analysis, the principle of autofeedback to stay on the path of progress.

Virgo is ruled by Mercury, the principle of intellect and transcendence. The clear intellect penetrates illusion to perceive deeper levels of Reality. Eventually it transcends all boundaries and reaches unbounded awareness, even if only for a micromoment. Repeated experience builds the platform of permanent unbounded awareness, the source of an inner fulfillment which will never fade away (cosmic consciousness).

Transcendence provides a powerful acceleration to growth and integration of opposites. This is one of the reasons Mercury is exalted in Virgo—the higher use of the intellect should serve as a synthesizing factor in understanding life. What is integrated is determined by the next sign, Libra.

The junction point between Virgo and Libra represents the turning point between involution and evolution. The first half of the cycle of time is the involution of spirit into matter, which begins in the fullness of unmanifest energy at the beginning of Aries, and progresses in steps of increasing specificity to the emptiness of transcendence at the end of Virgo. At this point transcendence is empty because it is cognized as separate from creation, separate from the subject-object duality of relative experience.

The second half of the cycle of time is the evolution of spirit into matter, which begins in Libra and culminates in the fullness of spirit and matter together in Pisces. The flat emptiness of transcendental consciousness starts to move into thought and matter. Diversity is transcended in Virgo. Transcendence is diversified in Libra. Pure consciousness begins to coexist with finite experience. This involution and evolution of individuality parallels the involution and evolution of the whole cosmos. As William Blake said, the entire universe is contained in every grain of sand.

Virgo loves precision, perfection, and detail. Romance and idealism wither and die in the microscopic analysis of Virgo. Thus Venus, the planetary lover, is debilitated here, along with attempts at positive thinking that fly in the face of cold, hard facts. But Mercury discovers in Virgo how to transcend its own thought processes and find perfectly pure and silent self-referral consciousness.

The danger of Virgo is becoming lost in detailed self-analysis and attached to the thoughts and beliefs one is meant to transcend. This danger can be averted through selfless service to others, especially in teaching and verbal communication. Where Sagittarius serves through action and Cancer serves through feeling, Virgo serves through penetrating analysis to remove confusion and contradiction.

The innocent virgin is also perfectly harmless. Thus Virgo is a sign of friendliness, kindness, gentleness, and joy, as well as obedience and service.

Favorite Fantasies: Do you dream of the perfect house in an ideal neighborhood, a spotless car, and perfectly behaved children? When the American dream becomes frozen and stereotyped, or one nit-picks for material perfection to the exclusion of emotional and spiritual values, a weak Virgo is indicated. On the other hand, a strong Virgo gives clear discrimination, allowing orderly progress in all fields of life. The strongest Virgo desire is discrimination into the ultimate of simplicity, the unified field underlying all existence. Such transcendence creates a firm foundation for the orderliness Virgo loves in her environment. Virgo also brings the ability to synthesize diverse streams of knowledge into a coherent whole. Do you dream of holistic knowledge, as we do? That is a high Virgo aspiration.

Key Idea for Education: Children must have the experience of transcendence as a central part of education. There are many techniques of transcendence. Young children, especially, may transcend spontaneously without formal training if merely encouraged to spend a few minutes in silence with eyes closed. Older children generally require training in a simple form of meditation. Silent time for prayer or meditation is a good first step when the legal and political environment of schools does not allow teaching specific techniques, which may be associated with religion.

Divinatory Message: Your answer lies in silence and meditation as a basis for clear discrimination. When cultivated in an effortless and natural way, inner silence leads to higher understanding, which restores a sense of perspective. What we thought was a mountain is seen as a molehill when we have inner silence and clear discrimination.

Relationship to Other Oracles: Virgo corresponds to the sixteenth principle in the other oracles. The corresponding Tarot card is the "Tower," a high vantage point which gives a broad view of the activity below, an excellent image of increased discrimination and transcendence of activity.

The Secret Dakini Oracle called "Holocaust" is illustrated by a burning house to indicate the purificatory power of transcendence. Some of the significations are "The material edifice of reality crumbles and burns," and "the loss of ego and the shedding of preconceptions."

The sixteenth hexagram of the I-Ching, "Enthusiasm," is a fitting description of the inner elevation which follows transcendence. "Here one moves along a line of least resistance," says the commentator Wilhem. Transcendence is always along the path of least resistance. This hexagram also relates to the need for obedience, service, and decorum, all qualities of the sign Virgo.

17

Libra: Balancing Polarities
—Action to Integrate Opposites

Creative Principle: Libra is the Scale of Justice which balances stability and adaptability. Integration of opposites is Virgo's strength. Thus integration properly belongs to both Virgo and Libra, Virgo more inner and Libra more outer. Virgo is the innermost letting-go of the relative and diving into the transcendent. Libra is emergence from transcendence with spontaneous integration of the polar opposites which are intrinsic to relativity.

Since Libra follows transcendence and transcendence gives skill in action, Libra represents skill in action. As we said in the commentary on Virgo, involution begins in Aries and culminates in Virgo; evolution begins in Libra and culminates in Pisces. This means that matter is at a maximum level of density in Libra, which is why the wheels of justice turn slowly.

Favorite Fantasies: Do you dream of perfect balance and harmony among all areas of your life, and shun conflict and strife? Are you willing to compromise to keep the peace? These are traits of Libra, who is concerned with keeping all the parts functioning as a harmonious whole.

Key Idea for Education: Education requires a balance of stability and adaptability. Lack of stability is seen in disciplinary problems, and lack of adaptability is seen in boredom. Interdisciplinary and multidisciplinary studies address both lacks, however they require integration of theory and practice through direct experience of transcendence, the transdisciplinary anchor of holistic education. To put it in other words, transdisciplinary education (the experience of transcendence) is the experiential basis of inter- and multi-disciplinary studies.

Divinatory Message: Face what the American Indian cultures understood as a basic problem of life: balancing our needs for stability and adaptability. For example, you may need to spend many years living in the same place, with very little travel. Then may come a counterbalancing period of change and variety, either through travel or relocation. Similar readjustments can take place in diet, friendships, hobbies, or any other area of life.

The danger of Libra is trying so hard to balance opposites that one becomes indecisive and vacillates between choices.

Relationship to Other Oracles: Libra corresponds to the seventeenth principle in the other three oracles. Its ruler, Venus, is the planet of high aspiration and maximum positivity. Marriage exemplifies Venusian idealism. As one anonymous wit put it, "Marriage is the triumph of optimism over experience." It requires a Libran integration between stability and adaptability. Stability is in the legal and emotional bond intended to last a lifetime. Adaptability is equally obvious—changes in the partner, as well as outer challenges of health, finances, etc.

These aspirations are evident in "The Star" in the Tarot and "The Island of Jewels," floating in the sky, in the Secret Dakini Oracle. The I-Ching hexagram called "The Following" focuses directly on the Libran leadership skill of responding to the needs of followers (adaptability) while maintaining a consistent and persistent path of action (stability).

18
Scorpio: Pleasure
—Sensory Gratification or Inner Bliss?

Creative Principle: As a result of the integration of stability and adaptability in Libra through the transcendence of Virgo, one gains increasing ability to enjoy action in Scorpio.

As we become increasingly centered in who we are, our actions spontaneously become more joyous. When we recognize our innermost nature as an ocean of bliss, all our activities become waves of bliss.

However, in our search for greater joy, there is a danger of sensual attachments. Such attachments only occur when we mistake outer objects as greater sources of pleasure than inner awareness, and we forget our inner unboundedness in pursuit of outer boundaries. The lower instincts of Scorpio are symbolized by the scorpion, which hides in small dark places and stings its prey—sensory attachments always have an element of pain! The higher instincts of Scorpio are symbolized by the eagle, which is passionate, yet flies high above any attachments to his nature. He swoops down to earth to catch his prey (enjoyments), but soars again in freedom.

Favorite Fantasies: Are you inwardly passionate in the extreme, whether pursuing earthly pleasures or heavenly bliss? Do you hide your passions, or share them with only a rare intimate companion? These are traits of Scorpio, who usually savors the sensory pleasures of the moment, but is capable of transforming the pursuit of pleasure into spiritual ecstasy.

Key Idea for Education: If children are bored in school they express their frustration in sensory indulgence or antisocial behavior. When education is individualized to meet each student's needs, and the narrow vision of isolated disciplines is replaced by the broad vision of inter-, multi-, and transdisciplinary studies, the joy of learning returns and negative behavior spontaneously declines.

Divinatory Message: Seek happiness through the pursuit of higher consciousness, not materialistic indulgence. Real happiness is felt not from a sense of duty, but an attunement to one's own inner bliss, the inner sense of fulfillment which is not dependent on outer events. Inner bliss results from the state of least excitation of consciousness, a steady state of contentment that is not affected by either pleasure or pain.

If we are not culturing bliss through daily spiritual practice, our life is wasted in the blind pursuit of pleasure and avoidance of pain. The consequent emptiness of spirit stings like a scorpion to remind us to fly high like an eagle toward inner freedom.

Relationship to Other Oracles: Scorpio corresponds to the eighteenth principle in the other three oracles. The enjoyment of Scorpio is symbolized by the Secret Dakini card "Soma," which represents a mythological plant cherished by the Gods for its divine bliss-bestowing nectar. Scorpio is also symbolized by the "Moon" of the Tarot. In the Vedic tradition, Soma is a name of the Moon. According to some commentators on the Tarot, the crescent Moon on this card should be dripping drops of nectar. The eighteenth hexagram of the I-Ching, "Work on What Has Spoiled (Decay)," indicates that it is the principle of joy which motivates the attempt to rectify a perverted sense of pleasure, which was the source of decay.

19

Sagittarius: Directed Action —Energy Focused on the Goal

Creative Principle: When pursued in a life-supporting manner, the enjoyment of Scorpio naturally takes us in the direction of more and more unbounded values of life. In Sagittarius we become the disciple of Spirit. Our aim is high and our ability to shoot an arrow and hit the target is both disciplined and spirited.

Webster defines evolution as "a process of change in a certain direction." Sagittarius gives clarity and focus plus enthusiastic execution to the evolutionary process. It allows us to plan concrete and systematic steps toward achievement of our objective. This is a more refined and detailed level of planning than Taurus, where the basic purpose of our action was defined but the steps were missing.

As explained previously, the first six houses represent the involution of spirit into matter, i.e., the growth of materiality and diversification. The last six houses represent the evolution of matter into spirit, i.e., the growth of spirituality and simplification. This simplicity of spirit is achieved through clear-cut boundaries. A disciple of spirit is disciplined on the spiritual path.

The danger of Sagittarius is that one's focus on the goal becomes too rigid, i.e., one develops a *sattwic* attachment to the goal and the means to achieve it.

Favorite Fantasies: Do you lay out intricate plans, anticipating every possible scenario? Do you create your own master plan and detailed subplans, as the leading management consultants advise? Sagittarius is the executor who maps out the means to achieve his ends in a free-spirited, freedom-loving manner.

Key Idea for Education: A school curriculum which is rooted in materialism cannot create disciples of the spirit. Sagittarius, the centaur, is half horse and half human. Man's quest requires a coordinated use of his animal and human natures in pursuit of dharma (ethical and evolutionary action). The joy experienced in Scorpio must be tempered by the moral awareness and one-pointed discipline of Sagittarius.

Divinatory Message: Bring the best qualities of a soldier and disciple to the problem at hand. One must have a clear aspiration and the dedication to take steps toward achieving that aspiration. All problems and issues should be viewed in the larger context of our role as spiritual disciples. Anything which doesn't serve that end should be discarded.

Relationship to Other Oracles: Sagittarius corresponds to the nineteenth principle in the other oracles. It is the "Phoenix" card of the Secret Dakini Oracle, representing the alchemical fire of transformation. It is the "Sun" card of the Tarot, which represents the same alchemical transformation. The nineteenth hexagram of the I-Ching, entitled "Approach," also symbolizes upward expansion in joyous, hopeful progress. The galloping horse of Sagittarius is seeking to approach the inexhaustible source of creation. The I-Ching even suggests that although joyous progress is certain, we must work with determination and perseverance to achieve it. All these qualities are characteristic of Sagittarius.

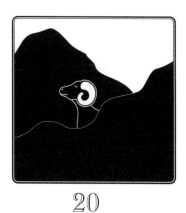

20
Capricorn:
Perseverance in the Ascent

Creative Principle: If the disciple in Sagittarius works with dedication and perseverance toward his spiritual goal, he achieves self-purification in Capricorn. This self-purification shatters the limited ego with all its boundaries, and one achieves the first enlightened state of awareness, cosmic consciousness. In summary, Sagittarius aims at the mountain top; Capricorn is the strong and determined mountain goat that finishes the ascent.

Capricornians excel at testing and executing the detailed plans devised by Sagittarians. Testing any plan provides the feedback necessary for refining the plan. As any test engineer knows, the best-conceived designs are usually riddled with flaws until thoroughly tested and revised. This "reality testing" is the "self-purification" of any scheme of implementation.

In the Vedic tradition the symbol for Capricorn is half mammal, half fish. This dual nature of reality is experienced in cosmic consciousness. There is a complete separation between the cosmic knower and the manifest creation he witnesses. This experience of witnessing is like the view from a high mountaintop, where one surveys the world below without being caught in it. It is a state of beauty, clarity, and broad vision unimagined from the world below.

Favorite Fantasies: Are you determined to surmount every obstacle? Do you concern yourself more with practical means than lofty goals? Concerned with "how" more than "why" or "what" to do? Capricorn overcomes difficulties through determination and seriousness of purpose. He patiently withstands a harsh environment, surviving through perseverance and self-control.

Key Idea for Education: Educators universally recognize that students need to apply knowledge in order to master it. However, education today is almost totally concerned with objective knowledge. Even psychology is taught as objectively as possible, with the physical sciences as a model for elimination of subjective responses.

The problem with a purely objective model of education is that students begin to feel like objects. Their subjective feelings and intuitions are unintentionally denied and suppressed simply because they are not part of the curriculum. Students often take psychology classes in the hope of better understanding themselves and others. The disease-based model they are generally taught excludes knowledge of higher consciousness, which is essential to human fulfillment. The proponents of humanistic and transpersonal psychology have rebelled against their profession's over emphasis on neurosis and psychosis, but have not gained much acceptance among mainstream psychologists.

The most important testing ground of subjective knowledge is one's daily spiritual practice. As the great Indian sage Shri Aurobindo emphasized, the world needs saints who integrate spirituality and activity more than solitary recluses in their caves. Periods of seclusion may be invaluable as preparatory steps, but higher consciousness is not complete unless integrated with activity.

There are innumerable ways of enhancing other subjective arenas, such as relating skills and career choice. Consultations in the Art of Multidimensional Living™ provide a holistic framework to help each individual identify which paths and practices will help him most in all eight fields (Part II Chapter 3).

Divinatory Message: This archetype cautions against the danger of Capricorn—excess rigidity. It also signals an opportunity to achieve your highest aspirations, if you have the concentration, perseverance, and devotion to surmount obstacles.

Relationship to Other Oracles: Capricorn corresponds to the twentieth principle in the other three oracles. The twentieth hexagram of the I-Ching, "Contemplation/View," indicates a prominent landmark such as a tower or mountain which affords a sweeping view. The corresponding Tarot card, "The Judgment" implies a renewal or change of a fundamental nature, an awakening of the dead, or the accomplishment of a great work of transformation. Webster says a judgment "involves forming an opinion about something through a careful weighing of the evidence." Here the final judgment is regarding the basic question first posed in Virgo, "Who am I?" It is both intellectual and experiential. The corresponding Secret Dakini card, "Transformation," indicates a fine level of self-development has been achieved.

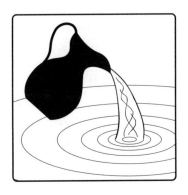

21
Aquarius: Disciplining the Parts for a Harmonious Whole

Creative Principle: When Self-awareness is gained, one is capable of turning toward creation to discover the deep underlying harmony which lies at its essence. This principle of harmony, whether we think of it as brotherhood or a more refined form of the self-discipline of Capricorn, is the keynote of Aquarius. However, for this harmony to arise, Saturn, the rule of Aquarius, may have to set things in their proper order. This implies the potential of a forceful reordering of our lives by Mother Nature.

Harmony is the reconciliation of opposites, be they love and discipline, seriousness and humor, male and female, or heat and cold. Harmony is not a blending of opposites to destroy difference, for diversity could not exist without tension between opposites. Rather, it is recognition of a deeper unity underlying all difference.

As we begin to experience finer and finer levels of the dance of creation, we spontaneously begin to act in a way which is always harmonious, because we appreciate the underlying unity in diversity. Eventually we learn to see God in everything and everyone, not as a lofty ideal, but as an integral part of every perception. This innocent and natural appreciation of the omnipresent divinity bursts the boundaries of our heart, and the floodgates of cosmic love overflow to nourish and harmonize our environment, like the water bearer pouring forth her healing liquid in the garden of life.

Favorite Fantasies: Do you dream of universal brotherhood and freedom? Are you disciplined enough for the hard work to achieve it? Where Libra dreams of peace and bliss, Aquarius knuckles down to make it happen. Libra is concerned with harmonious feelings, and shuns violent words and actions. Aquarius is more concerned that no one infringes on the rights of anyone else, and may use force to protect the innocent and oppressed. She is an altruist, but not a sentimentalist. She dreams of concrete steps to implement harmony.

Key Idea for Education: To raise a child properly, we must balance love and discipline and achieve a harmony between emotional nourishment and behavioral guidance. Wherever either quality is lacking, the other suffers. The impersonal environment of many modern schools discourages both values. Parents and teachers must discipline with love and love with discipline! This is easier to do when there are few enough students in each class for each to feel a personal connection to the teacher, and there are also well-enforced standards of behavior to prevent highly unsettled students from disrupting the whole class.

Divinatory Message: Seek a harmonious solution, one which anchors lofty egalitarian ideals with clear concrete boundaries. Sharing, conciliation and brotherhood are indicated.

Relationship to Other Oracles: To see why Aquarius corresponds to the twenty-first principle in the other three oracles we must realize that the "Joker" card in both the Secret Dakini Oracle and the Tarot properly belongs in the twenty-first position, although it is often listed as the zero card. (We use the conventional numbers for subsequent cards of the Tarot and SDO to avoid confusion with other texts.) Zero cannot represent a principle of Creative Intelligence. Zero represents the unmanifest out of which all the principles arise, just as in the mathematics of set theory all finite numbers and even infinity can be derived from zero.[6]

The twenty-first hexagram of the I-Ching, "Biting Through," is concerned with balancing opposites, such as punishment and gentleness, or discipline and love. The name "Biting Through" suggests that obstacles must be met forcefully, and forcefulness is characteristic of Saturn, the ruler of Aquarius.

22
Pisces: Completion
—Frustration or Fulfillment?

Creative Principle: Duality spins in a perpetual circle through the interplay of opposites, like two fishes chasing each other's tails. Pisces indicates the completion of a cycle. If one has mastered all the lessons of human incarnation, one achieves fulfillment in unity consciousness, the highest state of human awareness. If fulfillment is incomplete, one begins a new cycle in Aries. Any unfulfilled desires in Pisces become the seeds of new desires in the next cycle in Aries.

Pisces is also the sign of sacrifice. True fulfillment blossoms only when we sacrifice our egocentric desires to help others. When we let go of personal concerns for a higher good, we open ourselves to divine grace.

The water of Pisces represents the subconscious and superconscious. If your desires are not totally fulfilled in Pisces, then your subconscious drives you to a new cycle of creation in Aries. But if fulfillment is complete, then your subconscious is totally transformed into the superconscious. You are fully aware of your deepest desires, and those desires are fully in accord with Divine Will, so there is no conflict between what you want to do and what you should do. You are a perfect instrument of cosmic intention, and the infinite power of nature supports your every desire.

In this state you are no longer driven by hidden impulses. Conventional psychology is obsolete and incomplete because it does not go beyond the subconscious. Unity implies that the deepest, darkest regions of the subconscious have been brought to light. Unity consciousness has only been attained by a few individuals at this time in history. However, it is the long-term potential of all.

Favorite Fantasies: Do you dream of self-sacrifice for the whole of humanity? Are your underlying motives deeply emotional and connected to the collective subconscious? Do you try to emulate the life of Christ (symbolized by Pisces, the fish), as the supreme self-sacrificer?

Key Idea for Education: If children are not happy in school, something is drastically wrong in education! First and foremost, education should allow people to be happy. It cannot teach happiness, because happiness is the natural state of life. But it can allow happiness to blossom without impediment. Unhappiness is the symptom of deviation from what is natural.

When small children play, their happiness is unmistakable. The playgrounds of elementary schools are centers of harmony and joy that uplift their entire community, especially in the more enlightened schools. But by the time students reach high school, sports become so serious the recreative value of play is lost. When happiness depends on winning, it becomes fragile and vulnerable. Play requires nonattachment to the goal. Attachment begets obsessive seriousness. A healthy attitude toward sports lets one enjoy the game no matter what the outcome. Blissful nonattachment, plus purposeful focus, actually enhance performance!

Competition is healthy in the context of the whole. Both sides depend on each other's presence to make a game, just as the two fishes of Pisces need each other's tails to chase. The two fishes represent heart and mind, yin and yang, or any other fundamental duality.

The same loss of joy can be felt in the classroom when feelings are eliminated in the attempt to objectify studies. The dry, objective, rational approach to knowledge that dominates higher education today represents only one of eight major styles of thinking, a style characterized by the cold, dry logic of Saturn. (See Part II, Chapter 1.) The other six approaches are equally valid. Even more important are spiritual practices to cultivate the habit of swimming in the ocean of inner bliss.

Divinatory Message: Seek happiness through sacrifice and service. Dive into the depths of your unconscious to find a joyous way of giving from the heart. Pisces is ruled by Jupiter, who governs karma yoga, the path of selfless service. So look to helping others or serving God as your means to fulfillment.

Relationship to Other Oracles: Pisces corresponds to the twenty-second principle in the I-Ching and the twenty-first cards in the other two oracles. It is the "World" of the Tarot and "Earth-Bound" of the Secret Dakini Oracle. Both signify the completion of a cycle. The twenty-second hexagram of the I-Ching is called "Grace," which says that desires are satisfied through divine grace more than struggles and efforts on our part. Struggles and efforts may set up the conditions for grace, but grace is the primary determinant of the outcome. That is why the karma yogi follows Krishna's admonition in the *Bhagavad Gita*, "You have control over action alone, not over the fruits. Live not for the fruits of action, nor attach yourself to inaction." (II.46)

Summary of the Path through the Signs

In brief, FULLNESS (Aries), becoming PURPOSEFUL (Taurus), SPONTANEOUSLY (Gemini) TAKES A DIRECTION (Cancer) toward PROGRESS (Leo) and TRANSCENDS (Virgo), accelerating (also Virgo) the INTEGRATION OF STABILITY and ADAPTABILITY (Libra), and thus ENJOYS (Scorpio) EVOLUTION (Sagittarius) in SELF-PURIFICATION (Capricorn), HARMONY (Aquarius), and FULFILLMENT (Pisces).

Maharishi Mahesh Yogi gave ten principles of action in his Science of Creative Intelligence. We have adapted them to the behavior of the signs of the zodiac and added two more:

1. Follow the law of least action. (Aries)
2. Conserve time. (Taurus)
3. Engage only in useful action. (Gemini)
4. Engage only in effective action, i.e., action which has desirable results. (Cancer)
5. Act with fixity of purpose. (Leo)
6. Act in a way which brings no harm to others. (Virgo)
7. Act in a way which achieves maximum results. (Libra)
8. Act in such a way that action remains joyful. (Scorpio)
9. Plan one's actions in detail. (Sagittarius)
10. Execute the plan. (Capricorn)
11. Act in a way which is always harmonious with the environment. (Aquarius)
12. Act without attachment to the fruit and with a sense of service. (Pisces)

Introduction to the Lunar Mansions (Nakshatras)

The twenty-seven lunar mansions are elaborations of the first nine fundamental principles of Creative Intelligence, represented by the planets from Sun through Ketu. The nakshatras are divided into three divisions corresponding to the three *gunas*, or primordial attributes of nature—creation *(rajas)*, preservation *(sattwa)*, and destruction or transformation *(tamas)*. Everything in the universe, from subatomic particles to galaxies, from each thought you think to the thought-styles of entire civilizations, goes through stages of creation, preservation, and destruction. In fact, all three *gunas* coexist in various degrees at every level of mind and matter.

The nakshatras express how each of the nine planetary energies applies to each of the three *gunas*. There are nine *tamasic* or destructive nakshatras, nine *rajasic* or creative ones, and nine *sattwic* or balancing ones. The same ordering of the planets corresponds to each set of nine nakshatras: Sun, Moon, Mars, Rahu, Jupiter, Saturn, Mercury, Ketu, and Venus.

This relationship of the nakshatras to the *gunas* is not commonly understood by Vedic astrologers and may be disputed by some. We believe it is a true archetype, and one of the many important insights into the science of the stars which has been lost for thousands of years prior to the Astrology of the Eight Fields of Living™, an applied aspect of the Art of Multidimensional Living™.

The nakshatras are subdivisions of the signs. In a true astrology, the strength of each planet is determined primarily by the signs they occupy. Both signs and nakshatras also color the qualities of the planets. For example, Mars is strong and *tamasic* (destructive) anywhere in Aries, its own sign. Within Aries, it is most independent and hermetic in Ketu's nakshatra, Ashwini. It tends to be sensory-oriented in Venus' nakshatra, Bharani. And it takes on the Sun's leadership tendencies in the Sun's nakshatra, Krittika. We refer the serious student to Appendix A for a listing of the nakshatras' location with respect to the signs of the zodiac.

Relationship to Other Oracles: The Tarot has four suits of cards—Wands, Cups, Swords, and Pentacles. The first nine cards in each of the first three suits correspond to the nine nakshatras for each guna. Wands are the creative or *rajasic* principle—think of a magic wand to create whatever you want. Another symbol for wands is a growing young sapling, an expression of creativity. Cups (chalices) contain or preserve liquid. Thus Cups are the preservative or *sattwic* principle. Swords represent the destructive or *tamasic* principle.

The fourth and lowest suit is Pentacles. "Pentacle" means pentagram, or five-sided figure. The five sides correspond to the five elements—earth, water, fire, air, and space in the Vedic tradition, or earth, water, fire, wood, and metal in the Chinese tradition. Thus "Pentacle" implies something bounded and material. The houses are the most bounded and material aspect of astrology. They represent the last twelve principles of *The Global Oracle*.

According to the esoteric astrologer Alice Bailey, originally there were only ten houses of the zodiac, not twelve. The Pentacles correspond to the first ten houses. The last two houses have no corresponding card in the Tarot, but there are corresponding principles in the I-Ching and the Secret Dakini Oracle.

23
1st Lunar Mansion (Krittika) —Transformative Leadership

Traditional Name: "Star of Fire"

Planetary Rulership: *Tamasic* aspect of the Sun

Creative Principle: A leader must be able to cut or burn out all the impurities or wrongs in his domain, and give birth to purity, morality, and virtue. Krittika is the able commander in battles of any kind—legal, financial, emotional, spiritual, or military. He protects the good by destroying evil.

As a *tamasic* principle, inaction may be stronger than action for Krittika. It may only be necessary to start a fire to destroy impurity, like igniting a dilapidated and combustible structure, then managing the fire so that it does not burn out of control.

One potential weakness common to almost all governments is the tendency of manmade laws to outlast their usefulness. Governments throughout the world exhibit a chronic budget creep and perpetuation of outmoded programs. *Tamasic* leadership is needed to weed out the wasteful programs and outdated laws without damaging the useful ones. The useful and absolutely necessary facets of *tamas* are not to be confused with *tamasic* morals and habits, such as sloth, debauchery, dishonesty, etc.

Favorite Fantasies: Are you inspired by Alexander the Great, Charlemagne, Julius Caesar, and other great conquerors? Do you dream of being a leader in cutting all the waste, corruption, and injustice from government? Perhaps you have the same dream on a local level, hoping to reform your company, school, church, or family. The *tamasic* aspect of the Sun is better at eliminating outdated programs than creating new ones.

Key Idea for Education: Student leaders and school administrators must cut away the wrongs and impurities which can develop in schools. This is often difficult because of legal, financial, and political constraints. Educational institutions must be free to pursue higher knowledge without pressure from those who would require an economic or political justification for learning.

Divinatory Message: Be a leader in a *tamasic* solar way, such as bringing wrongdoers to justice, or protecting others from them. But like a true king, be careful not to harm the innocent in the pursuit of justice.

Relationship to Other Oracles: Krittika's cutting, *tamasic* quality is seen in the twenty-third hexagram of the I-Ching, called "Splitting Apart." Wilhelm says this hexagram indicates that inferior people will destroy the superior man's work by passive means. However, we feel that Wilhelm's usually excellent commentary misses one key point. Although it correctly captures the idea of destroying through passive means, it incorrectly implies that evil will destroy good, rather than vice versa.

This principle is also the Ace of Swords of the Tarot, which indicates using force in the pursuit of justice, while maintaining equilibrium between severity and mercy (Gray's commentary). It is also "Mother's Milk," the twenty-second card of the Secret Dakini Oracle, which represents "spiritual homesickness, the desire to get back to the Primal Source," and "the aspiration for nonduality." The imagery is not as paradoxical as it may seem. A mother's breast milk is gentle and nourishing, just the opposite qualities we have discussed for Krittika. However, anything that destroys ignorance (duality) is motherly, and the experience of unity (the sun) is the most gentle and nourishing experience of all. Impurity is the result of ignorance. Only by removing ignorance do we purify ourselves and our environment, return to our Primal Source, and nourish the highest values in life.

24
2nd Lunar Mansion (Rohini) —Emotional Purification

Traditional Name: The Star of Ascent

Planetary Rulership: *Tamasic* aspect of the Moon

Creative Principle: Rohini represents movement of life through the interplay of opposing forces. This movement, symbolized by the chariot, can trap us in Maya, or illusion, as we increase our tendency toward material enjoyments and all forms of sensuality. The recognition of our material entrapment can be the stimulus for ascending out of it to greater spiritual clarity and light.

The chariot metaphor is common in the Vedic literature. The horses represent the senses, which are powerful and unruly until tamed by the mind, or charioteer. The chariot, or body, is pulled by the senses, which can either pursue blind gratification, or follow the dictates of the mind to seek higher, more permanent values.

The Star of Ascent suggests that we can learn from our material attachments and aspire to pure spirit. Normally, Rohini implies ascending from matter to spirit. However, when weak, it could imply the reverse—spirit becoming increasingly lost in material pursuits.

Favorite Fantasies: Do you struggle to keep your higher aspirations alive when waves of impure emotion threaten to drown them? Are you motivated by heavenly hopes instead of earth-bound hormones? These indicate Rohini's positive desire to ascend from matter to spirit. However, if you have no interest in spiritual matters, and aspire only for emotional gratification from others, you reflect Rohini's negative potential for increasing emotional attachments, trying to hang onto bygone feelings.

Key Idea for Education: In the Vedic tradition there is a distinction between bhogis and yogis. Bhogis are caught in material enjoyments. Yogis have freed themselves from bondage to material attachments, or at least recognize such bondage and attempt to escape it.

It is a waste of time to try to convince bhogis to become yogis until they become disillusioned with the endless cycle of pleasure and desire. Material entrapments are bhogis' greatest teachers. They eventually bring disappointment and exhaustion, and thereby motivate the search for greater joy through nonsensory means.

Divinatory Message: Ask yourself whether your problem relates to an ascending or descending cycle of material attachment. Is your dependence on material gratification increasing or decreasing? You may decide to continue as a bhogi, pursuing sensory pleasures, or you may decide to be a yogi, foregoing sensory pleasures for spiritual development. Either choice may be appropriate for a time. However, if you choose to be a bhogi for now, try to maintain a sense of moderation. Eventually you'll tire of the endless pursuit of fleeting pleasures and will want to look for deeper joys.

Relationship to Other Oracles: Rohini corresponds to the twenty-third Secret Dakini Oracle card, "Maya, How She Spins." Maya is a classic symbol of the *tamasic* principle of the Moon. The image is an old woman who spins her webs of illusion to trap the ignorant in materialism.

This principle is also the Tarot's Two of Swords, which indicates some of the qualities of material entrapment, such as sensuality, laziness, dullness, and stagnation. It also carries positive qualities of the Moon, such as intimacy, compassion, and freedom from material attachments.

How do we get off the wheel of Maya? The twenty-fourth hexagram of the I-Ching, called "Return (The Turning Point)" indicates that we must use the *tamasic* principle of rest to return to the center or hub of the wheel, where we are not overly allured by material attractions on the wheel's periphery.

25

3rd Lunar Mansion (Mrigashira)
—The Power of Rest

Traditional Name: The Searching Star

Planetary Rulership: *Tamasic* aspect of Mars

Creative Principle: The traditional symbol for this lunar mansion, a deer's head, is very significant. A deer represents softness, sweetness, and innocence. The Sanskrit word for deer, *mriga,* is derived from "mri," which means both to search and to die—both searching and dying are related to this asterism. Mars, the ruler of Mrigashira, is a warrior and adventurer, who searches for adventure and is not afraid of death. Mrigashira suggests following a deer path through the jungle of obstacles and illusions we all face. In many traditions death is a state of rest, especially for the warrior who dies defending a just cause.

Mars also governs how we exercise will, or how we use our power. A *tamasic* will destroys others unless tempered by the sweetness and innocence of a deer.

Favorite Fantasies: Do you dream of being fearless in the face of death? This is an expression of the positive potential of Mrigashira. Do you want to die? This is a negative expression of Mrigashira. If you are tempted to take your life, turn the courage it takes to face death toward solving the problems presented by life!

Key Idea for Education: Learn to use power in a gentle and compassionate way—don't trample others in your search for fulfillment.

Divinatory Message: Exercise your willpower to destroy illusion or protect something you cherish. Sometimes it takes willpower just to resist being drawn into temptations of power, and sometimes it takes willpower to stop all activity and rest. Ask yourself if you are misusing power, or holding back on your efforts due to fear. Be bold and courageous, but ever vigilant to protect others' interests as well as your own.

Relationship to Other Oracles: Mrigashira is perfectly reflected in the twenty-fifth hexagram of the I-Ching, entitled "Innocence." It is also reflected in the twenty-fourth Secret Dakini card, called "Solar Return," which points to the need for a forceful will to confront obstacles and burn away undesirable karma—clear expressions of the *tamasic* power of Mars. The Three of Swords in the Tarot points to the strength needed in struggles and the possibility of division, rupture, and dispersion due to our misuse of power.

26
4th Lunar Mansion (Ardra) —Rebellious Righter of Wrongs

Traditional Name: The Oppressing One

Planetary Rulership: *Tamasic* aspect of Rahu (North Node of the Moon)

Creative Principle: The North Node of the Moon is a rebel, revolutionary, and outlaw. The lower meaning of this lunar mansion is someone who hunts down and cruelly oppresses or torments others. The higher energy of Ardra is someone who purifies wrongs and heals disease, going outside the law or convention to help the oppressed.

Robin Hood is a perfect example of this *tamasic* aspect of the North Node. He tormented wealthy persons who exploited others, and helped the poor and oppressed.

The Nodes of the Moon are invisible or shadow planets with no physical substance. Outlaws and rebels often work in secret, more comfortable in the shadows than the light of day. Their cause may be either just or unjust. Think of the underground resistance movement in Nazi-occupied France or the American colonists plotting their resistance to English exploitation prior to the Revolutionary War.

Another image of Ardra is the hunter. In a spiritual sense, he is the seeker who stays focused on the goal, and does not get caught up in flashy experiences on the path. In this sense he is eminently practical, wasting no time in distractions on the way.

Favorite Fantasies: Do you delight in deflating pompous people or ridiculing artificial conventions? Do you admire Monty Python, Mick Jagger, Bob Dylan, or a thousand other entertainers who spoof the establishment? The *tamasic* energy of the North Node of the Moon is better at destroying outmoded conventions and habits than creating new ones.

Key Idea for Education: Sometimes one must be a rebel in order to purify wrongs in the school system. The North Node of the Moon upholds difference and uniqueness, and destroys rigid or outmoded customs and conventions. However, the rebellion tends to be secretive. One simple way to exercise this principle is to do nothing when ordered to do something unjust—civil disobedience can be a nonviolent way to change society.

Divinatory Message: Be a rebel, but make sure it is for a useful cause. Take care that you only redress injustice and do not create it!

Relationship to Other Oracles: An outlaw lives in secrecy and seclusion. Separation from the mainstream lets him become a deeper outlaw in the sense that he grows stronger in his own uniqueness, rather than being shaped by societal norms. These qualities are seen in the Tarot's Four of Swords. Ardra also corresponds to the "Threefold Riddle," the twenty-fifth card of the Secret Dakini Oracle, which advises us to break through the subconscious, concealed part of our mind, where all our habituations and inculcations lay.

The twenty-sixth hexagram of the I-Ching, called "The Taming Power of the Great," also indicates the need for storing up one's creative powers through rest and quiet time, a key feature of *tamas*. It also points to the hidden treasures of the subconscious, which we discover by rebelling against the ego's desire to keep us ignorant of our higher Self. One who unlocks the vast power of the unconscious achieves "The Taming Power of the Great." Freud recognized that deep socially unacceptable instincts are buried in the subconscious. When we bring the light of awareness to them, we recover the huge power previously wasted in suppressing them. Then we can channel that energy to rectify wrongs in a just way.

27

5th Lunar Mansion (Punarvasu) —Renewal of Dharma

Traditional Name: The Star of Renewal

Planetary Rulership: *Tamasic* aspect of Jupiter

Creative Principle: The *tamasic* aspect of Jupiter, like every *tamasic* principle, implies rest and recuperation. Rest is the basis of activity, the time of renewal of all that has become deluded, distorted, or dilapidated. Punarvasu implies repeated return or restoration. Outmoded ideas, old buildings, old trees, old bodies, old stars, and even the whole universe must be periodically destroyed prior to renewal.

Tamas also implies destruction. Sleep is a *tamasic* state of mind-body, wherein waking awareness and activity are temporarily suspended in a period of quiet renewal.

Jupiter is nourishing, expansive, and socially oriented. Just as the disintegration of an old tree provides nourishment for younger ones, the disintegration of outmoded social conventions can nourish healthy new ones. For example, the dissolution of racial barriers frees people of different races to share common interests.

Two other symbols for this asterism are a quiver of arrows (a container of the instruments of destruction) and a bow, which turns a quiet arrow into a deadly missile.

The foundation of society is dharma—thought and action which uphold and uplift higher values in society. Jupiter, the significator of dharma, is generally associated with ethics, religion, and higher education. The *tamasic* aspect of Jupiter allows outmoded customs and conventions to die. For example, a strong dose of the Punarvasu principle might help India shake off two obviously outmoded customs—marriage dowries and the hereditary caste system.

The difference between this asterism and the previous one is great. On one hand, Jupiter acts in a very proper, respectful way; thus, the *tamasic* aspect of Jupiter, Punarvasu, reforms society by operating within its rules. On the other hand, the *tamasic* aspect of Rahu, Ardra, reforms society by breaking its rules. So Punarvasu tends to change from within without destroying the basic structure of institutions, while Ardra tends to change from without, rejecting the old structure entirely.

Favorite Fantasies: Do you maintain a healthy love and respect for institutions you want to change? Do you want to see outmoded conventions die with peace and dignity, not ridicule? Do you have a sense of service and generosity in your hopes of cultural reform? Do you dream of renewing ancient knowledge to its full glory? Then you have traits of Punarvasu, the asterism guiding revival of ancient wisdom and its institutions.

Key Idea for Education: The complex problems of modern education cry for fundamental renewal. In an age that is increasingly outward and object oriented, education must recognize that true knowledge comes from within. Schools need only draw this inner knowledge out of students, rather than impose it in ways that discourage or suppress inner fulfillment. When students are inundated with facts and techniques, and not encouraged to meditate or study the great spiritual traditions, they tend to suppress their own insights and inner experiences.

The men's movement in the West is largely an attempt to recover the universal rites of manhood which traditional societies used to usher in each stage of development. The initiation ceremonies themselves, the moral and religious preparation for them, and the coherent community spirit behind them are all Jupiterian significations. Spiritual feminism is similarly reawakening women's collective awareness of their spiritual strengths and the sisterly bonds.

Divinatory Message: Be prepared to fight any enemy of the truth in oneself or others. Some old beliefs, habits, or possessions must be destroyed in order to be renewed. This may include old moral standards and articles of faith which we have accepted without question, but which no longer serve a useful purpose. In contrast with the North Nodian outlaw approach to renewal in Ardra, Punarvasu achieves renewal in a very proper, socially respectable way.

Relationship to Other Oracles: Punarvasu corresponds to the twenty-sixth Secret Dakini card, "Mean and Heavy." The fearsome goddess Kali, protector of dharma, strides through the cosmos and destroys the enemies of truth and righteousness.

Punarvasu also corresponds to the Tarot's Five of Swords, which represents defeat and struggle. The lower meaning is the loss of something precious which formerly nourished us. The higher meaning is a fierce struggle to strip all unethical behavior from our lives in order to penetrate to higher spiritual planes of existence.

The twenty-seventh hexagram of the I-Ching, "The Corners of the Mouth (Providing Nourishment)," teaches us to choose our words carefully and be temperate in everything we do. These qualities are cultured in karma yoga, the path of selfless service ruled by Jupiter. (See Part II, Chapter 1, "The Eight Great Paths to God.") Care and temperance are Jupiterian expressions of *tamas* which purify and discipline. Although Jupiter is a *sattwic* planet, it has a *tamasic* aspect, as all planets do.

This hexagram implies that our greatest nourishment takes place through the *tamasic* qualities of rest and tranquility. Wilhelm says: "Words are a movement going from within outward. Eating and drinking are movements from without inward. Both kinds of movement can be modified by tranquillity. For tranquillity keeps the words that come out of the mouth from exceeding proper measure, and keeps the food that goes into the mouth from exceeding its proper measure. Thus character is cultivated." Character is dharma. What a perfect expression of the *tamasic* quality of Jupiter!

28
6th Lunar Mansion (Pushya)
—Simplicity and Discipline

Traditional Name: The Flourishing One

Planetary Rulership: *Tamasic* aspect of Saturn

Creative Principle: Saturn gives clear boundaries. We flourish when we have a clear purpose and a clear understanding of how to accomplish it. Saturn is more concerned with the means than the purpose. It simplifies our life by stripping away nonessentials and helping us focus on essentials. Saturn's power to strip away and set boundaries is most evident in its *tamasic* phase, called Pushya. The most obvious boundary of life is death. Hence our symbol of a gravestone with a clock to represent Pushya.

The ruling deity of Pushya is Brihaspati, the guru of the gods. A guru may discipline us and simplify our lives so that we do not waste time in distractions from our spiritual path. The arrow within the circle symbolizes this guidance and directionality.

We must stay focused on our path in order to flourish. The rational, step-by-step, "show me" attitude of Saturn rejects abstract specula-tion, emotionalism, and sensory distraction. But this cold, dry type of logic based on tangible evidence can become rigid and judg-mental. This is why the twenty-seventh card of Osho's *Neo-Tarot* says, "Judgement means a stale state of mind. And mind always wants judgment, because to be in process is always hazardous and uncomfortable. Be very, very courageous, don't stop growing, live in the moment, simply stay in the flow of life."

Favorite Fantasies: Are your dreams practical, down-to-earth, and rational? Do you disdain complexity, sentimentality, and fanciful speculation? Do you prefer a small, secure income to a potentially large but unpredictable one? Would you rather restore an old building than create a new one? Are you happiest when resting, physically and mentally? Pushya loves simplicity, stability, and tangible proof. This *tamasic* aspect of Saturn inclines one to act like an oldster, even when young.

Key Idea for Education: The cold, objective logic of Saturn is the bedrock of scientific reasoning and courtroom evidence. It gives clear, definitive boundaries in our thinking and activity. But this objective approach cannot rule all aspects of our life, or we dry up emotionally and spiritually, and turn into lonely, insensitive machines obsessed with the physical. So objective science and logic should not be taught without a subjective science. This is the main purpose of this book. Only a combined subjective and objective approach brings holistic education and fulfillment.

Divinatory Message: Try to clarify the means to reach your goals. Write down specific steps and a realistic timetable for achieving each one. Then stick to your plan, at least until you have a better one!

Relationship to Other Oracles: Pushya corresponds to the twenty-eighth hexagram of the I-Ching, "Preponderance of the Great," which lists many attributes of Saturn—standing alone, unconcerned, undaunted, and possibly renouncing the world. These qualities enable you to remain firm in your truth, unswayed by others' opinions.

The same concept of standing alone to see the world objectively is conveyed by the twenty-seventh Secret Dakini card, "Magic Carpet." The Tarot's Six of Swords also indicates success earned by hard labor and pragmatic thinking. It also indicates a journey, where guidance is needed. Whether this journey is pleasant or unpleasant depends on whether we use good judgment, or fall into judgmentalism.

29
7th Lunar Mansion (Ashlesha)
—Destroyer of False Identification

Traditional Name: The Clinging Star

Planetary Rulership: *Tamasic* aspect of Mercury

Creative Principle: Mercury, the ruler of this asterism, governs the intellect. Ashlesha represents the *tamasic* aspect of the intellect. It creates a deeply thoughtful and philosophical person with a tendency to austerity and reclusiveness. The lower use of such a *tamasic* intellect is hard, selfish, or venomous thinking. The higher use of this faculty is to penetrate deeply into the hidden aspects of life, just as snakes penetrate narrow holes and secret places inaccessible to others.

People ruled by this asterism can use the intellect to correct mistaken ideas, eliminating any untruth or distortions. As this is the *tamasic* intellect, it has more of a destructive than creative effect. Since this destructive power of the intellect can cause discomfort, this asterism also relates to poison, torment, burning, or pain. When one's most cherished beliefs are destroyed by such use of the intellect, one may experience torment. However, this torment lasts only until deeper truths are recognized and embraced.

A strong *tamasic* intellect grabs hold of a subject and does not let go until it is fully understood, like a boa constrictor that progressively tightens his grasp on his prey until it can be swallowed whole.

Mercury is also the planet of transcendence, which relates to the fundamental question, "Who am I?" In gyana yoga, the spiritual path of the intellect, one uses this *tamasic* aspect of the intellect to eliminate misidentifications. "Neti, neti" is the Sanskrit expression meaning "Not this, not this—I am not the body, I am not the breath, I am not the mind...." The finite attachments of one's smaller self are destroyed, and the infinite nature of one's higher Self remains.

Favorite Fantasies: Do you like to look at your own thoughts and feelings as if they belong to someone else? Do you see yourself and others as mere actors on the stage of life, while you maintain the dispassion of a spectator? These are useful techniques of knowledge which a person influenced by Ashlesha may practice spontaneously.

This asterism, like the previous one, does not fantasize much. But unlike the plodding, conservative Pushya, Ashlesha is quick and playful like his ruler, Mercury. Being *tamasic*, his play is likely to be traditional—do you enjoy classical music, drama, or literature? If you fantasize about improvising like J. S. Bach, or see yourself trading barbs with Shakespeare, you may have an Ashlesha streak.

Key Idea in Education: Give students the opportunity to question or even destroy your precious paradigms. And give them the opportunity to question each others' opinions, particularly after the age of fourteen, when the intellect becomes a strong force in the personality. Mercury is the teacher, and no great teacher feels threatened by different beliefs and ideas.

People identify with their beliefs to such an extent that more wars have been fought in the name of religion than for any other cause. Gyana yoga is the process of separating feelings from beliefs. However, very few people can dispassionately witness an attack on their deepest beliefs. Questioning must therefore be polite and respectful of people's feelings. Mercury is humorous, adaptable, and clever with words—use these skills to communicate in a truthful but nonthreatening way.

Divinatory Message: See if there is some assumption in the problem at hand that needs to be modified or destroyed. Try to start with a clean slate of understanding. Reexamine your assumptions and start over.

Relationship to Other Oracles: The twenty-ninth hexagram of the I-Ching, "The Abysmal (Water)," shows us how to teach without being thrown off our center. In other words, how to stay grounded in the Self. "Abysmal (Water)" is a symbol for the emotional turmoil that can ensue from stripping away beliefs we have clung to. Such a process increases self-acceptance and eventually leads to transcendence.

This inner awakening is described in the twenty-eighth Secret Dakini Oracle, the "Cosmic Carrot." The carrot contains the chakras, or spiritual centers along the spine. Spiritual development on any path awakens the chakras.

The Tarot's Seven of Swords suggests ways of intellectually destroying ephemeral relationships and ideas which keep us from true Self-understanding. Loss of material possessions and relationships often helps us let go of cherished beliefs and thereby find deeper sources of satisfaction. Ashlesha collects the scattered, many-pointed attention into a focused, one-pointed mind.

30
8th Lunar Mansion (Magha)
—The Heritage of Sacrifice

Traditional Name: The Glorious One

Planetary Rulership: *Tamasic* aspect of Ketu

Creative Principle: This asterism is ruled by Ketu, the South Node of the Moon. The *tamasic* aspect of Ketu always points to the past. So this nakshatra suggests the importance of gratitude to our ancestors and past benefactors.

Gratitude to ancestors is a form of surrender to the Divine Will. When we fully recognize our debt to our ancestors, tidal waves of love and gratitude fill our hearts and prepare us for further gifts. Surrender to ancestors prepares us for surrender to the Divine. Magha always brings the potential for divine gifts.

Our ancestors need our help and we need theirs. We promote our own progress and happiness when we pray for departed family members, as they invariably appreciate any blessings from this dense earth-sphere and return the blessings manyfold. However, our ancestors only bless us when we honor them. Although reverence for ancestors may seem strange in modern Western culture, it is a natural emotion when we understand the sacrifices our predecessors have made and continue to make to help us evolve in human form, especially in a society where we are free to pursue our own spiritual interests.

Ketu cuts through barriers, often in a dramatic, thunderbolt way. The biggest barriers to spiritual progress are attachments, whether material attachments like power and indulgence of the senses, or nonmaterial ones, such as clinging to gurus and ancestors. Magha enables us to let go of both kinds of attachments. We recognize our great debt to ancestors and teachers, while freeing ourselves of outmoded beliefs and lifestyles.

The traditional symbol of Magha, a palanquin, represents the contributions of the past which support the present and carry us into the future. Whether we know it or not, we are all kings and queens in our transcendent spiritual essence, whether cloaked as royalty or paupers.

Favorite Fantasies: Do you dream of private, respectful conversations with departed members of your family or spiritual heritage? Do you enjoy a sense of surrender to a great teacher like Christ, Buddha, or Shankara? Do you long for quiet time to study great figures in history? Magha is shy and secretive, so even if you have this reverence for the past, you may not want to talk about it.

Key Idea for Education: The study of great men and women is an important part of any profound educational system. Every tradition offers great historical figures to inspire students. Likewise, home life should instill deep knowledge and respect for one's own family. People who have no awareness of their cultural and family traditions suffer a deep sense of rootlessness and isolation. Those who know and revere their traditions feel connected to and supported by the immeasurable power of those traditions.

Divinatory Message: Call upon your ancestors, or the knowledge and values they held, to guide you in your present situation.

Relationship to Other Oracles: The thirtieth hexagram of the I-Ching, "The Clinging, Fire," teaches us to accept the conditions and limitations of the past. "Human life on earth is conditioned and unfree, and when man recognizes this limitation and makes himself dependent upon the harmonious and beneficent forces of the cosmos, he achieves success." (Wilhelm) This voluntary and joyous surrender to the Almighty power of Nature is the highest application of the *tamasic* aspect of Ketu.

The twenty-ninth Secret Dakini card, "Self-Preservation," shows an Egyptian mummy, which preserves the past as completely as possible. This card indicates the need for cherishing one's ancestors in order to progress in the direction of immortality. Ancient peoples who buried their dead rather than cremating them tried to protect and cherish the burial sites as a means of helping them in the afterlife and gaining their support. Non-Indians in the U.S. generally do not appreciate the importance native Americans attach to their burial sites, resulting in great injury to the natives' feelings over desecration of these sites.

Like the I-Ching's hexagram, the Tarot's Eight of Swords emphasizes restrictions, limitations, and dependencies created by our past, which we must learn to accept and use constructively. Sometimes the past limitations may seem heavy and overpowering, but the *tamasic* power of Ketu gives us the courage to surrender to the beneficent values of the past and discard the outmoded ones.

31
9th Lunar Mansion (Purva Phalguni) —Control of the Senses

Traditional Name: The Lucky One

Planetary Rulership: *Tamasic* aspect of Venus

Creative Principle: The *tamas* power of Venus gives discipline and control of the senses. Like many *tamasic* lessons, this discipline may seem like a loss at first. But as we grow in nonattachment, we learn to enjoy life much more!

This asterism may suggest that one has been lost in sensory pleasures, such as excess sexual passion, food addictions, and other attempts to overstimulate the senses. If you have been lost in sensory delights, Purva Phalguni can help you regain balance through sensory restraint and rest. A period of abstinence or dietary control may be the key to greater joy, a joy based on self-discovery and equanimity rather than sensory excitation. Keeping still within (resting in the hammock) prepares us for greater pleasures later.

Generally speaking, people under the influence of this asterism have the ability to control their passions, but also know how to enjoy the senses in moderation.

Favorite Fantasies: Do you feel scattered by too many sensory distractions, and just want to rest and collect your energies? Do you fantasize about past sensory pleasures, which you now idealize? Do you thrill to the romance of *Gone with the Wind* or *Romeo and Juliet* but wish they had a happy ending? Do you dream of dancing like Ginger Rogers and Fred Astaire? Purva Phalguni's tendency to idealize sensory pleasures comes from Venus, and its desire to revive the past reflects the *tamasic* principle of rest.

Key Idea for Education: Children today spend more time in front of a television than in class. Excess TV, movies, pop music, and even sporting events tend to overstimulate the senses and leave one feeling scattered and exhausted. There are uplifting examples in all the media, but they tend to be as rare as nutritious food in a candy store. This archetype suggests being more selective in the pleasures we pursue and resting the senses periodically.

Divinatory Message: Rest the senses and become centered within. Raj yoga is especially valuable to turn the senses inward in an effortless manner. Whether you are living the joy that comes from mastery of the senses, or suffering the frustration of uncontrolled desires, you are a "lucky one," as either way you will gain inner fulfillment by turning away from sensory pleasure.

Relationship to Other Oracles: Wilhelm captures the spirit of Purva Phalguni perfectly in his commentary on the thirty-first hexagram of the I-Ching, called "Influence (Wooing)." He relates it to the pleasures of courtship, marriage, and the mutual attraction between the sexes (all Venusian significations). "By keeping still within while experiencing joy without, one can prevent the joy from going to excess and hold it within proper bounds."

The thirtieth Secret Dakini card, "Castles in the Clouds," shows how our hopes and aspirations (Venusian significations symbolized by the high castles) may be obscured by fleeting pleasures (the clouds). The easiest way to master the senses is to keep focused on one's highest spiritual goal.

The Nine of Swords in Tarot points to the suffering and pain which can come from a life of uncontrolled sensory indulgence, and the value of a sensitive conscience to alert us whenever we are tempted to overindulge. This card also warns against the opposite type of sensory extremism: complete asceticism. The pleasures of Purva Phalguni are not to be lost in harsh denial of the senses. We are meant to be masters of the senses, not their slaves.

32
Pure Tamas:
The Old as a Basis for the New

Creative Principle: The *tamasic* nakshatras relate to destruction, trouble, misfortune, sickness, and death—the purificatory and transformative powers of nature. They also relate to rest, relaxation, and recovery, the descending phase after every wave which prepares for the next wave of activity. We must remember that nothing essential is ever destroyed, no matter how it may be transformed in appearance.

Thousands of years before the science of genetics, ancient peoples saw that an entire tree is contained in a single seed. The seed represents the *tamasic* principle, where the essential blueprint of a new tree can rest for years before the creative principle (*rajas*) provides the energy to sprout. Thus, *tamas* depends on *rajas*, and vice-versa, while *sattwa* maintains the balance between the other two. In this sense, none of the three *gunas* is good or bad. They are equal partners in weaving the web of life.

The way to enjoy this eternal dance of the *gunas* is to step outside their endless circle, to transcend all activity and rest in the perfect equilibrium of the Self, what Maharishi Mahesh Yogi calls the state of least excitation of consciousness. This is what Lord Krishna tells Arjuna in the *Bhagavad Gita*, "Be without the three *gunas*" (II. 45).

That is, transcend. Then, established in equanimity, perform dharmic (righteous) action (II. 48).

Favorite Fantasies: Do you dream of retirement, a time of taking it easy and enjoying the fruits of your life's labors? Do you enjoy late Fall, after the harvest, and Winter, before Nature wakes up in the Spring? Does a misfortune, such as the loss of a home, car, or job, lead to an aftertaste of sweetness because it completes a phase of your life and allows a fresh new beginning? Do you give thanks for all the blessings you have received, ever grateful for all the people who have helped you? These are all positive reflections of *tamas*.

Are you attached to the past and resistant to change? For example, do you yearn for a long-lost lover? Are you stuck in destructive habits? Do you resent people who challenge your old beliefs? Do you suffer from guilt and remorse? As with any of the archetypes, it is not necessary to try to substitute another archetype for one which is weak. Don't try to be anyone but yourself, just be more of what you naturally are. That means recognize your archetypes, strong and weak, and work on transforming the weak ones into strengths. If you feel negative *tamasic* emotions like guilt, remorse, and attachment to the past, work on developing forgiveness, thankfulness and nonattachment—forgiveness for mistakes, thankfulness for blessings, and nonattachment to your status quo.

Key Idea for Education: Each phase of development must be completed before the next one starts. A student must master algebra and trigonometry before tackling calculus. Similarly, in emotional and moral development there is a natural sequence of phases of growth. A preverbal infant develops an abstract sense of self not dependent on language. When children start to speak, they first refer to themselves in the third person, "Baby is hungry," etc. Only later do they refer to themselves in the first person. If language training and reading and writing skills are imposed too early, the child's sense of self and his ability for nonverbal thinking never fully develop. For further research on the natural phases of education, we strongly recommend Rudolph Steiner's books on the Waldorf school system which he founded.

Divinatory Meaning: There are two messages here: First, complete any tasks currently in process, otherwise the seed for new growth will not ripen. Second, be comfortable in loss, realizing that all things must pass, and that loss is the necessary precursor to renewal.

Relationship to Other Oracles: The thirty-second hexagram of the I-Ching is called "Duration," the culmination of a cycle. "The end is reached by an inward movement, by inhalation, systole, contraction, and this movement turns into a new beginning, in which the movement is directed outward, in exhalation, diastole, expansion" (Wilhelm). The thirty-first Secret Dakini card is "Just Passing Through," indicating that everything is transitory and must come to an end. The Tarot's Ten of Swords also points to an end and hopes for a new beginning.

33
10th Lunar Mansion (Uttara Phalguni): Dynamic Leadership

Traditional Name: The Star of the Patron

Planetary Rulership: Rajasic aspect of the Sun

Creative Principle: This star signifies the ability to deal with problems in a comprehensive, dynamic, and forceful way. Rajas is the creative force, and the creative solar person has the capacity and desire to act as the patron to all who come for help. Like a generous king, the patron may offer help in many ways. He is a born leader, and excels at integrating diverse forces, like a king who manages the different functions of his realm. He is confident in his strength and righteous in his mission. If not inwardly strong, he may be outwardly overambitious, showy, or hungry for publicity.

The great leader has the ability to engage in dynamic, creative activity while maintaining a calm center of rest within—thus the castle surrounded by a ring of fire. Uttara Phalguni, the *rajasic* aspect of the Sun, is more active, innovative, and excited by conquest than Krittika, the *tamasic* aspect of Sun, who is more interested in eliminating outmoded programs than creating new ones.

Favorite Fantasies: Do you dream of being a dynamic leader, managing myriad minions from your center of power and prestige?

Do you want to expand your empire, without worrying about holding onto present holdings? Do you suffocate in anonymity, and yearn for public acclaim and political power? Uttara Phalguni thrives in the expansion of power and glory, and wastes away in passive or servile roles.

Key Idea for Education: Be a leader, be self-sufficient. Don't just passively accept the political, social, and spiritual order in your school. Be active in creating the kind of order you want, but with an eye toward others' needs, rather than self-promotion.

Divinatory Message: Take an active leadership role in the resolution of your problem. Don't wait for others to take the lead. Plan your action to integrate all the necessary resources and balance the needs of everyone involved, then step forward as boldly as a king to carry out your plan. However, do not get sucked into excess egotism or obsession with power. A runaway *rajasic* Sun principle can develop into the autocratic tendencies of a Mussolini.

Relationship to Other Oracles: The thirty-second Secret Dakini card is "Shiva, Pillar of Fire." The pillar has a double signification. First, it is the quality of leadership that integrates the different powers of nature. Second, it is the Shiva lingam, the inexhaustible Self-created seed of creation, pure creativity itself in the form of a phallus.

The thirty-third hexagram of the I-Ching, "Retreat," carries two main meanings. First, the leader's need to stay centered in the midst of dynamic activity. Second, the knowledge of when to retreat, rather than press forward. This is the antidote to an overly *rajasic* Sun, which is so aggressive and domineering that it tramples others and ignores warning signs in its desire to shine in public.

The Tarot's Ace of Wands is also symbolized by a solar phallic symbol. The phallus represents pure creativity and the dynamic beginning of new enterprises. It is birth, creation, initiative, and impulse—powers stemming from the *rajasic* principle of the Sun.

34
11th Lunar Mansion (Hasta)
—Love in Action

Traditional Name: The Hand of Blessing

Planetary Rulership: Rajasic aspect of the Moon

Creative Principle: "Hasta" means "hand." It is the comforting hand that either heals or rules through the *rajasic* principle of the Moon, love in action. A mother's gentle and caring hands nurture her children. Mothering is an archetypal expression of the *rajasic* power of the Moon. Mothers throughout the world often overcome a lack of training in medicine and child rearing through an intuitive awareness of the children's needs and their own power to heal through love. Mothers also know how to take things into their own hands. If you love something enough, you can intuitively sense what is needed to help it, and have the energy to do so. Mothers have been known to perform seemingly impossible feats of strength, like lifting a car off their child, simply through the power of love.

This nakshatra also indicates the ability to use one's hands in many creative ways, whether handicrafts, handwriting, or hands-on healing. The hand is also a symbol of power. Hasta represents the power of love to overcome obstacles with gentleness, compassion, and receptivity.

The controlling power of Hasta can be a danger as well as a blessing if love becomes attachment, or the power to lead with love and gentleness turns into a desire to control others' behavior. If love is tainted with selfishness or has strings attached, it can turn into cruelty, characteristic of a weak or afflicted Moon.

Favorite Fantasies: Do you dream of becoming a mother, sheltering battered women, or starting an orphanage or hospice? These are positive potentials of the dynamic Hasta. She is Mother Theresa, helping the destitute and dying in the streets of Calcutta. She is Florence Nightingale, nurturing the sick and wounded. She is Mata Amritanandamayi (Amacchi), comforting hundreds of strangers every day as if they were her long-lost and absolutely precious children.

Do you try to control your family to satisfy your own emotional needs, oblivious to their needs? That's the negative potential of a weak Hasta. The common features of both positive and negative aspects of Hasta are the emotionality of the Moon and the dynamism of *rajas*.

Key Idea for Education: The enlightened educator, like the enlightened parent, rules through love, not force. Love heals all wounds and turns enemies into friends. A proper education nourishes students' delicate feelings and makes them sensitive to their fellow students. To avoid damaging students' self-esteem, competition must be balanced with cooperation. Everyone needs to feel needed, to be nourished in an environment of acceptance and appreciation (lunar qualities). The *rajasic* principle of the Moon suggests putting love into action.

Divinatory Message: Try to use the healing power of love to overcome obstacles. Use your intuition and sensitivity to help someone, especially a close family member.

Relationship to Other Oracles: The thirty-fourth hexagram of the I-Ching is called "The Power of the Great." "The hexagram points to a time when inner worth mounts with great force and comes to power." This power is so great there is danger of violating what is right. A mother has total power over her small children. The safeguard against misuse of power is the tenderness and active caring of Hasta.

The Tarot's Two of Wands also speaks of the proper use of dominion, or power. The thirty-third Secret Dakini card, "Eternal Life," focuses on the need to grasp eternal life in one's hand. The picture shows an ancient Egyptian God, Amen, firmly holding an ankh, a mystic looped cross symbolic of eternal life. It is the triumph of light over darkness through the power of love.

35
12th Lunar Mansion (Chitra)
—Courage and Passion for Adventure

Traditional Name: The Wonderful

Planetary Rulership: Rajasic aspect of Mars

Creative Principle: Chitra is the *rajasic* aspect of Mars, which indicates that striving for any great achievement (a gem) requires courage, inspiration, strength of will, and a willingness to take risks—all qualities of Mars. It also requires the strength of character to begin to carry out the enterprise in a strong and purposeful way.

This asterism has other significations. First, it gives precision in both planning and execution, and is therefore associated with technical achievements, such as construction, machinery, and, especially, tools of war, all ruled by Mars. Secondly, Chitra gives a passion, drive, and forcefulness, particularly sexual passion.

Favorite Fantasies: Chitra is the number one box-office hit of this age. He is Luke Skywalker, Rambo, the Terminator, Superman, the Incredible Hulk, and a thousand other fearless warriors of the screen. He is Joe Namath and Michael Jordan, superathletes who became invincible under pressure. He is George Patton and Douglas MacArthur, who lived to fight for their country. As the *rajasic* aspect of Mars, he is the most active and aggressive manifestation of the warrior-adventurer. So if you dream of scoring the winning touchdown, beating up thugs, or commanding your troops in battle, you dream with Chitra.

Key Idea for Education: Children need the challenge of applying their knowledge in truly creative ways. If schoolwork is purely theoretical and disconnected from students' life experience, students become frustrated. Their instinctive passions may turn outward to antisocial conduct, or inward to self-destructive tendencies. Because such challenges tend to be uniquely individual, teachers need to encourage each student to define personal goals to stretch the student's level of achievement.

The warrior/athlete/adventurer aspect of Mars is so overplayed in our culture that it's easy for students to lose sight of other constructive channels for Mars energy, such as engineering, mechanics, and construction of any sort. Encourage science projects and construction of buildings, cars, rockets, etc. Wilderness adventure programs such as the Outward Bound School are another great outlet for this energy.

Divinatory Message: Exercise courage, discipline, enterprise, and passion in achieving your objective. Weigh the risks like a general assessing a battle plan, then plunge ahead with strength and vigor.

Relationship to Other Oracles: This principle is the "Burning Bush: Lineage Tree," the thirty-fourth card of the Secret Dakini Oracle. The significations center around fiery, passionate, and technically demanding spiritual practices—all characteristic of Laya Yoga, the path of Mars, the spiritual adventurer's way to illumination. The thirty-fifth hexagram of the I-Ching, "Progress," emphasizes the rapid progress possible when one moves with confidence, enthusiasm, and purposefulness. The Three of Wands of the Tarot indicates someone beginning an enterprise with a creative perspective, using effort and strength to carry through the project.

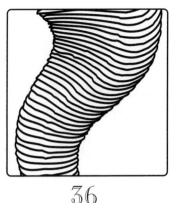

36
13th Lunar Mansion (Swati)— Independence and Innovation

Traditional Name: The Self-Going

Planetary Rulership: Rajasic aspect of Rahu, the North Node of the Moon

Creative Principle: This asterism represents dynamic movement impelled by rebellious desire. It is freedom-loving, independent, self-loving, and self-reliant. Such a person moves constantly, as if blown by the wind. Movement is a basic expression of *rajas*, and Swati is especially vigorous and active.

Swati expresses Rahu's intense love for freedom and discontent with confinement, convention, and conformity. He reacts to restriction in a creative, *rajasic* way. A *tamasic* Rahu (Ardra) passively resists intrusion and restriction, but the *rajasic* power of Rahu (Swati) actively rebels against anything that limits its individuality or freedom. However, since Rahu is a shadow planet, its rebellion is often underground or secret. Both the Nodes are experts in concealing their motives!

Favorite Fantasies: Are you audacious and outrageous? Do you want to drop your clothes in public, like Madonna, or use foul language for the shock effect? For an unevolved Swati, nothing is sacred, and authority is an invitation for rebellion. Gangsters, terrorists, and anarchists often express a crude form of this *rajasic* nature of the North Node of the Moon. However, a highly developed form of this archetype could be expressed in a way that benefits others. Thus the great tantric teacher Osho (Bhagavan Shree Rajneesh) mocked the phoniness of conventional religions, but only to reveal deep spiritual truths.

Key Idea for Education: The student rebellions of the sixties are an example of Swati energy, with both its positive and negative connotations. To avoid disruptive rebellions, educators must honor difference and let go of outmoded conventions. The way to assuage an agitated *rajasic* North Nodian is to recognize and rectify the hypocrisy or wrongs he is rebelling against. Don't be a Robert McNamara, Secretary of Defense during the Vietnam War, who waited twenty-five years before publicly acknowledging U.S. mistakes in that war. (In fairness to McNamara, we should mention that many of his peers, including Presidents Nixon and Johnson, never stopped defending their Vietnam fiasco.)

Divinatory Message: Your solution lies in rebelling against hypocrisy or falseness, and independently exploring better alternatives. Take care to focus on the good you can create, rather than the bad you want to destroy.

Relationship to Other Oracles: The Tarot's Four of Wands is best described by Alfred Douglas, who suggests that this card indicates decadence, or the qualities of an effete civilization which needs rectification. He also discusses the need for individualized approaches to living through culture and the arts.

The thirty-sixth hexagram of the I-Ching, "Darkening of the Light," says an active rebel must sometimes hide his inner light and remain outwardly yielding and tractable while secretly rebellious. The Chinese name of this hexagram literally means "the wounding of the bright," a perfect description of how the Nodes eclipse the luminaries (Sun and Moon). A *rajasic* Rahu often wounds the powerful.

What better description of a *rajasic* Rahu than the thirty-fifth Secret Dakini card, "As Above, So Below"? In the foreground is the flower of individuality. The lower background is a volcanic eruption—lava scourging the earth is a perfect expression of Rahu's intensely rebellious energy.

37
14th Lunar Mansion (Vishakha)
—the Sacrament of Self-Sacrifice

Traditional Name: The Star of Purpose

Planetary Rulership: Rajasic aspect of Jupiter

Creative Principle: This nakshatra indicates worship through action. The action may be a quiet, prayerful ritual, or dynamic service to family, school, nation, or God.

Since Vishakha's action is *rajasic*, it may be tainted with desire. There is danger of getting lost in the finite goal, forgetting the infinite goal, and hurting others in the haste to achieve one's purpose.

Ritual offerings, especially fire sacrifices, exemplify this creative, sacrificial energy of Jupiter, the lord of sacrifice and ritual. The habit of ritualistic offerings to God cultivates the sense of service in mundane action and helps keep us from getting lost in selfish little desires.

People with a strong *rajasic* Jupiterian energy know just the right means for accomplishing their ends, and they approach action in a sacrificial manner by surrendering it to the Divine.

Favorite Fantasies: Do you dream of building a glorious church, temple, or university building? Do you want to leave a legacy for future generations? Service to family, community, and religion are expressions of Jupiter's noble side, and the *rajasic* aspect of Jupiter means dynamic, creative action toward such ends. Vishakha, however, is not a dreamy altruist. He overcomes all obstacles in his quest for social upliftment, but if not fully developed, he can be ruthless in his fervor. The Crusades and Inquisition are sad examples of such untempered religious zeal.

Key Idea for Education: Children need to learn how to frame their goals and objectives within a larger context. In religious settings, that purpose can be using all actions as offerings to God. In secular settings, that purpose could be service to family elders or educational and historical institutions.

Divinatory Message: Review all your goals and place them in the context of sacrifice to the Divine. Although this is a total sacrifice, it is a balanced one, a subordination of small personal goals to broader transpersonal ones. It is not a call for martyrdom that denies your own individual worth. Such expanded vision actually enhances your individuality. Desires are normal and are to be honored, but put in the context of higher purpose. When we offer all our actions to God, we become reconnected to our Source and freed from identification with our actions and attachment to its fruits.

In the Vedic tradition there are four goals for house-holders: *kama* (sensory enjoyment), *artha* (career success and wealth), *dharma* (contribution to society and religion), and *moksha* (liberation). Spiritual development *(moksha)* is the most important. The others are designed to support spiritual development. Physical, mental and even financial health are great assets in the pursuit of enlightenment.

Relationship to Other Oracles: The thirty-seventh hexagram of the I-Ching, "The Family (the Clan)," focuses on another signification of Jupiter, the conscious emotions. We must not let the emotions which stem from relationships (the family) rule us. Unless we learn to master emotions, we are prone to hurt others in the pursuit of our own goals. In fact, a *rajasic* Jupiter indicates this very tendency to let emotions color our goals and motivate our actions out of self-interest, rather than sacrifice. The best way to master *rajasic* emotions like lust and anger is to offer them to God. Instead of venting them in a way that will hurt someone, direct the same passion into a work of service where your egotistical impulses are subordinated to helping others.

This principle is the "Guardian" of the Secret Dakini Oracle. The image is the fiery (*rajasic*) face of Mahakala, Great Time, who protects seekers and initiates them into the higher mysteries, a Jupiterian signification. It burns the illusion that there is an individual "I" who controls his own actions and deserves the fruits thereof.

According to A. E. Thierens, the Tarot's Five of Wands indicates self-centered action, taking no notice of others. Some commentators infer quarreling and fighting, which result from identification with a goal. Still other commentators point to more positive aspects of this asterism, such as focusing on plans, strategies, and the means to achieve them. In summary, some commentators show the lower aspect of Vishakha, and some the higher aspect. The majority address the concepts of goals and purpose, and either sacrifice to higher principles, or the opposite—suffering as a result of a selfish, narrow vision.

38
15th Lunar Mansion (Anuradha)
—Detail, Discipline, and Self-Denial

Traditional Meaning: The Star Calling to Activity

Planetary Rulership: Rajasic aspect of Saturn

Creative Principle: Anuradha indicates disciplined physical activity, especially the spiritual application of physical purification, such as fasting, hatha yoga, and Tai-Chi, or just long periods of silence and solitude. It also governs the field of law, which binds people to their promises.

What do legal matters and the physical purification have in common? They are both defined by Saturn, which governs boundaries and objective, logical thinking based on tangible evidence. So Anuradha indicates the need for boundaries on the path to freedom. The faster you drive, the more careful you must be about staying on the road.

Saturn loves silence, and the *rajasic* aspect of Saturn expresses silence in activity. Saturnine activities are simple, repetitive, mechanical, plodding, and servant-like—all within well-defined boundaries. Saturn excels at cleaning up. That is why this nakshatra is often associated with excrement, a by-product of bodily cleansing.

Saturn rules hermits and renunciates, people who simplify life to the maximum and spend long periods in total silence. Saturn is also related to obstacles. The *rajasic* aspect of Saturn overcomes obstacles with slow, plodding persistence, wearing them away over time. Anuradha means finished or completed. It finishes projects through perseverance and attention to detail.

Some authors relate Anuradha to friendship, allies, and coworkers. This is a misunderstanding, unless we consider infinite silence as our greatest friend. Saturn loves solitude, not the complexity of social interactions.

Favorite Fantasies: Do you dream of climbing mountains or taking long solo journeys to remote lands? Do you want to expand your ranch, not for the pride or money, but the sense of privacy and security? If you have the determination to finish detailed physical, logical, or legal endeavors, you express this *rajasic* aspect of Saturn.

Key Idea for Education: Children need both love and discipline. A potter needs two hands to make a pot. The hand of love expands the pot from within, while the hand of gentle discipline shapes the pot from without.

Saturn governs legal process. Although the U.S. legal system is one of the strongest in the world, it has certain weaknesses which tend to tie the educators' hands. Touch a child with tenderness and affection, and risk accusations of child molestation. Touch a child in discipline, and risk accusations of violence or discrimination. The real problem here is a social malaise which both abuses children and overreacts to any accusations of abuse. Educators need clear guidelines (a Saturn signification) on the limits of acceptable behavior, both in display of affection, and in the exercise of discipline. Then they need the freedom to address each child's needs within those guidelines.

Divinatory Message: Simplify your life! Eliminate all nonessential activities, and focus on simple, practical, down-to-earth procedures.

This may mean cutting the budget, socializing less, eating less, or cutting out frivolous or time-wasting activities.

Relationship to Other Oracles: The thirty-eighth hexagram of the I-Ching, "Opposition," relates to the value of boundaries and obstacles as teachers. The Tarot's Six of Wands also points to opposition and how it can either defeat us or strengthen us. The thirty-seventh Dakini card, "Fire of Sacrifice," also expresses the need for disciplining body, speech, and mind, and the need for renunciation as a tool for successful activity. Please note that the higher sense of "renunciation" is action performed in silence, free of attachment. It does not mean permanent renunciation of action, although periods of retirement and solitude are useful on the path of Saturn.

39
16th Lunar Mansion (Jyestha)
—Illumination Through Discrimination

Traditional Name: The Chief One

Planetary Rulership: Rajasic aspect of Mercury

Creative Principle: Jyestha, like Lord Vishnu's divine discus in many great Hindu myths, destroys ignorance and falsehood and clears the way to full illumination. It is the power of the intellect to cut through obstruction, especially lack of verbal clarity and other barriers to communication. Any obstruction, whether intellectual, emotional, or physical, can help to throw the awareness back on itself in the Self-referral of transcendence.

Mercury is the great synthesizer, integrating disparate pieces of knowledge into a coherent whole. Jyestha is ruled by Indra, Lord of the Devas, who has unlimited power, and who is governed only by himself. In this case the power of Indra is the power of the intellect to make profound decisions and communicate them in a clear, unambiguous manner. A clear intellect expresses its power in organizing and synthesizing all the different factors in a complex decision, and expressing that decision to others.

The danger of Jyestha is disclosing truths before people are ready to hear them. Premature teachings can harm the listener, even if offered with good intentions. This is why Lord Krishna, an incarnation of Vishnu, tells Arjuna in the *Bhagavad Gita,* "The wise do not delude the ignorant (with knowledge they cannot understand)." If you are bothered by a friend's negative habits and criticize him without invitation, there is little chance that he will change his habits, but great likelihood that you will hurt his feelings. If his heart is crushed, the harm is much greater than any potential benefit from making him aware of the deficiencies.

This principle applies to all teachings in gyana yoga, the spiritual path ruled by Mercury. The gyani helps you destroy illusory beliefs that hide your infinite Self. But the wise master only offers knowledge when the student is ready to appreciate it. Someone who does not want to understand himself will only resist the truth and become inwardly defensive, even if outwardly cooperative.

Favorite Fantasies: Do you dream of solving the ancient riddles of metaphysics and philosophy? Want to cut through life's illusions with your intellect? Those are spiritual aspirations related to the *rajasic* aspect of Mercury. Do you ache to write the Great American Novel, rival Shakespeare in verse, or titillate your cybercomrades with clever quips on the Internet? If so, you express the more mundane side of Jyestha.

Key Idea in Education: Students need to respect others' sensitivities and not confront them harshly in the name of truth. We see this basic principle of respect violated in many of the popular talk shows on TV, where the moderator frequently triggers an emotional confrontation of opinions, with no room for deeply intelligent answers.

Divinatory Message: The key to solving the problem is better communication, or clearer expression of the problem and alternative solutions. Exercise strength and confidence to make an intelligent decision.

Relationship to Other Oracles: When we face "Obstructions," the thirty-ninth hexagram of the I-Ching, we must put ourselves under the leadership of a great man (Indra) to overcome the obstacles. Here the great man is the intellect, either our own or that of a wise adviser.

"Amusement," the thirty-eighth Secret Dakini card, teaches us that awareness of the power of desire is the key to overcoming attachment to desire. When we refine desire and eventually transcend it, we gain equanimity in pleasure and pain, loss and gain. This process of transcendence clears obstructions, both physiological and conceptual. "Amusement" also refers to the Mercurial power of humor to transcend barriers to understanding.

The Tarot's Seven of Wands teaches the importance of good communication and skillful exchange of ideas in making decisions. Thus it also refers to the *rajasic* nature of Mercury.

40
17th Lunar Mansion (Moola)
—"Let Go and Let God"

Traditional Name: The Root One

Planetary Rulership: *Rajasic* aspect of Ketu

Creative Principle: *Moola* means "root," and this asterism refers to the foundation or root of things. In the highest sense it leads us to our spiritual source in an objective way. Just as roots sustain the visible aspects of a plant from beneath the ground, the inner life represented by Moola nourishes and anchors the outer aspects of life while remaining unseen and unheard.

Ketu, the South Node of the Moon, is generally associated with death and transfiguration. In the spiritual life we must let old beliefs and habits die, and even let go of our most sublime experiences. For example, in cosmic consciousness we experience unbounded Self-awareness, but ordinary sensory awareness. Our infinite subjectivity contrasts with finite perception of objectivity. Ketu lets us surrender our unbounded inner bliss to penetrate to the roots of objectivity. Our perception is refined until we see all life as a celestial dance and play. Our hearts expand in vast tidal waves of love, and everything we perceive becomes intensely personal and intimate. This requires death of the expanded ego of cosmic consciousness, and rebirth in the celestial awareness of God-consciousness. As many saints have said, one goes through a dark night of the soul in order to experience the Divine Life, where there is no separation between the lover and the beloved.

Ketu sweeps away anything that keeps us from surrendering to God, all things that bind us to material life—any intellectual, emotional, or material attachments that keep us from complete surrender. In cosmic consciousness we experience unbounded subjectivity, but have not fully developed our perception through the senses. Ketu gives the ability to surrender, and thereby opens us to the far greater glory of God consciousness.

Moola reminds us that in time all material needs and attachments will be cut away through the power of Divine Grace. Sometimes the *rajasic* power of this grace, like the Hindu Goddess Kali, may frighten us unless we realize that our loss is a blessing in disguise. Just as a surgeon removes a gangrenous leg to save a life, so the Divine cuts off precious attachments to save our spirit. Like all the cards related to Ketu, this one is inauspicious for material endeavors and auspicious for spiritual ones.

One way to experience the transformation power of Ketu is a style of meditation found in many in cultures: Sit still and breathe in all the world's negativity and suffering, and breathe out the same energy transformed to joy and bliss. Breathe fully and freely in this way, then note how your perceptions change after meditation. This is Ketu's power—to transform negativity into positivity and purify the perception.

Favorite Fantasies: Have you ever lost something you thought you needed, then realized you neither wanted nor needed it? Have you had an accident or illness that turned out to be a blessing? When we reflect about how bad luck is just good luck in disguise, and how no one is free of mishaps, then it becomes easier to develop an attitude of acceptance and surrender. This is Ketu's key to transforming negativity into positivity. When we completely "let go and let God," we see more than the proverbial silver lining on every cloud. We see through the clouds to the unbounded expanse of sky.

Key Idea for Education: The mass media condition us into thinking that we NEED things. The best-selling song of the '60s, "Satisfaction," by the Rolling Stones, captures the inevitable frustration of chasing illusory needs, especially those created by the media. Educators rarely have control over their students' exposure to the media, and parents may find television a convenient babysitter. So weaning children off the tube is a delicate issue. The best approach will vary from child to child, but no approach is likely to work unless the parents set an example themselves.

Another way to experience simplicity is to camp out. Forget the RV and warm shower. Take a pack trip into the wilderness, and learn to live in harmony with the elements with a minimum of conveniences.

Divinatory Message: Surrender to Mother Nature. Forget your vested interest. Transformation comes from remaining open to grace, not insisting that things happen your way. Let go and let God.

Relationship to Other Oracles: The Nodes of the Moon are generally depicted as a snake or dragon. Rahu is the head and Ketu the tail. The thirty-ninth Secret Dakini card, "Serpent Power," is a clear symbol of the transformative power of Ketu and an awakening of our latent abilities. The fortieth hexagram of the I-Ching, "Deliverance," gives similar indications—resolution of tensions and complications, and periods of sudden change: "Just as rain relieves atmospheric tension, making all the buds burst open, so a time of deliverance from burdensome pressure has a liberating and stimulating effect on life."

The Tarot's Eight of Wands also refers to a lightning transformation from death to a new birth, and a new sprouting based on a firm root.

41
18th Lunar Mansion
(Purva Shadha)—
Positive Thinking, Positive Action

Traditional Name: The Invincible One

Planetary Rulership: *Rajasic* aspect of Venus

Creative Principle: Purva Shadha brings success through positive thinking and creative visualization. This asterism is associated with water, and suggests the ability to flow like a river toward the ocean, drawn by ever-increasing charm in the direction of more and more. Venus is the most beautiful, charming, harmonious, and alluring planet. She governs dreams, aspirations, and positive fantasies— those charming mental functions which are free of the drabness and rigidity of physical constraints.

Creative fantasy can be a great regenerative tool to prepare us for the boundaries of daily life. The danger of Venus is getting lost in dreams, escaping into fantasies to such an extent that we suppress practical matters and cut ourselves off from the world. The fine arts are an invaluable means of allowing Venusian creativity to flow, while strengthening our awareness of the physical world.

A vigorous imagination can be a great aid in enduring hardship. Jewish prisoners in Nazi concentration camps who talked of sumptuous holiday meals had a much higher survival rate than other prisoners who passively accepted their starvation rations. One gains the power of an elephant through positive thinking and creative visualization.

Favorite Fantasies: Do you dream of losing yourself in dance or music? Do you envision a utopian society free of war, crime, and disharmony? Do you have vivid sexual fantasies, unfettered by the inhibitions and imperfections of real interactions with a mate in the flesh? All these varied daydreams reflect the *rajasic* aspect of Venus.

Key Idea for Education: The arts play an important role in expressing healthy fantasy and imagination. There is an increasing tendency in primary and secondary schools to reduce or eliminate art and music programs. This is a dangerous development, especially for the ages seven to fourteen, when learning is best effected through the imagination and aesthetic sense.

Divinatory Message: Maintain positivity and clearly visualize achievement of your highest ideal. But don't avoid mundane obligations or set goals beyond your reach. Picture, hear, and feel something beautiful. Then, like a musician who translates an abstract inner melody into physical interaction with his instrument, express your vision in a concrete form. It could be an artistic expression, such as a drawing, song, or poem, or it could be a written plan to implement your dream.

Relationship to Other Oracles: The fortieth Secret Dakini card, "Blow Your Mind," teaches us not to become entrenched in old habit patterns, but open our minds dramatically through the power of healthy fantasy and visualization. The Tarot's Nine of Wands is interpreted by Felix Guirand as the desire to attain the realms of the psyche which go beyond physical limitation, i.e., to explore with an imagination unfettered by material constraints.

At first glance, the forty-first hexagram of the I-Ching, "Sun/Decrease," sounds contrary to the expansive and visionary

Venusian quality of Purva Shadha. We feel this hexagram expresses Purva Shadha's imaginative power to overcome or endure hardship and loss. Wilhelm describes the value of material decrease and scanty resources in developing inner strength and truth: "One must draw on the strength of the inner attitude to compensate for what is lacking in externals; then the power of the content makes up for the simplicity of form. There is no need of presenting false appearances to God. Even with slender means, the sentiment of the heart can be expressed."

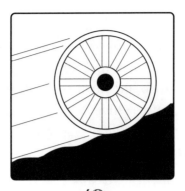

42
Pure Rajas:
Creativity Blossoms

Creative Principle: Desire leads to action and action leads to achievement. These are all expressions of *rajas*, especially desire and action. Pure *rajas* gives the ability to engage in dynamic action. *Sattwa* allows us to enjoy and preserve the achievement. *Tamas* takes it away and allows for rest.

The nine *rajasic* principles indicate different forms of dynamic growth. There are also dangers with every principle. With excess *rajas*, one could be an overzealous religious fanatic, a businessman obsessed with continued expansion, or a soldier who only knows how to attack, unable to rest or retreat. If *rajasic* tendencies are really extreme, one may become cruel and oppressive in one's obsessive haste to reach the goal, or just exhausted by lack of rest.

Favorite Fantasies: Do you dream of being the superhero, the superathlete, the superscientist, or the superlover who responds to every situation with dynamism and creativity? The desire to "be all that you can be" is a basic expression of the fundamental nature of life to grow to higher levels of achievement and fulfillment. The dynamism of *rajas* is the essence of great drama, but must be balanced (*sattwa*) by rest and relaxation (*tamas*).

Are you anxious about the future? Worried about your own life, your loved ones, or the whole planet? A healthy *rajasic* principle anticipates the future with eagerness and confidence, ready to adapt to unforeseen twists in the road. A weak *rajas* is terrified by change. An overstimulated *rajas* is swept away by desires. If the *rajasic* element is both overstimulated and too weak for follow-through, one experiences periods of manic excitation, with no power of execution.

Key Idea for Education: Do not force children into a mold, expecting them to achieve by your standards of academics, athletics, music, etc. Many of the most successful people are self-educated in their chosen field. Abraham Lincoln taught himself law. Microsoft chairman Bill Gates dropped out of Harvard to play with computers and eventually became the richest person in America. We're not encouraging dropping out. The key is helping each student discover his own unique talents, which are always immensely satisfying to unfold.

Divinatory Message: What is your personal creative gift? Don't follow popular conventions. Find your own niche. As Joseph Campbell said, "Follow your bliss!"

Relationship to Other Oracles: The forty-second hexagram of the I-Ching, "Increase," teaches hard work in times of progress in order to make best use of favorable times. This is the hexagram of increase and self-improvement through dynamic activity.

The Tarot's Ten of Wands also speaks of *rajasic* qualities, such as dynamism, executive ability, the uses of power, changes in activity, and even the cruelty, repression, and revenge that can come from excess *rajas.*

The forty-first Secret Dakini card, "High Tension," shows a muscleman's body, with lightning bolts escaping from the headless neck. Excess *rajas* can make us act forcefully, but as if we had no head!

43

19th Lunar Mansion (Uttara Shadha) —Omnipresent Light

Traditional Name: The Universal One

Planetary Rulership: *Sattwic* aspect of the Sun

Creative Principle: This asterism indicates a penetrating vision for leadership and the *sattwic* qualities of peace, harmony, stability and universality. Uttara Shadha is the universal one; people under its influence see the big picture and honor both universality and difference. Such people take the lead in integrating unity and diversity, part and whole. In home life they uphold the family unit as more than the sum of its members. In society they inspire the diverse factions to work together for a common good. They may use force, tempered by the desire for harmony, or they may motivate through charisma—all qualities of the Sun.

But here the Sun's leadership is for protection and solidification (*sattwa*), rather than growth and expansion (*rajas*) or rest and destruction (*tamas*). The danger is *sattwic* attachments, such as holding onto a leadership position past one's useful period of service, or preserving anything too long and retarding needed transformation (*tamas*). In terms of political careers (a solar signification), *rajas* governs the expansion of fame and glory, *sattwa* governs the period of maximum power, and *tamas* governs retirement and rest in one's later years.

Sattwa is also the principle of balance. People under the influence of Uttara Shadha have the ability to consider all sides of a problem and balance the conflicting interests with fairness and firmness.

Favorite Fantasies: Do you dream of being a fair and just leader and balancing conflicting interest groups? That suggests a strong Uttara Shadha. If your dreams are to hold onto power in order to dominate and exploit others, it suggests a weak Uttara Shadha. Integrating diverse interests, be they spiritual, commercial, academic, or athletic, and receiving public recognition—all these relate to Uttara Shadha.

Key Idea for Education: A key element of childhood development is learning to nurture, support, and sustain others without losing one's own identity. A true leader gains a stronger self-identity by helping others and considering their interests before his own. Henry Ford exemplified this principle. He realized that by looking after the welfare of his workers, he cultivated a skilled and loyal workforce who contributed to his own welfare.

Divinatory Message: Try to see your problem in relation to all the people it will effect, and see how consideration of their interests contributes to your own self-interests. For example, if your child is worried about how he will be accepted by other kids in his new school, you might suggest that it won't be a problem if he helps the other kids feel like more of a group.

Relationship to Other Oracles: The forty-third hexagram of the I-Ching, "Break-Through (Resoluteness)," achieves unity by balancing strength and friendliness. But this friendliness must never be a compromise with evil. *Sattwa* cannot coexist with evil, since *sattwa* is light, peace, and harmony, and evil is just the opposite.

The Tarot's Ace of Cups speaks clearly of the *sattwic* qualities of the Sun—abundance, good cheer, joy, contentment, and all the other qualities which bring a feeling of universality. The forty-second Secret Dakini card, "Wave of Bliss," indicates the fruit (*sattwa*) of any prior action achieved in harmony with others.

44
20th Lunar Mansion (Shravana)
—Learning Through Loving

Traditional Name: The Star of Learning

Planetary Rulership: *Sattwic* aspect of the Moon

Creative Principle: The Moon governs emotions, especially subconscious emotions. It attunes us to our innermost feelings, others' feelings, and even the collective subconscious. Shravana, the *sattwic* aspect of the Moon, gives us the ability to turn negative emotions into positive ones. Fear and hatred turn into acceptance and love. Signposts of this love are: complete acceptance of others with no agendas for who they should be or what they should do; sensitivity to others' feelings before they express them verbally; a stable, contented state of mind that feels completely nourished and supported; absence of guilt and condemnation; and universal bliss and goodwill toward all.

Favorite Fantasies: Do your fantasies relate to deep feelings, rather than words or actions? Do you want to tune into the collective subconscious, or intuitively sense how others are feeling? These are lunar tendencies. When they have a smooth, easy, relaxed and contented tone, they relate to a healthy *sattwic* aspect of the Moon. When they relate to anxiously controlling or holding onto others emotionally, they relate to an unhealthy Shravana. Such emotional dependence can be heard in thousands of pop songs with lyrics like "Baby, don't leave me," "I can't live without you," etc.

Key Idea for Education: "Shravana" means listening, specifically the respectful attentiveness of an eager and receptive student. There are two key lessons for education related to Shravana:

1. You must first win someone's heart before winning his or her mind. Communication begins from the heart—creating harmonious feelings between teacher and student or parent and child.

2. To receive knowledge from another, you must be able to listen without preconceptions or emotional attachments. Learning requires an open heart and an open mind. This principle also applies to all communication in the classroom of life. Only an open-minded, open-hearted person can hear what another is saying.

Rudolph Steiner said that veneration of truth and knowledge is the first prerequisite for spiritual development. Early in the twentieth century he wrote: "Our civilization tends more toward critical judgment and condemnation than toward devotion and selfless veneration. Our children already criticize far more than they worship. But every criticism, every adverse judgment passed, disperses the powers of the soul for the attainment of higher knowledge, in the same measure that all veneration and reverence develops them."[7]

Divinatory Message: Listen from the heart and speak from the heart! For example, if you are deciding which house to buy, ask yourself which one you feel most settled and content with, including all factors—cost, location, aesthetics, etc. If you are deciding which career to pursue, make sure you're comfortable with the emotional side of the work.

Relationship to Other Oracles: The Tarot's Two of Cups represents reciprocity, reflection, harmony, affinity, concord, and understanding—all qualities of a *sattwic* Moon. The forty-fourth hexagram of the I-Ching, "Coming to Meet," reflects the same ideas, especially meeting in concord. It concerns both the benefits of concord and the potential dangers, such as the subordination of one's own needs for the purpose of peace.

The forty-third Secret Dakini card, "Mount Meru, Center of the Universe," indicates a place of great power and stability, a holy site where an individual can center himself and listen to the Divine. Great teachers often spend years in high mountains, or other lonely natural settings, where they can listen in silence to the quiet vibrations in the heart. Mount Meru also signifies the integration of inner and outer worlds, which takes place only when we listen with the heart to both our own innermost feelings and others', too.

45
21st Lunar Mansion (Dhanishta)
—Power to Protect the Prize

Traditional Name: The Star of Symphony

Planetary Rulership: *Sattwic* aspect of Mars

Creative Principle: The *sattwic* aspect of Mars uses the will to uphold harmony. Some significations are charity, royal virtues, and the ability to use the will as a spiritual tool. Mars is the great achiever, the commander-in-chief who inspires and directs his army. In this case, he is neither attacking nor defending, just maintaining a vigilant guard on achievements already gained. Thus Dhanishta is associated with enjoying the spoils of war, such as gems and other treasures.

A *sattwic* Mars uses its strength to protect others and promote harmony. Mars also governs the deeper levels of sound. (Venus governs the outer levels.) Enlightened music is a powerful tool to promote harmony and protect society from negative thinking. If we know how to use music in a life-supporting way, we gain the support of nature and uphold society. If we use it in a harsh way, we undermine society.

An even subtler use of Dhanishta is mantra, or primordial sound for healing mind, body, spirit, or environment. Thus mantra techniques, both verbal and silent, can be considered a subtle form of music.

Mars always connotes the discipline of a warrior. Mars governs Laya or Kundalini yoga, the spiritual path of the will. The Laya master may discipline his students severely, but this discipline must be based on love. Thoughtful discipline strips away bad habits while strengthening body, heart, and mind.

Another Mars signification is fire sacrifice, performed to generate coherence in the community and win the support of gods or ancestors.

Favorite Fantasies: Do you dream of being a great defender of Freedom, Justice, or Truth? U.S. foreign policy has attempted to protect weaker countries from aggressors for most of the twentieth century, although our government's actions are often perceived as aggression. At present (1995), NATO is playing a similar role in Bosnia, attempting to prevent the slaughter of one ethnic faction by another. Do you jump to the defense, verbal or physical, of your friends, family, school, or religion? The *sattwic* aspect of Mars stands up for whatever it treasures. Another Dhanishta manifestation is defending your wealth against thieves. The National Rifle Association's campaigns to resist gun control may reflect this impulse for self-protection.

Key Idea for Education: Music and environmental sound have a powerful influence on us, but schools are generally impotent to deal with this issue if it degenerates into a debate over freedom. We are not arguing for censorship here. We would prefer to see community forums and parent-teacher discussions on the social effects of music. We also suggest that students be exposed to uplifting and harmonious music as part of their cultural education. As far as environmental noise, soothing natural sounds such as birds or running water tend to settle the mind, while abrasive machine-based sounds like traffic, jets, and hard rock music tend to have the opposite effect.

A little-understood quality of Mars is the ability to heal emotional wounds. Mars is commonly associated with the cause of trauma. It can also aid the cure. When we suffer physical injury, as in a car accident, battle, or fire (Mars significations), we generally go into a period of shock before we consciously experience the full pain. When we experience emotional trauma, the shock may last a lifetime. We have elaborate defense mechanisms which keep the full emotional pain from our awareness.

The ego has elaborate defenses to keep us from feeling emotional pain, because anything that makes the ego feel weak, vulnerable, or worthless threatens its very survival. Unless we consciously decide to reexperience our emotional injuries, we subconsciously exert great energy to hide from them. We stagger through life with vague complaints and general dis-ease, feeling disconnected from our infinite source, armored against attack and emotionally frozen in the fear that opening our hearts could invite an enemy into our fortress.

Dhanishta, the *sattwic* or harmonizing aspect of Mars, gives us courage to deal with physical and emotional pain. It allows us to revive repressed memories and bring the dead pieces of our soul back to life. No matter what has damaged our sense of Self, a calm and detailed review of the traumatic event, with full forgiveness of all parties, allows us to heal the wound. Psychic wounds fester in denial, but they mend with loving attention.

Although Mars is widely feared, he can heal whatever he harms. Although he rules the will, he can heal the heart through the ability to release painful emotions without fear. In this way he can open the heart, normally associated with the Moon.

Divinatory Message: Exert your will toward your goals in a harmonizing way. Express your joy and satisfaction in music, or organize others in a celebrative, harmonious way. Remember that Mars' role is to protect others, especially weaker persons, so never adapt means contrary to this end. If your problem is emotional, use your will to face your deepest emotions with courage.

Relationship to Other Oracles: The Tarot's Three of Cups speaks of using the will in a way which brings not only abundance and plenty, but also hospitality, joy, and merriment—all *sattwic* qualities upheld by Dhanishta. The forty-fifth hexagram of the I-Ching, "Gathering Together (Massing)," talks of the leadership needed to bring people together, and the need for vigilance against danger: "Precautions must be taken, ... we must arm promptly to ward off the unexpected. Human woes usually come as a result of unexpected events against which we are not forearmed. If we are prepared, they can be prevented."

The forty-fourth Secret Dakini card, "Heart-Drop," relates to Dhanishta in two ways we have discussed. First, it gives the power of attention to appreciate the subtle sound values of music and mantra, both of which can unlock the treasures of the heart. Second, it gives the courage to face deep emotional trauma and unfreeze old blocks in the heart.

46
22nd Lunar Mansion (Shatabhisha) —Snaking Around Obstacles

Traditional Name: The Veiling Star

Planetary Rulership: *Sattwic* aspect of Rahu

Creative Principle: Rahu is always a rebel, but the form of rebellion varies according to the dominant guna. The *tamasic* aspect of Rahu, Ardra, presents passive resistance to outmoded laws and conventions, such as Gandhi's passive resistance to British rule in India. The *rajasic* aspect of Rahu, Swati, prefers a more active, aggressive form of attack, like the student rebellions of the '60s in the U.S. The *sattwic* aspect of the North Node, Shatabhisha, balances the active and passive forms of rebellion. It prefers working around obstacles rather than directly confronting them.

Rahu is always destructive, but its *sattwic* aspect creates peace and harmony by destroying evil and impurity. Thus Shatabhisha relates to physicians and other healers. A dramatic example of spiritual application of Shatabhisha energy is the teachings of Bhagwan Shri Rajneesh (Osho), who attacked all the outmoded religious conventions of his day and reveled in controversy.

At the same time there is an aspect of this asterism which covers, screens, surrounds, or holds captive—"the veiling star." What is being veiled is outmoded conventions or practices which have become detrimental. Dick Gregory and Lenny Bruce might be examples of comedians who satirize damaging elements of the social order, in a sense veiling or diminishing their light.

This principle also implies the ability to push upwards in a vertical ascent toward spiritual illumination through *sattwic* use of the rebel energy. In order to gain enlightenment, it is usually necessary to shake off many self-limiting beliefs and habits ingrained in us by society. Nobody becomes enlightened by following convenient, socially-accepted norms or lifestyles. Most of the great sages in history had to rebel against the dominant religious and cultural order, yet do so in a way which stimulates social change while preserving order in society. Jesus, Buddha, Shankara, and countless others—in fact, most of the great religious leaders in history—have reformed society without destroying it.

Favorite Fantasies: Do you resist oppressive obligations by quietly ignoring them? Do you quietly break small rules just for fun, and go out of your way to violate convention, not to be noticed, but for the novelty and sense of freedom? If your rebellion has the smooth and harmonizing quality of *sattwa*, then it expresses the Shatabhisha archetype.

Key Idea for Education: It is important to realize that rebellion against outmoded conventions in schools can be done in a way which is so flexible and adaptable that it does not create illwill or disharmony. The blade of grass pushing around a rock does not offend the rock. Many such blades growing all around the rock can completely hide it. This principle is valuable to remember when one is tempted to attack negativity in a fit of anger (*rajas*) or passive despair (*tamas*), as a *sattwic* reform usually does not raise as much resistance as a *rajasic* approach, nor is it likely to be as frustrating and slow as a passive, *tamasic* rebellion.

Divinatory Message: You are meant to find a way to change your present circumstances through a gentle rebellion which manages to preserve the fundamental integrity of the group or social structure you are dealing with. For example, if you want to replace a high official in your organization and he's likely to resist you, then try to guide him adroitly toward early retirement or a better job elsewhere.

Relationship to Other Oracles: The forty-sixth hexagram of the I-Ching, "Pushing Up," indicates a plant pushing upwards through the earth, adapting itself to obstacles by growing around them. This is a clear representation of Shatabhisha.

Grimaud's interpretation of the Tarot's Four of Cups is an agreement reached after some difficulty, adjustment, or compromise, and subsequent abundance. Some of the other commentators focus on the failure to properly use a *sattwic* North Node, and the resulting discord and estrangement.

The forty-fifth Secret Dakini card, "Like a Bubble," focuses more on the vertical ascent made possible by a *sattwic* North Node, and the relaxed attitude needed before peace and harmony can arise in pure awareness. It also points to the ability to let go of all preconceptions, and open the mind to its original spontaneous pure nature.

47

23rd Lunar Mansion (Purva Bhadra)
—Sustaining Satisfaction through Sacrifice

Traditional Name: The First of the Scorching Pair. The following lunar mansion, Uttara Bhadra, is the second.

Planetary Rulership: *Sattwic* aspect of Jupiter

Creative Principle: Who are the scorching pair which burn on contact? They represent the twin aspects of desire—the process of being driven by a desire to fulfill something and, very often, the let-down after satisfying the desire, which creates the seed of a new desire. A higher understanding of the scorching pair is the burning nature of desire and its transformation into a sacrificial offering to the Divine. The *sattwic* aspect of Jupiter, Purva Bhadra, represents the satisfaction of desire, whether spiritual or mundane. (Please refer to the next lunar mansion, Uttara Bhadra, which represents the aftermath of desire.)

In Vedic fire sacrifices one offers precious objects like flowers, foods, and gems into the fire, which transforms them into gifts fit for the gods. This transformation through sacrifice is symbolic of the whole practice of karma yoga, governed by Jupiter, where we sacrifice our personal desires to the Divine. Only the *sattwic* aspect of Jupiter is capable of fully performing this sacrifice, balancing *tamas* and *rajas*. The burning of the material objects is the destructive side, and the heavenward ascent of the purified essence of the offerings is the creative side.

"Ask not what your country can do for you. Ask what you can do for your country." This statement, popularized by John F. Kennedy, is a perfect expression of Purva Bhadra. It could be applied to one's family, school, or religion, as well as to one's nation.

Ancient astrologers related this asterism to pain by heat, torture, and oppression. When modern astrologers say that someone ruled by Purva Bhadra will burn, torture, or oppress others, they are very mistaken. The asterism actually refers to fire of self-sacrifice that burns away selfish desires. If done gladly without guilt or masochism, self-sacrifice leads to tremendous joy and abundance. He who gives gets back tenfold!

Favorite Fantasies: Do you burn to preserve your religion, family, or school? Do you bristle with indignation when any of these are insulted? Do you dream of sacrificing yourself for a higher cause? Are your fantasies formal, proper, and righteous? These indicate the *sattwic* aspect of Jupiter, called Purva Bhadra.

Key Idea for Education: Students need to see that sacrifice is essential for success, especially nonmaterial success. Heartfelt sacrifice is rewarded manyfold, while mechanical sacrifice with no feeling is wasted. This principle is illustrated in the lives of all naturally unselfish men and women. Those who serve the needs of their times in a deep and natural spirit of selfless service tend to be very happy people! They find both inner contentment and support from Nature for their good deeds. Such people are able to work for a universal principle without consideration for their own personal welfare, yet they find their own welfare is well taken care of.

Divinatory Message: See how some sort of self-sacrifice can help solve your problem. It might be channeling the power of anger and outrage into action to correct a wrong. Or it might mean financial sacrifice, which cuts us free of monetary attachment.

Relationship to Other Oracles: The forty-sixth Secret Dakini card, "Abundance," shows a chalice overflowing with precious coins. "The chalice represents the Self, or a position which is being offered to the Self. The golden coins symbolize inner riches, either literally or alchemically as the transformation of spiritual light." If we take a narrow view, "abundance" seems to be the opposite of self-sacrifice. However, if we understand the law of cause and effect, sacrifice is a means to both inner and outer wealth.

The Five of Cups also refers to a gift or inheritance, or a victory over obstacles after a struggle. On the other hand, the forty-seventh hexagram of the I-Ching, "Oppression (Exhaustion)," focuses more upon how to overcome obstacles and deal with oppressive desires by surrendering those desires to higher ideals. When a strong person meets with adversity, he remains cheerful despite all danger. This cheerfulness becomes the basis of success because it attracts support of nature and motivates him to rise above adversity.

Jupiter is the planet of abundance and good cheer. He maintains this good cheer by nonattachment to small personal desires, and derives joy from the happiness of others. As with many of the oracular principles with menacing titles, "Oppression (Exhaustion)" refers to the danger of ignoring the relevant principle. In this case one becomes exhausted if one remains attached to the fruit of desire and fails to sacrifice personal desires for the greater good of community or divinity.

The final meaning of "Oppression (Exhaustion)" in the I-Ching is that what oppresses us is desire itself. We become exhausted if we are slaves to desire. As Osho said in commenting on this principle, "It is time for you to stop seeking outside yourself for that which would make you happy. Look inside."[8] Oppression is nothing other than the scorching pair of desire and subsequent let-down!

48
24th Lunar Mansion (Uttara Bhadra) —Contented Renunciation

Traditional Name: The Second of The Scorching Pair

Planetary Rulership: *Sattwic* aspect of Saturn

Creative Principle: This lunar mansion denotes the ability to quench desire through endurance, perseverance, and detachment. This is why this asterism suggests journey to a distant place, leaving everything behind, renouncing worldly pleasures, and wandering about as a hermit. It also shows the wisdom, knowledge, and ability to control fiery emotions, such as anger, envy, or sexual passion.

As mentioned under the previous lunar mansion, the first of the scorching pair represents the satisfaction of desire. This lunar mansion, the second of the pair, represents the aftermath of desire. If we hold onto desires (a weak Saturn), we feel a loss and kindling of new desires with the satisfaction of each old one. However, if we let go of desires (a strong Saturn), we feel an even deeper satisfaction from within.

Uttara Bhadra also implies the power to perform austerities (tapas). As previously mentioned, *sattwa* balances *tamas* and *rajas*. The self-abnegation and austerity of this asterism achieves both self-purification (*tamas*) and nourishment of others (*rajas*). Even the most sincere seeker gets stuck in small personal concerns if he focuses only on his personal evolution, and ignores the welfare of others. This is why yogis in remote regions of the Himalayas and hermetic saints in all parts of the world attenuate their own desires and work to purify world consciousness.

Another signification of this asterism will be a powerful spur toward your detachment: Uttara Bhadra gives the power to quench desires here and now, without waiting for some nebulous future. Look at the futility of chasing fulfillment through sensory and egoic stimulation. Simplify your life and experience the equilibrium (*sattwa*) of perfect silence in solitary meditation.

Favorite Fantasies: Would you rather have a solitary hut in the mountains than a mansion in the city? Are you a Henry Thoreau, content with simple food, simple clothes, a simple home, and simple social life? Are you easily satisfied, accepting whatever comes to you? Uttara Bhadra reflects *sattwic* contentedness in Saturn's simple surroundings.

Key Idea for Education: Students must learn that less is sometimes more. Create exercises to let them experience how they are happier with a simple, quieter life, rather than an excitement treadmill which spirals in the direction of ever greater cycles of stimulation and depression. For example, compare a week of minimum stimulation (lots of rest, no TV, movies, or raucous music; moderate diet, extra meditation, etc.) with a week of heavy stimulation (lack of rest, overexertion, excess socializing, etc.)

Since Saturn governs cold, dry, rational thinking, this is a wonderful opportunity for practical applications of scientific methodology. Keep a notebook to record daily experiences, such as quality of sleep and meditation, efficiency at work, relationships with others, etc. Then look for correlations after the observation period.

Divinatory Message: Ask yourself whether each of your goals is something you really need to be happy. If you don't need it, drop it. It's that simple!

Relation to Other Oracles: The forty-seventh Secret Dakini card, 'Horseplay," indicates the importance of play as part of the spiritual path. We can only play when we let go of worldly preoccupations: "evoking the feeling of play within the heart liberated from worldly concerns, just as on the threshold of the apparent world the inner Spirit plays." The renunciation of Uttara Bhadra is a peaceful and contented one, inspired by the dual recognition of the ephemerality of desires and the lasting joys of pure spirit.

Saturn governs deep, hidden, underground places, both physical and spiritual. The forty-eighth hexagram of the I-Ching, "Going to the Well" shows how we refresh ourselves by drinking deeply of pure consciousness. Some of the other planets, especially Jupiter, can transcend in activity, but Saturn transcends only in silence. This silence may be for just a few minutes, or may extend for many years of blissful renunciation. Although long-term austerities and renunciation sound like torture to people addicted to sensory gratification, to the truly Self-sufficient they are just another form of play!

The Tarot's Six of Cups places strong emphasis on what we need to renounce—clinging to the past or worrying about the future—rather than staying centered in the present. A *sattwic* Saturn gives this ability to live in the eternal now. Unfulfilled desires pull us into the past and future. Living contentedly in the present, without remorse for the past or worry for the future, is the truest form of renunciation.

49
25th Lunar Mansion (Revati)
—Observe the Observer

Traditional Name: The Keeper of Flocks

Planetary Rulership: *Sattwic* aspect of Mercury

Creative Principle: Revati shows how the flocks (thoughts) are nourished, supported, and protected by the shepherd (a *sattwic* intellect), capable of distinguishing friend from foe and truth from falsehood. The *sattwic* intellect is usually quiet and watchful, like a shepherd tending his flocks. But he is capable of sudden leaps of progress, like a shepherd bounding over obstacles to protect his sheep—the ability of a *sattwic* intellect to transcend.

Mercury governs the spiritual path of Gyana Yoga, the path of discrimination. Revati is not the more active, *rajasic* thinking of Jyestha, nor the *tamasic* thinking of Ashlesha, which either blows holes in false ideas, or rests the intellect in transcendence. Revati governs a balanced discriminative faculty *(buddhi)* which spends most the time in quiet vigilance, watching sheep (thoughts) move (express creativity) in a direction (intelligence). He can bolt with lightening speed when necessary, cutting through a thicket of false notions, but he generally prefers to be a silent witness to the mind.

The danger of this nakshatra is hushing up to keep the peace when one should speak out boldly.

Favorite Fantasies: Do you enjoy friendly debate, word games, and other light mental gymnastics? Do you laugh at your own fantasies and play with your own thoughts? Do you imagine yourself a great trickster, and know that imaginations are only the ego's tricks to disguise itself? Any such light, sweet inclinations of the intellect reflect the *sattwic* aspect of Mercury.

Key Idea for Education: Too often students are taught to use the intellect solely in a competitive (*rajasic*) or a destructive (*tamasic*) way. It is important to learn a *sattwic* use of the intellect, which nourishes others by clarifying key concepts and enhancing friendly communication.

Modern education creates a busy, hyperactive intellect that may be adept in facts and figures, but flounders on deeper questions of higher purpose and metaphysical truth. When their discriminative faculty *(buddhi)* starts to awaken around age fourteen, students can benefit by pondering the nature of life in an atmosphere of freedom and even levity.

Even more important, students need to transcend the intellect, using gyana yoga to increase awareness of Self and others. Higher knowledge begins with the recognition that words and concepts can never capture the absolute truth of life. One must transcend thoughts to experience their source. This transcendence requires a Mercurial sense of joy, play, and spontaneity. We are but actors who have become so serious about our roles that we have forgotten that life's drama is just a tragicomic game, and our life roles are just guises we assume for a short period of entertainment. One of the best ways for students to learn to observe their own roles is for them to role-play the various archetypal roles expressed in this book, especially the planetary roles.

Divinatory Message: Seek to resolve your problem, not on the level of the problem, but through transcendence. Leave the problem for half an hour or an hour and meditate. The meditation itself can be in accord with any of the eight major paths to God. (See Part II, Chapter 1.) The optimum path depends on your own innermost strength of personality.[9]

Next, try to express the problem clearly in different terms. A clear understanding of the problem, including your feelings toward it, always helps in the resolution, even if the problem seems to be someone else's understanding, not your own. One approach of ayurveda, the ancient Indian system of health care, is that all problems are based in "pragyaparad," or mistake of the intellect. Donald Epstein, the founder of Network Chiropractic, cites J. Krishnamurti, the Indian philosopher, "(who) often said that to help someone with a problem, all you had to do was understand it without judgment and see it clearly; in time this understanding will be transmitted to the person with the problem. The same holds true when a part of your body—a part of your being—experiences a problem or symptom."[10]

Relationship To Other Oracles: Transcendence through the intellect, symbolized by this asterism, is represented by the forty-ninth hexagram of the I-Ching, "Revolution/Molting." Wilhelm cautions that one must be free of selfish aims in order to help people. Such freedom from selfishness is not possible unless the small ego is softened through a regular practice of transcendence.

The Tarot's Seven of Cups also points to imagination and vision, resulting in some temporary attainment. Transcendental consciousness is temporary illumination, and cosmic consciousness is transcendence made permanent and integrated with activity.

The forty-eighth Secret Dakini card, "White Lady: Mother of Pearl," points to detachment and transcendence through discrimination, and the danger of getting lost in occult studies and magical powers. "Her path is not of the heart, but of the man's desire for rational knowledge.... Understand her as a glyph of the analytical mind." The state of transcendence, like the white lady, is beyond life and death, unbounded and untouchable. It can be glimpsed only by those who are attracted to her pearls of wisdom, and unattracted to the pearls of transient pleasure. What could be more *sattwic* than this?

50
26th Lunar Mansion (Ashwini)
—The Grace of the Cosmic Surgeon

Traditional Name: Star of Transport

Planetary Rulership: *Sattwic* aspect of Ketu

Creative Principle: Ashwini represents the power of grace to save and heal us and cut away any impediments which block the flow of grace into our lives. It is this grace which inspires us to be helpers and healers of others. Many people who survive great trauma find satisfaction in helping others with the same afflictions.

The ruling deities of Ashwini are the two Ashwins, the celestial healers, symbolized by two horses. The name is derived from *ashwa,* or horse, a universal symbol of power and speed. In oriental medicine, such as Chinese acupuncture and Indian ayurveda, disease is merely a symptom of blocked energy. Healing occurs when we allow the energy to move, especially when we allow trapped impurities to be cleared from the mind-body.

Ketu cuts deep, as a surgeon who must destroy part of the body to save the whole. Again we see a *sattwic* principle represent both destruction and healing creativity.

Favorite Fantasies: Do you dream of performing figurative self-surgery—giving your love-life a coronary bypass, amputating your addictions, or giving your social skills a face-lift? Do you remain unruffled when you wreck the car and the house burns ? Do you want to heal others by allowing grace to flow through you, without taking credit for its miracles? When strong, this *sattwic* aspect of Ketu understands the sweetness of silent surrender to the Divine. When weak, it cuts blindly without knowing how to heal.

Key Idea for Education: Modern education emphasizes the doer, controller, or agent of action. Students must learn the other side of action—how to surrender to the force of grace and win the support of Nature. This need not be seen in religious terms, but in terms of everyday life. Grace may be good weather, good teachers, good food, or good luck in any form. Or it may be a quality of the heart, such as increased sensitivity and compassion for the suffering of others.

Over 2,000 years ago Ecclesiastes wrote about grace: "... the race is not to the swift, nor the battle to the strong, neither yet bread to the wise, nor yet riches to men of understanding, nor yet favor to men of skill; but time and chance happeneth to them all."

Divinatory Message: Don't expect the answer to come so much from your own efforts as through the grace of God. Nature's bounty may come in painful ways, cutting away some precious belief or possession in order to open our hearts. The path to compassion, although sometimes painful, results in deeper joys of the heart.

Relationship to Other Oracles: The forty-ninth Secret Dakini card, "Cutting Through," shows two hands carrying large scissor-like choppers, which give us discriminative wisdom to sever our false notions and free us from the cycle of death and rebirth. The fiftieth hexagram of the I-Ching, "The Cauldron," is represented by a bronze pot for preparing ritual offerings. It symbolizes the nourishment, both physical and spiritual, which we receive when we allow Ketu's fire to transform our blessings into a form we can use ourselves or offer our Creator. Grace often comes through prophets and holy men, who in sacrificing to God, allow God's grace to descend on earth.

Finally, the Tarot's Eight of Cups also points to the need to leave material success in or order to achieve something higher, and the great joy and happiness which results from that process.

51
27th Lunar Mansion (Bharani)
—Harmonizing through Inner Charm

Traditional Name: Star of Restraint

Planetary Rulership: *Sattwic* aspect of Venus

Creative Principle: The *sattwic* aspect of Venus raises the interesting question of how to best discipline or control the senses in a way which brings realization of Self or God. Venus rules the senses and governs the spiritual path of Raj yoga, the path of increasing sensory charm. In Raj Yoga one leads a life of sensory restraint. But rather than trying to suppress the senses, one leads them within through the increasing charm of subtler levels of awareness. For example, the right mantras, used properly, can draw the attention from ordinary surface awareness to finer and finer levels, until the mantra disappears and the awareness is open only to itself. This is transcendence, the state of pure consciousness, being awake inside with no thought and no object of experience separate from the subject.

The traditional symbol of Bharani is a special water pot used for ceremonial bathing of sacred statues. It is in the shape of the female sex organ, or *yoni,* a clear signification of Venus. Pouring water from it symbolizes offering the subtle senses to the Divine.

Favorite Fantasies: Do you like to soak in a hot bubble bath, dreaming of soft, sweet romantic encounters? Do refined music, a gourmet dinner under candlelight, and charming company tickle your fancy? Do you peacefully dream of an ideal society, free of crime and disharmony? All these suggest Bharani, the *sattwic* aspect of Venus, but only if they exhibit restraint, moderation, and control of the senses.

Key Idea for Education: In an age such as ours where hyperstimulation of the senses is the norm, it is especially important for students to learn how to escape the treadmill of excitation. There are two *sattwic* ways of stepping off the treadmill. First, in the pursuit of outer pleasures, focus on ideal beauty in a simple, contemplative way, such as admiring one great work of art for extended periods, or listening to a great piece of music repeatedly with no distractions or interruptions. Second, and more important, establish a daily routine of leading the attention within through the principle of increasing charm. The Transcendental Meditation (TM) program of Maharishi Mahesh Yogi is an example of such a Raj Yoga program.

Divinatory Message: Try to let your aesthetic sense guide you to a decision. What is most charming, beautiful, and harmonizing to others, as well as to yourself?

Relationship to Other Oracles: The fiftieth Secret Dakini card, "Recall/Memory," shows conch shells, often used in religious ceremonies. Conches are used both for blowing like a trumpet to attract good and repel evil, and as ceremonial pots for offering water to the deities.

The Tarot's Nine of Cups represents both the happiness and contentment from fulfilling Venusian wishes and the troubles and difficulties that accompany unfulfilled desires. Our desires are never completely fulfilled as long as we stay on the treadmill of sensory gratification and ignore our inner unboundedness. Optimum evolution requires a balance of inner and outer pleasures.

The fifty-first hexagram of the I-Ching, "The Arousing (Shock, Thunder)," is another caution against denial of inner awareness. When we pursue sensory gratification in an outward or mechanical way, we are inevitably shocked and shaken by the result. Fear of sensory deprivation and disappointment after sensory saturation are beneficial, for such suffering makes us look deep for more permanent joy and bliss.

52
Pure Sattwa
—Enjoying the Fruit

Creative Principle: *Sattwa* is the principle of preservation. Rajas creates, *sattwa* preserves, and *tamas* destroys. Whenever growth gets out of hand, balance is lost. Athletes who take steroids to stimulate muscle growth compromise their long-term health. Likewise, if destruction is too fast, trauma can result as useful values are destroyed along with unuseful ones. Revolutionary wars invariably destroy far more than their instigators intend. *Sattwa* restores the balance between creation and destruction, and gives us a chance for savoring success.

Sattwa is also purity, clarity, truthfulness, and joy. Neither pleasure nor pain is lasting. They are part of a larger cycle of the three *gunas*. The last nine nakshatras show us how the nine planets function in a preservative, harmonizing way.

Favorite Fantasies: Do you dream of being a Buddha, sitting in a peaceful, self-collected state? Do you dream of a happy balance between active duty and passive rest? These indicate a strong principle of *sattwa*, capable of balancing rest and activity.

On the other hand, a weak *sattwic* principle oscillates from one extreme to the other without ever finding a comfortable equilibrium in the middle. We saw that in the emotional arena, a weak *tamas* (archetype #32) dwells on the past and wallows in guilt, remorse and depression. Similarly, a weak *rajasic* principle (#42) tends to be manic, living in expectation of a future rewards, so excited about tomorrow that it denies yesterday and today. A weak *sattwa* is bipolar, swinging between depression (weak *tamas*) and mania (weak *rajas*), without ever finding the sweet balance point in between. That is why spiritual teachers throughout the world teach us to live in the present, accepting the way things are, content with the infinite blessings we already have. In other words, practice pure *sattwa*, enjoying the moment, while thankful for the past (strong *tamas*) and attending to future duties (strong *rajas*).

Key Idea for Education: Children today are caught on a pendulum swinging between hyperexcitation and destructive forms of rest and relaxation like alcohol and drugs. Movies, TV, and passive spectator sports often exacerbate the disequilibrium. They are passive forms of entertainment (*tamas*) that often over stimulate the mind (*rajas*). They can be balanced by meditation and participatory activities, such as making music, active nonviolent athletics, and group building projects.

Divinatory Message: Center yourself between the extremes of hyperactivity and passive withdrawal. This is best done through meditation, which may be either inward and silent or outward and active. Outward meditation is moderate activity with full self-awareness.

Relationship to Other Oracles: The fifty-second hexagram of the I-Ching, "Keeping Still (Mountain)," teaches us the key to *sattwa*: proper meditation. Only a deep inner calmness allows us to turn outward into activity without losing our center. We become a mountain of silence, even in activity. Wilhelm says, "While Buddhism strives for rest through an ebbing away of all movement in nirvana, the *Book of Changes* (I-Ching) holds that rest is merely a state of polarity that always posits movement as its complement." Rest is *tamas*, movement is *rajas*, and *sattwa* is the balance between the other two. This is why either extreme—all activity with no meditation, or all meditation with no activity—is incomplete. Lasting peace and fulfillment come only through a balance of inner silence and outer dynamism.

The fifty-first Secret Dakini card, "Deep End," shows a mermaid, half-woman and half-fish, diving deep into the unconscious. The fish tail gives her the power to swim in the ocean of pure consciousness while she retains her human nature, i.e., she lives the divine and mundane simultaneously.

The Tarot's Ten of Cups indicates perfected success, total contentment, and the burning need for spiritual progress, as well as spiritual fulfillment. The fulfillment of *sattwa* comes from the proper balance of rest and activity.

Introduction to the
Houses of the Zodiac

Creative Principle: In the trinity of experience (experiencer, object of experience, and process of experience), the houses of the zodiac correspond to the object—the outer aspect of the three. The position of each planet by sign and nakshatra determine one's inner gifts and strengths. If, when, and how those inner gifts find expression is determined by the houses.

For example, an exalted Sun generally confers power, fame, and influence. However, if it is in the twelfth house, the house of material loss, then it leads to loss of that power, fame, and influence. (Caution: Do not rely on conventional methods of drawing an astrological chart, either Eastern or Western. We feel that they are based on hearsay and superstition, and do not reflect the methods of the ancient masters, who intentionally omitted key secrets to drawing and interpreting charts. Such is the practice of all great spiritual and esoteric masters —the deepest secrets are never put in writing. They must be discovered in consciousness, usually with the help of a perfected master.)

Relationship to Other Oracles: The twelve houses of the zodiac are clearly reflected in both the I-Ching and the Secret Dakini Oracle. It is only the Tarot, which uses ten rather than twelve Pentacle cards, where there is a discrepancy. As mentioned in the introduction to the Nakshatras, this could reflect either the fact that originally there were only ten houses of the zodiac (the view of some esoteric teachers, such as Alice Bailey). Or, it could be an accommodation to principles of symmetry for designing what is essentially a game: Since there are only ten relevant cards in the other three suits, there should only be ten Pentacle (earth) cards as well.

This question is further complicated by the fact that the Tarot adds sixteen other principles (four kings, queens, knights, and pages), which correspond to the sixteen subdivisions of a horoscope. We omitted them from this book because they are not essential and might confuse most readers.

The houses of the zodiac have many significations in astrology. We only deal with the primary ones here.

53
First House
—The Emergent Self

Traditional Meaning: The House of Self

Creative Principle: The first house relates to physical appearance and self-image. Our self-image determines how we project ourself in public. It shows how our self-love tends to expand into the environment. Strong planets related to the first house give a strong, charismatic physical presence. Such presence becomes an asset for whatever we seek.

Favorite Fantasies: Do you daydream about how much people admire you? (Strong first house) Or do you worry about what people think of your complexion or belly? (Weak first house) Do you have poise and confidence in public, or do you freeze in front of a crowd of two? If you can accept and be grateful for your body, no matter how it looks, you have mastered the first lesson of the first house. If you can project yourself with confidence and charisma, you have mastered the second lesson.

Key Idea for Education: Contrary to advertising by the health and beauty industry, the key to projecting a healthy self-image is not physical appearance. It is Self-love based on Self-awareness. When we live the bliss of Self-awareness, our hearts naturally flow in love.

We enjoy sharing our love and joy with others, and never hold back our appreciation of others.

Self-image naturally evolves as a child matures and gains confidence from new achievements each year. However, the same aging process tends to ossify self-limiting beliefs. Physical ailments and slumped posture are symptoms of a negative self-image; vigor, vitality, and good posture reflect a positive self-image.

Children develop self-image problems when they feel their worth is based on impersonal outer factors such as test scores or athletic performance, rather than inner factors such as equanimity and concern for others. There are many ways to enhance self-image. The first and most import is spiritual practice in tune with one's innermost strength of personality. The second is knowing one's unique mission in life, and serving in accord with that mission. Personal readings in the Art of Multidimensional Living ™ can clarify both in a very dramatic way.

In all cases "follow your bliss!" Listen for the whisper of inner fulfillment as your consider your life's alternative. Bliss is felt in the body as a restfully alert sense of balance and well-being. Its opposite, denial of your inner nature, is experienced as tension, lack of feeling, or a vague sense of being off balance and out of touch with oneself. Bliss is centering and calming. Non-bliss is unbalancing and unsettling. The greatest bliss is found in opening one's heart in unbounded love. If a thousand ego-oriented self-help programs have not brought you happiness, try giving some joy to others, expressing yourself in whatever way is most natural and uplifting.

Divinatory Message: Let your sense of physical well-being be a guide. Listen to the infinite wisdom of the body, but don't cave in to grosser physical urges that tend to undermine your dignity or respect for others. Use your physical presence in a nonthreatening way. For example, if you want to buy a house, spend time inside it to see how you feel there. If you want to woo someone in romance, forget the phone and letter approach. Get together physically, but with enough space so that you can listen to the quiet cautions and comfort levels before you get swept away in a tidal wave of sexual hormones and ego needs.

Relationship to Other Oracles: The fifty-third hexagram of the I-Ching, "Development (Gradual Progress)," emphasizes the gradual nature of any sort of maturation. Our self-image cannot be overhauled in weekend seminars or crash diets. It takes years of perseverance and patient attention to our inner bliss.

In the fifty-second Secret Dakini card, "Rose Garden," budding roses symbolize self-development. The soft, fragrant petals suggest delight in subtle sensuality. Dr. Deepak Chopra, an endocrinologist turned ayurvedic doctor and spiritual teacher, suggests that inner bliss is a very sensual experience.

One of the major meanings of the Tarot's Ace of Pentacles is gift or inheritance. Our body is a gift from our parents and ancestors, and the physical foundation of our self-projection.

54
Second House
—Wealth in Harmony with Nature

Traditional Meaning: The House of Wealth

Creative Principle: This principle indicates our ability to accumulate wealth, whether as inheritance or money we earn ourselves. Accumulation of wealth often depends more on our ability to hold onto it than to earn it. The second house also relates to our physical resource in childhood—the basic necessities, such as food, clothes, and shelter.

The second house can also be called the house of nourishment. It relates to family life during childhood, and anything that passes through the mouth in either direction, primarily food and drink going in, and words coming out. Wealth is financial nourishment, so this understanding is consistent with the first.

Favorite Fantasies: Do you fantasize about food? Do you have an eating disorder, such as anorexia, bulimia, or habitual overeating? Do you dream of affluence, or the security of always having adequate food, clothing, and shelter?

Key Idea for Education: Schools are an extension of a child's home life. Many public schools have become cold and impersonal, and do not provide the basic sense of security and nourishment every child needs. This is one more argument for decentralizing education and making it more of a family and community experience.

Divinatory Message: Make sure you have the resources to realize your goals. These may be physical, monetary or the emotional support of your family. This card may also indicate you need to pay attention to earning and preserving wealth.

Relationship to Other Oracles: The Tarot's Two of Pentacles gives some of the following significations which relate to the second house: financial dexterity, building good fortune, using economy in displaying one's forces, and just plain wealth and money!

The fifty-fourth hexagram of the I-Ching, "The Marrying Maiden," shows the need for affectionate, voluntary relationships in the world, particularly relationships between young and old, which develop in the context of a nourishing and supportive family. The name "Marrying Maiden" relates to the fact that in ancient cultures a girl becomes part of a new family when she marries.

The fifty-third Secret Dakini card, "Tree Spirit: Yaksha," indicates that we also live within the greater family of nature herself. We need to harmonize with nature's cycles if we want to be truly nourished. True wealth is not money in the bank, but all that nourishes and sustains life.

55

Third House
—Competition Cultivates Competence and Confidence

Traditional Meaning: The House of Siblings

Creative Principle: The third house shows how we develop relating skills and courage through cooperation and competition with our siblings and close companions. Just as lion cubs play-fight in their instinctual development of hunting skills, children develop courage, coordination, and communication skills by interacting with their siblings and other playmates. Parents are often scared by the intensity of sibling rivalries, but the siblings generally know better than their parents when play-fighting ceases to be play.

Favorite Fantasies: Do your fantasies often involve brothers or sisters? Is there a playful element in your dreams of adventure? Do you feel a sense of competition with siblings or close friends, needing to prove yourself against them? If you feel you must outperform your siblings in sports, school, or career, then you reflect third house significations.

Key Idea for Education: Friendly competition is a healthy way to develop confidence, courage, and prowess. Genuine play develops friendship and equanimity. Seriousness (attachment to winning) leads to enmity and mood swings—elation on winning, deflation on losing, and anxiety about the outcome.

Competitors at play enjoy each moment. They strive hard to win, but their attention is fully in the present. They watch the ball, not the crowd's reaction. When we are fully absorbed in the moment, both inner fulfillment and outer achievement are maximum.

The basic principle behind competition should be that friendship and goodwill are more important than winning. When the competition turns nasty and spawns jeering or fights, it's clear that this principle has been violated.

When a student is so preoccupied with an exam that he cannot concentrate on the questions, or an athlete is so preoccupied with winning that he loses mental poise, achievement is undermined. Many great athletes have said that when they are "in their zone" and playing their best they are totally absorbed in the moment. There is often a sense that they are not acting. The sport is played through them, but they are the witness, not the actor. These peak or "in the zone" experiences are the times of most exceptional performance—the athlete gets the best of both inner experience and outer achievement. "The inner makes the winner!"

Divinatory Message: Display your prowess in action you enjoy. It is not enough to plan great deeds. Actualize them in a courageous way. It may be useful to seek the cooperation of companions and siblings to achieve your purpose.

Relationship to Other Oracles: The Three of Pentacles emphasizes qualities like skill, workmanship, rank, power, and earned esteem. Among children, especially siblings, there is a definite sense of rank, power, and esteem.

The fifty-fifth hexagram of the I-Ching, "Abundance (Fullness)," suggests that abundance needs both stability within and movement without, or courage and skill. The idea of movement without is especially tied to the third house concept of skillful and spontaneous activity. Inner stability supports outer courage and strength. Thus both inner and outer are needed for an integrated state of abundance.

Just as the I-Ching recognizes the need for balance between stability and movement, the fifty-fourth Secret Dakini card, "Asylum," indicates a balance between rest and activity. A unicorn rests in a tree overlooking a beautiful field. It suggests imaginative contemplation to gain clarity and strength prior to action in the field below, a time of recreative fantasy and play, free of worldly cares. Childhood and childlike play are an excellent way to regenerate our creative powers.

56
Fourth House
—The Heart at Home

Traditional Meaning: The House of Home and Domestic Happiness

Creative Principle: The fourth house relates to land and property, and our ability to acquire them and gain emotional satisfaction from them. It also indicates our vehicles (our moving homes) and general quality of family life. In a deeper sense, it indicates our subconscious and superconscious, which are inseparable from our home and family.

Favorite Fantasies: Do you dream of a beautiful house surrounded by a white picket fence? Feel at home in your car? Yearn for the company of your natural mother or another motherly figure? Look forward to family reunions on the old homestead? A modern fourth house fantasy would be to take Mom and Dad on vacation in a giant RV.

Key Idea for Education: Students must feel at home in school. Sterile, barren classrooms and a cult of information and heartless objectivity make students feel homeless and insecure. Decorate schools to convey warmth and life. Trees, gardens, indoor plants, natural sunlight, birds and other wildlife, streams and fountains, uplifting art and architecture—all these contribute to students' vitality and psychic comfort.

When students are recognized only for objective metrics like grades, test scores, and athletic performance, and subjective values like compassion, intuition, and aesthetic sense are ignored, their inner development is stunted. They learn to treat other people as objects, evaluating them as a potential source of money, power, sex, etc., or as threats to any of the above. One goal of the fourth house is to see "the world is my family." Even if a family member is a threat to others, we wish him health, happiness, and peace.

There are many means of honoring subjective values in schools, such as shared goals, older students helping younger ones, charitable projects, teacher-student friendships, and dramatic reenactments of uplifting myths. In India, whole villages stage dramas taken from their great epics, the *Ramayana* and *Mahabharata*. It's a wonderful way of inspiring young and old with higher values, and creating deep communal bonds.

Divinatory Message: Look to home and family as either the cause of or the solution to your problem. For example, if you are looking for someone to marry, this archetype could indicate either that your family could help you find the right person, or that overdependence on your family is somehow obstructing your search for a mate.

Relationship to Other Oracles: The fifty-sixth hexagram of the I-Ching, "The Wanderer," talks of someone who has no abode. His home is the road. Homes are potential prisons when we are attached to them. Wandering is a way to remove this attachment.

The Tarot's Four of Pentacles also indicates enclosures, possessions, a sense of security, and other qualities relating to the fourth house. The fifty-fifth Secret Dakini card, "Totally Bananas," emphasizes more the inner home, the subconscious, and awareness of primal emotions through fantasy.

57
Fifth House
—Creativity to Honor the Creator

Traditional Meaning: The House of Creativity, Children, and Education

Creative Principle: The fifth house indicates our ability to gain the full fruits of our creative potential. The most basic form of creativity is having children and educating them creatively.

The fifth house also governs our creative expressions through art, music, and literature. Creative potential is determined by signs and planets, but the ability to express that potential fully is governed by this house.

Another basic form of creativity is related to our relationship with the gods, the most primal and powerful expressions of Creative Intelligence. The fifth house governs sacred ritual to contact the gods. We humans are the children of the gods, yet in many cultures the gods are as dependent on us as we are on them. Our devotions feed the gods. Lord Krishna says in the *Bhagavad Gita*, "Through *yagya* (sacred ritual) you sustain the gods and those gods will sustain you. By sustaining one another, you will attain the highest good." (III.11)

A similar type of ritual is worship of ancestors, which we discussed under the nakshatra Magha.

Favorite Fantasies: Do you dream of higher degrees from a prestigious institution? Do you want to perpetuate your family line with children and grandchildren? Do you express yourself through art, music, or writing? Do you worship with your family? These fifth house significations have creativity and education in common—we learn through parenthood, the fine arts, and educating others.

Key Idea for Education: In this age it is becoming increasingly difficult for parents to bridge the generation gap with their children, due to planetary influences which foster intense rebelliousness. This rebelliousness is both a cause and effect of a widespread sense of personal isolation. Large institutions—government, commerce, health care, education—tend to treat people as inanimate, anonymous, bio-economic machines, not unique human beings, each with vast untapped genius, love, and creative energy. Schools that abandon the fine arts, minimize personal contact between teacher and students, and otherwise mechanize the process of education only exacerbate the isolation and resulting rebelliousness.

Two antidotes are best administered in the home. First, let the family worship together, both at home and in temples or churches. Second, imbue children with a sense of family history, so that they see themselves and their relatives in the context of a family chain. It is ideal for the whole family to study its genealogy together and for older members to share elevating stories with the younger generation. Stories from great epics and the lives of great men and women are a wonderful way for a family to share inspiration while connecting to their cultural roots.

A few aids for creativity in education are: small class sizes; art, drama, and musical performance; the study of history with an eye toward honoring great men and women; and any form of creative expression, such as individual science projects or hands-on building projects, where students design and build something useful, like a boat or classroom.

Divinatory Message: Focus your creative gifts in a way that others can enjoy, such as the fine arts, sports, or public speaking. Or spend time helping your children or grandchildren express themselves. If this seems too abstract or difficult, pray. Honor God through activity, either in formal worship or in your own creative way.

Relationship to Other Oracles: The fifty-sixth Secret Dakini card, "Elixir Fruit: Essence," uses ambrosia and sweet fruit to symbolize tasting the sweet essence of things. As mentioned, parenthood and the creative arts are a powerful way to satisfy the senses. However, any activity that stimulates your creativity and absorbs you in joy can have the same effect.

The Tarot's Five of Pentacles relates to all the creative gifts, such as lovemaking, affinity with others, children, etc. The fifty-seventh hexagram of the I-Ching, "Sun/The Gentle (The Penetrating, Wind)," signifies our ability to penetrate to the essence of things. It cautions that these creative gifts must be disciplined and not allowed to degenerate into irresolute license. Since the I-Ching is always concerned with leadership, it also speaks about how to use power creatively and spread it amongst the people.

58

Sixth House
—Perseverance Overcomes Adversity

Traditional Meaning: The House of Enemies, Disease, & Debts

Creative Principle: This house relates to all forms of adversity, especially enemies and disease. It also relates to suffering inflicted by enemies, such as fights, torture, and imprisonment.

This house also relates to the hard work and sense of service needed to overcome such impediments. Protecting one's health and maintaining friendships can be hard work, just like maintaining a strong national defense. But hard work is a two-edged sword. If not balanced with deep rest and creative play, it can lead to disease. Debts are another form of adversity requiring hard work and perseverance.

Favorite Fantasies: Do you have an illness, injury, or debility you dream of overcoming? Does adversity stir you to try harder (strong sixth house), or blow the wind out of your sails (weak sixth house)?

Key Idea for Education: Although Western medicine is effective in preventing infectious diseases through inoculation, it is not so effective in preventing degenerative and chronic diseases related to lifestyle. The medical industry's focus on cure rather than prevention is reflected in the public school system, where holistic and preventive medicine are minimal. Thus the job of holistic health education, like spiritual education, falls on the parents' shoulders because schools are unwilling or unable to assume the role.

In many high schools and even junior high schools, handguns and drug-related violence create a suffocating environment of fear and mistrust where both learning and friendship struggle for air. We support the efforts of law-abiding citizens to banish drugs and weapons from our schools. But programs which fail to deal with the fundamental causes of drug use are doomed to failure. The popular "causes," such as poverty, illiteracy, and evil drug lords, are only fodder for political campaigns. No amount of money spent to fight crime and drugs can eliminate the spiritual bankruptcy they depend on.

In a nation founded on the separation of church and state, the benefits of spiritual instruction can be gained without using religious language. Interdisciplinary education connects each individual to all others, each field of knowledge to all others, and each individual to the source of all knowledge, the transcendental field of pure consciousness. When we add transdisciplinary study (spiritual practice in accord with our most natural path), we have both a theoretical and experiential basis for true spirituality.

Although this book uses theistic language, the same underlying principles can be taught in a nontheistic context. If parents want to tie the key concepts to God, that is always their prerogative. The concept of an infinitely just and loving Creator is a precious cornerstone of faith to billions of people throughout the world, but holistic education can omit worship and religious dogma in the secular classroom. With increasing ethnic and religious diversity in the global village, it is beneficial to study questions of ultimate concern in a context that honors all religions and cultures.

When we see our interdependence on others, we must see that any enmities only undermine our individual and collective strength.

Lack of such connectedness indirectly creates enemies. When one feels isolated and alone, one regards others with suspicion rather than warmth. So the current fragmented, mechanized educational system is actually contributing to the problem. If you doubt this, ask yourself if all the most highly educated people you know are significantly more loving and less angry than those with less schooling.

Divinatory Message: Overcome adversity through hard work and service to others. This may be through following Christ's admonition to turn the other cheek, or turn an enemy into a friend by sensing his needs and helping to fulfill them.

If your problem is debts or chronic illness, this card suggests hard work and perseverance. If your query is whether to follow a certain course of action, this card suggests great danger through potential enemies, debts, or illness.

Relationship to Other Oracles: The Tarot's Six of Pentacles indicates charitable actions, gifts, debts, and ruin—all sixth-house significations. The fifty-eighth hexagram of the I-Ching, surprisingly enough, is called "The Joyous, Lake." Here the I-Ching is calling for firmness, strength, steadfastness, and gentleness—qualities needed to deal with sixth house adversities. Dealing with enemies requires inner strength and (except in war) outer gentleness. The ideal way to deal with enemies is to convert them into friends.

There is another way to interpret this hexagram. If we are tempted to overindulge in pleasures, we reap disease, debts, and enemies. If we get carried away by pleasurable diversions, we must suffer accordingly. "If a man is unstable within, the pleasures of the world that he does not shun have so powerful an influence that he is swept along by them." This is the great danger—that so called "joys" overpower us and destroy our inner balance and direction.

The fifty-seventh Secret Dakini card, "Temptation," takes exactly the same slant. A snake pokes its head between the temptation of worldly pleasures and the lure of cosmic knowledge. We incur sixth-house problems when we get lost in worldly pursuits. Note that none of these oracles ever says that all desires are bad and must be squelched. It is only losing one's purpose and equanimity in desire that causes suffering.

59
Seventh House—
Unimpaired Partnerships

Traditional Meaning: The House of Marriage and Partnership

Creative Principle: This is the house of relationship, or the self in society. It includes marriage, business, partnerships, and other formal or legal relationships. Since interaction implies movement between two persons or places, it is also the house of journey and travel. But love can turn to war, thus this house can indicate quarrels and disputes between partners.

Favorite Fantasies: Is there anyone who has never fantasized about the perfect partner, the ideal friendship, or dream journey? When marriage does not follow the dream plan, do you fantasize (and maybe act out) a war with your partner? Have you ever started a business venture with grand dreams of success? A weakness in seventh house matters leaves one vulnerable to advertisements to get rich quick or find instant romance.

Key Idea for Education: Students should work in pairs and small groups to learn cooperation and relationship skills.

Divinatory Message: Form alliances or partnerships to achieve your objective. Learn the value of adaptability and compromise, so necessary in any partnership.

Relationship to Other Oracles: The Seventh of Pentacles is not clearly seen by most commentators on the Tarot, but A. E. Thierens hits the nail on the head with the following significations for this card: friendship, concord, cooperation, and natural outcome to what was previously sown. A. E. Waite brings in other seventh house ideas—business, barter, and altercation.

The fifty-eighth Dakini card, "Chameleon," is all about adaptability, the key ingredient for lasting relationships and prevention of war. The fifty-ninth hexagram of the I-Ching, "Dispersion (Dissolution)," also talks of qualities necessary to healthy relationships: courteous communication without repression ("... when a man's vital energy is dammed up within him, ... gentleness serves to break up and dissolve the blockage"); dissolving of divisive egotism; and collective celebration of sacred rites to arouse "a strong tide of emotion ... shared by all hearts in unison." Devotion to a higher ideal, especially in a group, is one of the most powerful ways to strengthen relationships.

60
Eighth House
—Unlimited Acceptance of Limitations

Traditional Meaning: The House of Death, Destruction, and Impediments

Creative Principle: This house indicates our longevity and how and when we are likely to die. It is also the house of disease, impediments and obstructions in the achievement of our goals.

The obstacles of the sixth house are more clearly self-created, and may be overcome through perseverance, whereas eighth house obstacles are born of our interactions in society, and therefore are more difficult to surmount through individual effort. They may be best handled by acceptance and the creative use of limitation. For example, many blind musicians have found that lack of sight actually sharpens their hearing, and thereby enhances their musicianship.

These distinctions between the sixth and eighth houses are relative, not absolute. In general, the first through sixth houses relate to the self, and the seventh through twelfth houses relate to relationships and society.

It is a common misconception to think of the inauspicious

houses—the sixth, eighth, and twelfth—as wholly bad or negative. The obstacles and losses indicated by these houses have two great values. First, they inspire us to dive deeper into our inner resources and come up with more creative solutions. The world mythology is replete with heroes whose greatness is expressed by conquering seemingly insurmountable obstacles.

Second, those obstacles which are not meant to be overcome teach us the invaluable lesson of grace. Only when we fully accept our lot in life can we recognize our infinite intimacy with every atom of creation, and open ourselves to immeasurable blessings from the Creator.

The eighth house is also associated with past and future. How are these connected with the other eighth house significations? Insurmountable obstacles, especially death and disease, are meant to teach us acceptance. Fleeting joys can be achieved through effort, but lasting bliss is only gained by acceptance. As long as we dwell on the past and future, we miss the bliss of the present. Obstacles pull us out of fantasy land into the here-and-now. Acceptance of the eventual demise of the body frees us from escapism and fear, and lets us enjoy the timeless bliss of Self-awareness. So, like the sixth and twelfth houses, the "negative" traits of the eighth are only with respect to material progress, and are invaluable aids to deeper understanding when used wisely.

Favorite Fantasies: Although the eighth house is associated with death, it is only associated with the wish for death if very weak or afflicted. The purest eighth house fantasy is for total acceptance and understanding of our physical, mental, and environmental limitations. This does not mean passive resignation to all obstacles. "Give me the strength to change the things I can change (sixth house), the courage to accept the things I cannot (eighth house)."

Key Idea for Education: The lesson of the eighth house is acceptance, not blame. This does not mean passive resignation, but learning to use obstacles to your advantage. For example, if you cannot afford a course you want to take, find free sources of knowledge, such as friends or libraries.

Divinatory Message: Transform your guilt and blame into forgiveness and acceptance. If you are trying to decide whether to do something, realize this card implies great impediments to success. Do not proceed with your plans unless you can joyfully accept great material limitation in the venture.

Relationship to Other Oracles: The sixtieth hexagram of the I-Ching, "Limitation," discusses setting limits on all things—energy, expenditures, and even limits on limits. "To become strong, a man's life needs the limitations ordained by duty and voluntarily accepted." The challenge of the eighth house is to know when the limitations are too great to be overcome, so that one does not exhaust one's energy in futile efforts.

The Eight of Pentacles gives some of these same ideas: prudence, economy, chastity, and intelligence lovingly applied to material matters—all ways of conserving energy.

The fifty-ninth Secret Dakini card, "Pearls Before Swine," indicates the need for discrimination to appreciate the pearls of wisdom which are lost to ignorant people. Discrimination shows us that we need not suffer due to limitation. We can accept outer constraints without limiting ourselves internally.

61
Ninth House
—Good Dharma Brings Good Karma

Traditional Meaning: The House of Dharma and Fortune

Creative Principle: The ninth house signifies dharma, our moral fiber and duty to society. It also governs religion, philosophy, and law, which are related to our ethical and social behavior.

When we follow our dharma we are rewarded with good fortune. Thus the ninth house is traditionally associated with good fortune. We feel that the good fortune of the ninth house is limited to matters of dharma, such as receiving good spiritual training, or enjoying the company of enlightened souls. The ninth house is also associated with elders and preceptors, from whom we learn dharma, and religious pilgrimages, where we honor dharma.

Favorite Fantasies: Do you dream of finding the perfect spiritual teacher? Do you want to build a church, mosque, or temple? Are you filled with gratitude to your parents, grandparents, or religious teacher for the high values they inspired? Do you dream of a pilgrimage to the Holy Land, the Himalayas, or the sacred sites of Native Americans? Are you righteous, respectful, and law-abiding in your fantasies? These all suggest a strong ninth house.

Key Idea for Education: Dharma is that which upholds society. In traditional cultures religious institutions were the main vehicles for upholding dharma outside the family. In fact "religion" is one meaning of "dharma." Even in nondenominational schools the values of dharma can be taught as the moral glue that holds society together while allowing each individual freedom to develop his own gifts. Many religious moralists are reluctant to admit that atheists can be highly ethical and theists can be just the opposite. No group in history has ever had a monopoly on virtue, although many have implied as much to keep followers in their fold.

Divinatory Message: This card is a positive indication for good fortune in what you seek, but it strongly cautions you to pay strict attention to ethical implications. It also encourages the study of religion, philosophy, and moral principles for helping you decide a right course of action. For example, if you are tempted to take unfair advantage of someone, this would be an admonition against such unfairness.

Relationship to Other Oracles: The sixty-first hexagram of the I-Ching, "Inner Truth" is a good definition of dharma. Wilhelm's commentary on this hexagram abounds with dharmic principles such as law and justice.

The Tarot's Nine of Pentacles emphasizes luck significations, such as gain, inheritance, and fate. It also points to religious and spiritual practices needed to align oneself with dharma and thereby achieve good fortune.

The sixtieth Secret Dakini card, "Taking Up Arms," shows the God Vishnu, the protector of dharma, as He incarnates in the world to destroy evil. It is a position of great strength and fearlessness because one has the invincible power of dharma on one's side. Divine incarnations are not a one-time event. God takes on different incarnations in different world cycles to destroy the wicked, protect the innocent, and restore dharma and balance in nature.

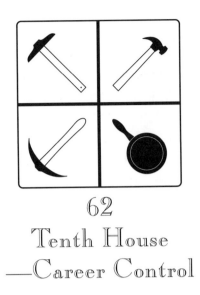

62
Tenth House
—Career Control

Traditional Meaning: The House of Career & Worldly Action

Creative Principle: This house indicates our action in the world. It is normally thought of as one's career or vocation, as well as professional success and recognition. (We feel that it can relate to work in any of the eight fields of life, but we will limit our discussion to professional life, and let you infer what you can about other fields of life. (Please see The Eight Fields of Living, Part II, Chapter 3.) Since professional success depends on training, if this house is weak or afflicted, we have difficulty surviving in a competitive world. If it is strong and unafflicted, we rise above difficulties in our career.

The tenth house indicates satisfaction and recognition in our career. The eleventh house indicates earnings. So if the tenth house is weak and the eleventh strong, it would suggest a lucrative but frustrating professional life. If the tenth is strong and the eleventh weak, it would suggest professional satisfaction and recognition, but limited income from work. (Note: We offer these tips on astrology only to clarify the basic archetypes, not as a guide for chart interpretation. Any book that pretends to teach chart interpretation is only misleading you into thinking that the real inner keys to prognostication can be learned from books.)

The tenth house is traditionally associated with one's father. Prior to the Industrial Revolution, sons apprenticed to their fathers. Although this direct transmission of skills has been mostly lost in modern societies, parents still make great sacrifices to help their children develop good careers. There is a less obvious connection between profession and our parents. Children are drawn to parents who can nourish their creative gifts. Heredity does not determine genius; it provides a channel for its expression. Johann Sebastian Bach and Wolfgang Amadeus Mozart were both sons of musicians, and showed precocious musical skills from an early age.

There are many basic symmetries in a horoscope. For example, the tenth house (father and profession) is opposite the fourth house (mother and home life). The first house (self-image and body) is opposite the seventh house (partnership and marriage, i.e. looking at another instead of oneself). The second house (nourishment and other things that support life, especially in childhood) is opposite the eighth house (old age, death, disease, and things that destroy life). The third house (competition, self-assertion, and siblings) is opposite the ninth house (obedience to legal and religious authority, wherein we subordinate our own desires to elders' wishes or higher principles). The fifth house (creative expressions and offerings to God) is opposite the eleventh house (gifts from God as some form of gain). The sixth house (obstacles which are meant to strengthen our perseverance and determination) is opposite the twelfth house (losses, including loss of the body, which teach us the total acceptance required for grace to flow through us).

Favorite Fantasies: Do you dream of lording over your business as a great king rules his kingdom? (The tenth house is also associated with kingship.) Are you willing to work long hours to achieve your professional goals? (The tenth house is also the house of action.) Do you dream of making you father proud of your professional success?

Key Idea for Education: Schools today are increasingly oriented toward job training. This is to be commended, but it has drawbacks. When job training is the only purpose of education and all the other studies that open the heart and mind are ignored, then both individual and society suffer greatly. The Golden Age of Greece was built with an educational system that honored the Platonic ideal of drawing knowledge out of a student, rather than imposing it from without. Body, mind, and spirit were developed together. Nowadays students are prepared to be consumption/production machines with limited appreciation for the fine arts, philosophy, and literature. Liberal arts colleges try valiantly to preserve cultural values, but lack the interdisciplinary and transdisciplinary keys that are the most effective means of achieving their end. Students often graduate with technical skills, but without interpersonal skills or a strong sense of self. Even the most highly educated professionals exhibit high levels of angst, anger, and alienation.

Career training must be in the context of service to society and the need for many different professions to create a balanced economy. Career planning should begin by asking "What can I enjoy doing that will contribute to others' well-being as well as my own?"

Divinatory Message: This card suggests that your answer lies in actualizing your dreams in the competitive world. It is time to stop speculating about what could be done. Take a pragmatic approach that meets others' needs as well as your own. Act now, without hesitation or procrastination.

This card favors outer action, not inner reflection. It further implies success in the world if one undertakes action.

Relationship to Other Oracles: The sixty-first Secret Dakini card, "Survival," gives an image of tenth-house significations gone astray. The picture is a few green shoots surviving in the middle of vast industrial waste. So it is for the serious seeker trying to survive in the spiritual wasteland of our postindustrial economy. Our work expresses a fundamental need to survive. This principle implies that spiritually motivated, socially conscious workers can survive and even thrive in spite of a polluted economic environment.

The Tarot's Ten of Pentacles suggests career-related significations such as success, wealth, and building a stable home in the world of action. It also points to the possibility of a reversal of fortunes if this principle is weak. A.E. Thierens summarizes the meaning of the tenth house well: "It is the good ripe fruit of karma, the fullness of nature at its height." In other words, this house signifies fulfillment of our actions in the world.

The sixty-second hexagram of the I-Ching, "Preponderance of the Small," may sound contradictory to dreams of a great career. Actually, it is a caution by the Chinese sages about the dangers of flying too high and achieving too much success too early. In other words, don't get lost in wordly action at the expense of higher values in life.

63

Eleventh House
—Aspirations Answered:
Cashing in on Karma

Traditional Meaning: The House of Gain

Creative Principle: The eleventh house is the house of income, profit, and abundance. Any planets placed here are deemed favorable, and become more favorable later in life. It also relates to a general ability to fulfill all desires in an easy and effortless way.

Eleventh house gains may be either material or spiritual. In either case, the gains may lead to excess. Excessive indulgence and vanity are obvious dangers of sudden material wealth, but spiritual pride is equally pernicious. That's why all valid spiritual traditions teach us not to be infatuated with flashy experiences or paranormal powers.

Western astrologers emphasize the group tendencies and proclivities of this house, whereas some Eastern astrologers emphasize its individualistic and egoic tendencies. Our feeling on the matter is that a study of the eleventh sign, Aquarius, indicates a combination of individual and collective tendencies. (There is some correspondence between the houses and signs of the zodiac.) Aquarius maintains a certain individualistic and independent quality, while at the same time seeking to uplift society and treat everyone as brothers and sisters.

As we said in the previous principle, both the tenth and eleventh houses are related to professional success. The tenth house indicates happiness and contentment in one's career, and the eleventh house indicates gains through career, investments, or friends. Both ninth and eleventh houses relate to good luck. The ninth house is good fortune in religious and spiritual development, whereas the eleventh house is more related to financial and material rewards, and a general ability to fulfill all desires.

It takes action to capitalize on good fortune. We cannot collect eleventh house gains from tenth house work unless we do the work, whether spiritual or material. Even collecting on a winning lottery ticket requires watching for the winning number and turning in the lucky ticket.

Favorite Fantasies: Do you dream of winning the lottery or breaking the casino? Or making lots of money at work? If your desire is for honest gain, and you take the steps necessary to allow it to flow to you, it suggests a healthy eleventh house. If you don't feel worthy of affluence, it suggests a weak eleventh house.

Key Idea for Education: Children need to learn prosperity consciousness in a natural way. Prosperity most often comes through patient pursuit of realistic goals and clear, firm aspirations. These aspirations may be spiritual, material, or a combination of both.

Divinatory Message: The indications are very favorable for gain in whatever undertaking you are contemplating. However, be careful of easy success which can lead to complacency or overindulgence.

Relationship to Other Oracles: Since there are only ten Pentacle cards in the Tarot, and since we are in a slightly different ordering phase in each oracle, one can question whether the last two principles of the I-Ching and of the Secret Dakini Oracle relate to the last two houses of the horoscope. Our best judgment is that they do, but we leave it to you to decide for yourself.

The sixty-third hexagram of the I-Ching, "After Completion," implies the fulfillment of desires and a state of peace, which are in danger of becoming upset and undone through the very cyclical nature of life. The sixty-second Secret Dakini card, "Dangerous Pussy/The Past," connotes "the seductive and dangerous aspects of the raw female energy." The danger of the eleventh house is in being seduced into complacency by our own success. With every gain there is risk of loss, and with the fulfillment of every desire there is risk of losing the source of fulfillment.

64

Twelfth House—Lose the World and Gain the Universe

Traditional Meaning: The House of Material Loss and Spiritual Gain

Creative Principle: Each house builds on the material actualization of the prior house. We start in the first house with the basic personality seeking expansion. The second house gives the material comforts and resources needed for security. That security provides the basis for the courage and confidence which develop in the third house. These qualities provide a foundation for harmonious family life in the fourth house, which in turn support creativity in the fifth house. But creativity invites obstacles and enemies in the sixth house.

The challenges of the sixth house teach us the adaptability so necessary for harmonious relationships in the seventh house. Even the most harmonious relationships meet with further obstacles and limitations in the eighth house. In the ninth house we align ourselves with natural law or dharma to deal with those limitations. Performing our dharma is the foundation of career success in the tenth house, which in turn brings the profit and income signified by the eleventh house. But material gain is always a temporary thing which must eventually vanish in the twelfth house. Material loss and suffering provides the impetus for spiritual emancipation, the culmination of human development, also governed by the twelfth house. In this sense the twelfth house is the most important house in the zodiac, as it indicates our ability to gain enlightenment.

The twelfth house is traditionally associated with enemies, expenses, loss, and death. No wonder it is often considered the unluckiest house! We feel that a totally negative reading of this house reveals how far astrology has descended into ignorance. Although this house is rightly associated with material loss, it is very auspicious for spiritual matters. When we are stripped of material attachments we are freed to focus on the deeper questions of life.

Favorite Fantasies: Fear of death and disaster indicates a weak twelfth house. Desire for enlightenment indicates a strong twelfth house. In some traditions, enlightenment means stepping off the wheel of birth and rebirth. We prefer to see it as freedom from suffering and misidentification, and empowerment to help others.

Key Idea for Education: Material abundance should not be thought of as contrary to spiritual attainment. It is natural to want two hundred percent of life—fullness of both material and spiritual aspirations. However, it is equally important to clearly see how material loss can actually be a great boon to spiritual evolution.

Children should be taught that although they have a body-mind complex, they are not that body-mind complex. Any material gain or loss, i.e., anything that affects the body-mind complex, is merely one more play of Mother Nature that does not touch the deep inner essence of the Self.

Divinatory Message: Be very careful of what you are seeking. This archetype implies a likely loss relating to your material aspirations or possessions if you proceed on your contemplated course of action. It also signifies that this action may be a great spiritual boon.

Should you pursue your plans? If your question relates purely to spiritual matters, then you are receiving a resounding "yes." But if your desire is primarily a material one, then you are receiving a resounding "no."

Relationship to Other Oracles: The last hexagram of the I-Ching, "Before Completion," is a clear indication of the completion of a life cycle. The time is the end of winter, when lakes and streams are beginning to thaw. One must move warily, like an old fox walking on thin ice. One must use deliberation and caution to avoid falling through the ice before reaching the other shore. "The conditions are difficult. The task is great and full of responsibility. It is nothing less than that of leading the world out of confusion back to order." It takes a highly enlightened person to lead the world from confusion to order. Our material foundations may crack like ice in springtime, but with care and caution we can utilize this time for great spiritual freedom.

The sixty-third Secret Dakini card, "Centering/The Present," shows complete spiritual illumination in the form of the Shri Chakra, a powerful yantra (geometrical image for meditation). It symbolizes the integration of male and female, inner and outer, microcosm and macrocosm, and the presence of all the deities in every iota of creation. It is truly an image of the enlightenment gained through the twelfth house.

Note: The last Secret Dakini card (the sixty-fourth), called "Last Laugh/The Future," appears to be a commentary on all the houses as a whole, in particular, not getting caught in wrongful identification with the significations of any one house. This card may also be a summary of the whole Secret Dakini Oracle deck—one must see each principle as part of a greater whole. Use the deck for guidance, but don't get caught in the process. Life is nothing but the play and display of Creative Intelligence. Once we see the transitory nature of existence and our role in it, we can only laugh!

Part II

The Art of
Multidimensional Living

Introduction to Part II

The Art of Multidimensional Living™ is a new approach to holistic living with four major branches. The first branch, interdisciplinary learning (the sixty-four fundamental archetypes), was covered in Part I. The other three branches are covered in Part II:

Chapter 1
   Transdisciplinary learning—The Eight Great Paths to God™

Chapter 2
   Multidisciplinary learning—the twenty-four archetypal disciplines

Chapter 3
   Holistic living—The Eight Fields of Living™

1. The Eight Great Paths to God™

by Douglas Grimes

"What is my spiritual path?" This may be the most important question we can ask. With traditional social order unraveling at the seams and the environment in ever-deeper distress, the highest good we can perform is to take recourse to the only source of ultimate harmony and order, our own spiritual nature. It is the link between humanity and divinity, the finite and the infinite. But the so-called "spiritual" and new-age marketplace is noisy and crowded, and many seekers remain terribly confused by the options.

The concept of different paths for different psycho-physical-spiritual types is common to all the great religious and spiritual traditions throughout the world. There are different ways of organizing the various systems and practices. The one that I have found most comprehensive and effective is a planetary model developed by my coauthor Edward Tarabilda, founder of the Art of Multi-Dimensional Living™. I give Ed 100% of the credit for this paradigm. Whatever understanding of the planets I present here comes from him.

The eight paths correspond to the eight levels of human life:
1. The physical body, ruled by Saturn
2. The senses, ruled by Venus
3. The mind *manas,* ruled by Jupiter
4. The intellect *buddhi,* ruled by Mercury
5. The will, ruled by Mars
6. The heart, ruled by the Moon
7. The integrating factor or sense of "I-ness," ruled by the Sun
8. An independent, iconoclastic factor, ruled by the Nodes of the Moon.

Although all eight levels are found in everyone, each individual has just one which is most suitable as an avenue for spiritual development. The first seven levels are found in classic descriptions of the personality from both Eastern and Western spiritual schools. The eighth is necessary to explain the rebel tendency which everyone has, expressed or not, in some area of the personality.

These paths are presented here as fundamental archetypes, not as taught by particular teachers or schools. Many teachers and schools rightly or wrongly mix paths as we define them here. The seven planets plus the nodes symbolize the first eight principles of Creative Intelligence, the unmanifest basis of existence and consciousness. They are the basic organizing principles behind both subjective and objective creation.

The eight paths are:
1. Hatha Yoga, the path of physical culture, ruled by Saturn
2. Raj Yoga, the path of sensory refinement, ruled by Venus
3. Karma Yoga, the path of action, ruled by Jupiter
4. Gyana Yoga, the path of discrimination, ruled by Mercury
5. Kundalini or Kriya Yoga, the path of will, ruled by Mars
6. Bhakti Yoga, the path of devotion, ruled by the Moon
7. Surya Yoga, the path of integration, ruled by the Sun
8. Tantra, the path of the spiritual rebel, ruled by the Nodes of the Moon. We set it apart from the others because it is a completely different category than the yogas.

Here they are in more detail:

1. Hatha Yoga, the path of physical culture, ruled by Saturn:

Saturn rules the physical body, boundaries, hierarchy, detail, and structure. Although modern marketers of hatha yoga promote books and coed classes full of sleek models in scanty bathing suits or leotards, true hatha yoga is the most private, reclusive, and conservative of all spiritual disciplines, as Saturn is the shyest, slowest, and most reclusive planet.

Hatha Yoga is far more than physical postures and purificatory regimes. It requires great restraint in all areas—physical, mental, and emotional. The hatha yogi seeks simplicity and solitude. He always restrains his senses, and regularly fasts in different ways, abstaining from food, sleep, sex, social interaction, and any form of sensory indulgence. This is the most austere path for the serious seeker, and the most universal one for the casual seeker because anyone can benefit from some physical purification, if not taken to extremes.

Breathing techniques (pranayamas) are an important part of hatha yoga, and play a preparatory role in other paths, especially kundalini yoga. Breath is the delicate bridge between mind and body, the subtle link between subjectivity and objectivity. Breathing techniques offer great potential for purifying both mind and body, but malpractice can cause untold damage. Advanced pranayamas cannot be learned from books. They require a skilled master. Unfortunately, there are few, if any, masters competent to teach them today. It is safer to be moderate in pranayama and ease off as soon as you experience negative side effects, such as headaches, irritability, or disorientation.

We our born with empty lungs. Our first act in this life is inhalation. Our last act at death is exhalation. For the yogi, every inhalation is a birth and every exhalation a death. Retention of full breath is suspension of life. Holding the lungs empty is suspension of death. Holding the breath is one of the easiest ways to stop the mind cold. However, mere lack of thoughts without expanded awareness is of no spiritual benefit. Depriving the brain and heart of oxygen can only be deleterious in the long run.

Hatha yogis are also the greatest skeptics, trusting concrete evidence and cold, dry logic more than speculative ideas or ever-shifting emotions.

The Saturn path loves silence, secrecy, and seclusion. For guidance in the physical postures of Hatha Yoga, the Iyengar approach expresses the meticulous attention to detail necessary for proper practice of this path, although some of its adherents make the mistake of prescribing one "universal" set of postures for all people, rather than tailoring the practice to individual needs. The Native American vision quest—a period of fasting, seclusion, and prayer in the wilderness—is another perfect example of Saturn's approach to spiritual unfoldment. Several Roman Catholic monastic orders also exemplify the Saturn path in their outer behavior, such as the austere Franciscans and silent Trappists.

Each of the yogas has its own characteristic form of meditation. One Saturn meditation is just being empty, sitting very still and doing nothing, as in typical Zen practice. The meditator may just observe his breath, or count each stage of breathing in a very slow, deliberate manner.

The irony of the Saturn path is that it uses the body to transcend the body. Through assiduous attention to purifying the gross material sheath, the hatha yogi becomes aware of the nonmaterial realm of pure spirit.

For all the yogas there are both a danger and an antidote for the danger. The general antidote is awareness of the validity of different paths for different people, and practice of the path most suited to one's unique personal spiritual nature. Since Saturn governs boundaries and the body, the greatest danger in the Saturn path is becoming mentally rigid or preoccupied with one's own body.

2. Raj Yoga, the path of sensory refinement, ruled by Venus:

Venus is the sweetest, loveliest, and most positive planet. She governs the senses, the fine arts, and refined manners. Raj yogis favor sweet talk, sweet food, sweet music, and idealistic plans for global harmony. They avoid danger, confrontation, debate, and tend to underestimate the efforts needed to implement their lofty ideals. In terms of spiritual practice, outer Raj Yoga involves refined art and music, and inner Raj Yoga involves refinement of the inner senses, primarily through simple sounds, or mantras, chosen to attune the individual to the cosmic harmony. The name "Raj," or "king," derives from the fact that kings are born into a life of material ease, where refinement of the senses is most easily pursued.

Several centuries before Christ, the great sage Patanjali captured the seed ideas of Raj Yoga in his *Yoga Sutras*. As Venus is the planet of ease and comfort, Raj Yoga should be the easiest of the yogas, but often it has been taught as just the opposite. This is not to imply that the Raj yogi can be a hedonist, indulging every sensory desire without restraint. On the contrary! Many people try to practice the outer behavioral disciplines of Raj Yoga without a simple inner technique of transcendence—the old cart before the horse. It is easier and more effective to put primary emphasis on change from within. Behavioral change will follow.

There is a common misconception that Raj Yoga is the universal yoga. Many people think that Patanjali taught integral yoga because he discusses eight different levels of practice (outer prohibitions and observances, physical postures and pranayamas, sensory restraint, and three types of inner practice—concentration, meditation, and absorption). Misunderstandings arise with Patanjali because he was addressing two different issues in his *Yoga Sutras*—eight limbs which are common to all yogas, and details specific to Raj Yoga. Each yoga takes a different approach to all eight limbs.

The senses draw the attention away from the bliss of Self-awareness, so all the yogas require restraining the senses to some degree. Life in the body is not possible without some sensory experience. And the senses are unruly, like powerful wild horses pulling the mind from object to object. So how do you pursue Self-awareness while the senses pull you away? How do you minimize the struggle and maximize the bliss?

We have desires related to each of the eight levels of life. The planetary ruler of each yoga sublimates desires on both an outer and an inner dimension. The outer dimension is purification of action and surroundings to better reflect our infinite nature. The inner dimension is leading the attention away from outer objects of physical experience to subtler levels of inner spiritual experience.

Venus, the ruler of the senses, governs the desire for sensory pleasure. She can choose to either indulge in sensory pleasures, or sublimate those desires for suprasensory bliss, the calm and lasting inner fulfillment that is not associated with any specific experience. On an outer level, she avoids conflict by building an environment of beauty and harmony. On an inner level, she refines the senses to transcend the senses.

Maharishi Mahesh Yogi is a perfect example of a great modern Raj Yogi. His Transcendental Meditation (TM) Program and the TM-Siddhi Program are classic Raj Yoga at its best, naturally fluid and effortless. The TM practice uses the sense of hearing. One experiences finer and finer states of a meaningless and harmonious sound to seduce the awareness away from the outer senses, until the sound disappears and the time-space boundaries of experience dissolve in the boundless bliss of the Self.

Just as Venus is the great peacemaker, the proper practice of Raj Yoga is a great antidote to stress and violence for both individual and society. As hundreds of scientific studies have shown, TM is very restful and uplifting to mind, body, and environment. It is also one of the easiest and safest paths for many diverse people to practice.

Although the path of action (karma yoga) and the path of the heart (bhakti yogi) are the most explicitly devotional, there is a devotional aspect of every path, even without belief in God. In Raj Yoga devotion is through appreciation of harmony and beauty. Maharishi gives the analogy of a great artist whose perfect sculpture adorns a public setting. Many people see the sculpture everyday without giving it much notice, but one man is so captivated by it that he comes daily and is spellbound by its beauty. The art lover naturally dreams of meeting the great artist, and the artist is naturally delighted to meet the rare soul who really appreciates the beauty of his handiwork. In the same way, the Creator of the universe showers love and blessings on those who truly appreciate the infinite beauty of creation.

The danger of mispractice on the Venusian path is a dreamy sort of pseudospiritual narcissism, where one is attached to positivity and avoids dealing with the sometimes harsh "realities" of daily life. As with any path, the dangers are least for people naturally suited to the path.

3. Karma Yoga, the path of action, ruled by Jupiter:

This is the path of selfless service. The true karma yogi enjoys giving without thought of reward. Unattached to his action and the fruit thereof, he gladly does his duty to God and man.

On an outer level, that duty may be violent, as in the case of Arjuna and other warriors, or it may be nonviolent, as in the case of Gandhi and Martin Luther King. It may be religious work—Jupiter rules the priesthood and sacred ritual, or it may be secular—great philanthropists like Andrew Carnegie express Jupiter's generosity and abundance.

Spirituality in all its myriad forms requires transcendence, and transcendence generally implies silent awareness. How is it possible to transcend in activity? It appears to be a contradiction in terms. Jupiter, the guru of the devas, knows that the infinite dynamism of creation coexists with the infinite silence of its Source. How does He incorporate silence in activity?

To answer this question, we must understand *manas,* the aspect of the mind which turns percept into concept and concept into action. It is distinguished from *buddhi,* the discriminative intellect. *Buddhi* is the seat of higher reason, the ability to probe to the core meaning beyond the surface value of words. When we say Einstein had a great mind, we are referring to his *buddhi,* not his *manas.* The vast majority of our thoughts occur in *manas.* For most of us, *manas* is forever spinning, blindly chasing desire, trying to relive the past or anticipate the future, and only dimly aware of the eternal beauty of the present.

Until we awaken our higher faculties, we live in a perpetual cycle of action, impression, and desire. We have no control over our actions because we have no control over our desires. As soon as we begin an action, a new wave of impressions floods the senses, and a new wave of desires wells up beyond control. Our daily lives become habitual repetitions of the same patterns of thought and action we've followed for years.

The first great faculty that makes humans so different from animals is the ability to use symbols and reflect on their own thoughts— qualities of *manas.* Animals have limited *manas.* Their physical and sensory capacities, ruled by Saturn and Venus, respectively, are more highly developed in some species than in humans, but even the most intelligent animals have limited ability to conceptualize, consider, and plan their actions. They act automatically and instinc- tively, with almost no self-awareness and little use of symbols. An animal learns to determine whether a rustling in the brush is friend or foe, predator or prey. But with the possible exception of the higher marine mammals, animal vocabularies and symbolic skills are minute compared to human.

Humans, on the other hand, are richly endowed with symbolic skills they use in language, art, science, and technology. We could describe the whole of human civilization as symbol systems. By means of *manas* we translate our impressions (percepts) into symbols (conceptual expressions) and actions (physical expres- sions). Our symbols take on enormous power of their own. We fight wars over slogans, sacrifice health and wealth in the pursuit of ideals, and organize our societies around the shared symbols embodied in our political, educational, and economic institutions.

Why are we caught in this cycle of desire, action, and impression?

Why is most of our mental energy wasted dwelling on the past and future, barely tasting the eternal glory of the present? Because of desire, say the sages. Not that desire is bad. Life is not possible without desire. Suffering and imbalance arise only when we let desires overshadow our inner fullness and our intimate connection with all life.

The central teaching of karma yoga is nonattachment to the fruit of action. Jupiter is very generous and expansive. The essence of karma yoga is selfless service, giving without thought for reward. In the *Bhagavad Gita* Krishna says, "You have control over action alone, not over its fruits" (II.47). The Karma Yogi says his prayers and does his duty to the best of his ability, but does not worry about the outcome, as that is out of his hands. The archer can only pull back his bow, point his arrow, and release. He cannot control any sudden gusts of wind which may blow his arrow off target.

The karma yogi takes control of the cycle at the only point where it can be managed, the gap between impression and desire. *Manas* organizes the raw data of sensory impressions into meaningful images and abstracts them into symbols (words, pictures, music, etc.). The sensate mind of animals has minimal symbolic skills. Symbolic skills give us the power to rise above our lower passions and selfish tendencies. The most obvious human symbolic skill, language, opens up boundless possibilities related to Jupiter. It lets us learn ethical standards to guide our thoughts and actions. It preserves knowledge from generation to generation. It lets us share our joys and sorrows and celebrate together to strength our common bonds.

One type of karma yoga is sacred ritual, symbolic action to elevate the mundane to the divine and express appreciation to the higher powers of Nature. It purifies the whole cycle of action-impression-conception-desire. Ritual requires sacrifice. Selfish desires are sacrificed for a higher purpose, such as service to God, country, alma mater, or the needy.

For many people, ritual has the dual effect of elevating the worshipper's awareness and winning support of the supersensible beings operating behind the visible world. Just as great heads of state are receptive to citizens who approach them with the proper protocol and respect, the higher powers of nature listen patiently to people who honor them in ritual, especially heartfelt rituals and ancient rituals which have survived the test of time. Although the major world religions have lost most of their knowledge of tran-scendence, they have all maintained certain ceremonies which continue to have power, especially for those who have done the inner work necessary to appreciate their significance.

There are many levels of ritual. Suffice it to say that empty ritual, without feeling or understanding, is of little value. Heartfelt ritual, with rich symbology and understanding, stimulates the deepest wellsprings of life and thrills the higher powers of nature, who reward the worshipper generously for his offerings.

With regular practice ritual becomes habitual. We cultivate the habit of offering all our actions to the divine. All our thoughts become prayers, our words blessings, our actions services. Then action, which has been a means of bondage, becomes a means of liberation.

Jupiter rules scripture and gurus. Karma yogis know from the study of scripture and the example of great sages that silence and activity are two sides of the same eternal Reality. The karma yogi follows the example of great saints, scholars, and philanthropists, and conducts his daily life in a manner that reminds him of the Almighty. He treats all life with reverence, as even the most wretched of sinners is a perfect expression of cosmic order. He is also inspired to visit sacred sites where he can meditate or worship in an environment enriched by enlightened beings.

Although the karma yogi may find deep rest and relaxation in silent meditation, his primary vehicle for evolution is selfless service. As his mind develops, he becomes increasingly sensitive to the needs of others and his own unique gifts for helping them. Rather than acting out of some onerous sense of duty, he learns to respond spontaneously, intuitively, and joyously. He learns to rest in activity. As he becomes attuned to nature, his thoughts and actions become superfluid, and deep knots of frustration and conflict evaporate. He discovers through experience something psychologists are only beginning to understand, that all neuroses are rooted in attachment. Releasing our surface attachments removes hidden obstacles to fulfillment of our deeper desires, those inspired by cosmic intelligence.

The karma yogi gains maximum benefit from meditation techniques he can use in activity, followed by a brief period of silence to complete the cycle of rest and activity. The late great Kashmiri saint, Lakshman Jee (a.k.a. Lakshman Joo), said that an active meditation is a thousand times more powerful than a silent one for the karma yogi. Again, a word of caution—for yogis of other paths, trying to remember a mantra in activity may just divide the mind. An exception applies to people on the path of the heart, where remembrance of the names of God becomes spontaneous and automatic.

Jupiter also governs morality. As a practical teacher, he knows that most people have neither the time nor the inclination to spend all day in worship. They need guidance in daily life to prevent gross mistakes that could derail their evolution or disrupt society.

Morality is often confused with spirituality. All the universal principles of moral behavior are necessary to prevent physical, emotional, and spiritual damage. But spirituality is transcendental, not behavioral.

The ash heaps of history are full of seekers who fell prey to temptation and violated basic standards of morality. If we practice surface morality, without inner inspiration, we suffer a constant tension between what we want to do and what we ought to do. Indulge your desires, and remain their slave. Suppress them, and suffer all kinds of frustration. Either way, you are divided. So what do we do? If we are yogis, we are very selective in the desires we follow. We don't deny desire; we learn to redirect the energy of life-damaging tendencies and purify our minds and bodies so that all our desires become spontaneously life-supporting.

Inner practice does not relieve us of the need to watch our outer behavior, but it facilitates the process enormously. Even a good night's sleep makes it much easier to speak and act rightly.

No matter what our path, as our consciousness develops, our desires flow more and more with the stream of evolution and gradually gain the infinite power of Nature for their fruition. The gap between our "want's" and "should's" disappears as individual life joins the current of cosmic life. Paradoxically, in surrendering our surface desires, we finds fulfillment of all our needs, physical, mental, and spiritual.

There is one danger in all spiritual practices—attachment to the path to the extent that one loses sight of the goal. This attachment takes a different form in each of the great paths. In karma yoga, it may take the form of attachment to one's own guru or religion, or a pompous piety and surface morality. The antidote is under-standing how different forms of action, good and bad, are a neces-sary part of the cosmic plan. Saints would never realize their potential for saintliness without sinners to test them!

4. Gyana Yoga, the path of discrimination, ruled by Mercury:

As a surgeon wields a scalpel to cut away a malignant tumor, the gyan yogi uses reason to cut away ignorance and misunderstanding. He knows that the ego's attachment to false belief is a veil to one's own true bliss, so he delights in exposing false conditioning and blind assumptions. The ego is revealed as a fiction, a nonentity which survives only as long as one clings to the belief that one is separate from the universal order. When the ego disappears, only the bliss of Self-awareness remains.

Modern education tends to distract and numb the intellect with a glut of unconnected information. Students become bored and frustrated because schools emphasize objective knowledge and suppress the need for subjective exploration into one's own consciousness. Today's education reinforces what Dr. Deepak Chopra aptly calls "the superstition of materialism," the belief that matter is primary and spirit is secondary or nonexistent.

A true education enhances discrimination between that which never changes, the Self, and the ever-changing mirage of phenomenal existence. It is more concerned with quality of consciousness than quantity of surface information. Three of the most powerful tools of education are transdisciplinary learning (techniques of unfolding consciousness), interdisciplinary learning to show the fundamental principles of creative intelligence that link all fields knowledge (Part I of this book), and multidisciplinary learning (next chapter). All three are almost completely absent from secular education today.

Like Saturn, Mercury is a skeptic and shuns blind faith. Saturn requires concrete facts and figures, and dominates modern materialistic education with its emphasis on form rather than substance. Mercury probes deeper, looking beyond the obvious surface values for subtler truths and higher causes. Saturn prefers silence, whereas Mercury delights in word play and excels in debate. The greatest of all gyanis, Adi Shankara, defeated the best-known philosophers of his time in great public debates with thousands in attendance.

Mercury, the planet of transcendence, uses language to connect matter and spirit. He employs words to transcend words. As Lao Tsu said, "The Tao that can be put in words is not the Tao." The intellect cannot identify ultimate Truth. It can only cut away falsehood. The Sanskrit term is *neti, neti,* "not this, not this." So the gyani questions everything, especially his own identity. He strips away false identification with his body, senses, mind, intellect, will, feelings, and finally, his sense of I-ness. Eventually he realizes the ultimate answer is beyond words, beyond conception, beyond thinking and feeling.

His mind does not spin in the attempt to discriminate. He just quietly and patiently observes the different levels of his personality, and the ego flees his inner gaze, trying to hide in the shadows of unexplored corners of consciousness. He silently witnesses his life, observing how the senses, mind, and feelings function. The analysis component is secondary to the witness value. Nonjudgmental, neither active nor passive, just watching the mind churn, watching the ego judge and justify. Eventually the churning slows and stops, and the mind collapses into no-mind. Then ego disappears, for it can exist only in the active mind. The ego cannot live in silence. It cannot survive in light. It cannot breathe without duality, comparing self to nonself to justify its own fictitious existence.

Our beliefs shape our experience, not vice versa. We attract experiences based on our belief systems. If we believe the universe is impersonal matter controlled only by the mechanical laws of Newtonian physics, we experience tremendous worthlessness and despair. Our physical powers are so ridiculously puny and short-lived compared to the forces that create and destroy galaxies. However, if we deeply believe that all life is connected and we are an integral part of a cosmic plan that comprehends all the parts in the whole, then we find every moment of the day infinitely rich and joyous.

No matter what our level of education, the intellect tries to maintain the ego's sense of separateness, by means of beliefs which we may be only dimly aware of. In ignorance the intellect is slave to the ego, working feverishly to maintain a sense of separateness. When serving a fragile ego, it is defensive, elusive, fragmented, and inconsistent. It either attacks blindly or retreats by avoiding the serious questions that might expose its master's mirage.

The gyani uses the intellect to cut the bondage to conditioned beliefs. By merely observing the ego's machinations without judgment, he frees himself from the painful belief in his own mortality and separateness.

Belief in God is not a prerequisite to any yoga, especially Hatha and Gyana Yoga. Gyanis of different cultures often see creation as a manifestation, an impersonal absolute, not a personal God who loves and protects all His or Her billions of children. Gyani philosophers typically say that it is simply the nature of the absolute to periodically manifest and periodically dissolve the manifestation. Some, like Adi Shankara, are also devotees of a personal God. Others, like many Buddhist and Jain philosophers, see no need to posit a personal God behind the creation. They may have very different views of the universe as either real or unreal. What they share in common is the primacy of Absolute Truth—that nondual Ultimate Reality which never changes and can never be put in words.

Shri Ramana Maharishi was one of the best-known Indian gyanis of the first half of this century. His main technique was simply asking "Who am I?"—the ultimate question every gyani must ask himself intensely and repeatedly. Contemporary gyanis include Jean Klein, and Ramesh Balshekar, a student of Shri Nisargadatta Maharaj. Other great gyanis in recent Western tradition include Rudolph Steiner, Martin Heidegger, and Paul Brunton.

Since Gyan is the path of the intellect, it is often thought of as the path for educated intellectuals. Actually, gyan requires no more formal education than any other path. Ramana Maharishi never finished high school, and Nisargadatta Maharaj had even less schooling. They also read little, but their brilliant reasoning disarmed the mightiest intellectuals.

Another common misconception about the path of the intellect is that it makes one dry and heartless. It is true that the intellect must be free of emotional bias to cut to the essence of any question, but right practice of any yoga only opens the heart. It is fashionable in some circles to drop platitudes about how all life is one, all people one, all paths one, etc. To the gyani, such talk is nonsense. The clear intellect recognizes difference. To truly love and respect someone, honor his or her uniqueness. You only insult greatness by homogenizing it with mediocrity, like mixing clear water with mud.

Another common misconception about Gyan Yoga is that it is only for recluses, not active people in the world. This idea has two sources:

First, many people think that by realizing the ephemerality of worldly things, one must become disillusioned and disgusted with them and retreat to the forests. It is true that most saints pass through a "dark night of the soul" where ordinary concerns are seen as empty, but the inner vacuum left by disillusionment with finite dreams is just a preparation for spiritual fulfillment, a cleansing of the inner receptacle prior to full enlightenment. Periods of solitude may be a prerequisite for enlightenment, but most enlightened persons eventually return to an active life in society.

Second, Adi Shankara, the most influential philosopher in Indian history, has unfortunately been misinterpreted as a proponent of the recluse way of life. There is a deep misconception in India that materiality and spirituality are opposed, that you have to renounce one for the other. People who are meant for a recluse way of life demonstrate tremendous emotional self-sufficiency from early childhood, shunning society for the joys of solitude and contemplation. They are a small percentage of the population. The widespread belief that one must renounce the world to find God has led millions of seekers into an abnormal reclusiveness which requires total denial of their desires. Such suffering in the name of enlightenment is like swimming in ice water to warm up.

All forms of yoga involve some restraint, but enlightenment comes from following one's own nature, not denying it. The important thing is to follow one's nature in the aspiration for the Supreme, and not squander this precious life in a preoccupation with petty wants.

The danger of Mercury's path is self-infatuation and indifference to others. Such defects are only indicative of incomplete insight into the path of Gyana. The true gyani grows in love as he grows in discernment of how everyone and everything is unique and perfect in the context of the whole.

5. Laya, Kundalini, or Kriya Yoga, the path of will and the warrior, ruled by Mars:

Why do some people enjoy risky adventures like climbing mountains, racing cars, jumping off cliffs with a hang glider, or even going to war? These are outer expressions of Mars energy. He is the commander-in-chief of the planetary army, the adventurous risk-taker, the master tactician and technician. The spiritual warrior carries Mars' love of adventure into exploring uncharted realms of consciousness. Mars rules fire, both physical and spiritual. Kundalini Yoga awakens the primal fire at the base of the spine. The kundalini yogi uses this fire to transform carnal instincts into spiritual awareness, just as fire transforms dense, heavy matter into rarified gasses rising toward heaven.

Kundalini yoga usually begins with preparatory physical postures and pranayamas (breathing exercises) and strict control of diet and behavior. The goal is to awaken the dormant primal force in the sacrum and direct it upward through the central channel of the spine, called the *shushumna,* and pierce the various spiritual centers, or *chakras,* along the spine and until it bursts into the top *chakra* in the head in a blaze of light and power. Since Mars is technically oriented, kundalini techniques can be very complex. *Bandhas* (postures that lock the breath in different energy centers), *mudras* (hand gestures) and concentration on the *chakras* with specific mantras and images are often used together.

Fast breath exercises are one way to fan the primal fire. Saturn likes slow, measured breathing. Mars prefers fast breathing (hyperventilation), possibly alternated with sudden, brief breath stops, just like a soldier who fights intensely, then suddenly stops to reassess the enemy, and jumps back into battle again and again.

The physical techniques of kundalini yoga are most effective if combined with inner practice, such as concentration on the chakras with appropriate mantras. An experienced guide is needed!

Lest we become enamored by the thrill potential of such practices, let us quote from Swami Rama's book, *Choosing a Path*:

> "In my opinion these exercises are but preparation for awakening kundalini. I would like to warn students not to waste their time and energy in using physical techniques for awakening kundalini. I practiced these methods in my youth, but did not derive much spiritual benefit.... Sometimes these techniques can injure the nervous system by disrupting the pranic vehicles. Excessive pranayamas and mudras can lead to ill health."

Mars rules the will, and willpower is the key to mastering the primal fire. This is certainly not the only path that can open the chakras—others do so indirectly—but it is the most direct and aggressive. The spiritual warrior seeks a high-voltage charge that will not quit, but he must have the discipline to control the wild physical and emotional blocks it can release. He must also be humble and unattached to any powers that may appear.

The primal fire flowing downward is experienced as sexual desire. Flowing upward it is experienced as higher awareness. In order to redirect the flow, celibacy is essential, at least during periods of intense practice. Of course, celibacy has always been a hot topic in religion. There are many simple guidelines that make celibacy easier, but most religions only teach outer control, not inner development, so celibacy remains a strain for most people. It is unnatural for most people to try to be celibate for a whole lifetime, but there are periods in everyone's life when it is necessary to abstain from sex, especially when learning to master the primal fire.

Sometimes the wise warrior uses stealth and surprise, rather than direct frontal attack. This side of the Mars path is seen in sorcery and shamanism. Carlos Castaneda's books are fascinating adventures in native Mexican shamanism, and excellent reading for all spiritual warriors.

In the great epics of India, the *Ramayana* and *Mahabharata,* battles are waged with powerful magic and illusion. Likewise, the spiritual warrior learns to play with perception and deception, manipulating reality to his will. And just as the good soldier serves a higher master, the spiritual warrior surrenders his own will to the cosmic will. This is the irony of the Martian path—one learns to assert his will only to surrender it!

Some excellent teachers, such as Paramahansa Yoga, prescribe "kriya" techniques to raise the kundalini, but their gentle, soothing manner is really more akin to the Venusian path. The true Mars type shuns the soft and dreamy platitudes of Venus. He wants challenge, not rest and relaxation. Mars also loves variety and experimentation. His path allows plunging into one technique after another, just as a recreational adventurer may go from skydiving to whitewater kayaking to hotdog skiing. One Babaji kriya yoga teacher in Canada, Marshall Govindan, imparts 144 different techniques.

Another word of caution: The casual dabbler in Mars practices is like reckless Rambo who charges into battle without a strategy. The successful spiritual warrior spends years in training and study. He knows his own strengths and weaknesses, as well as the enemy's. The real Mars yogi is the disciplined commander-in-chief of his own mind, body, and will, not a thrill-seeking soldier of fortune. As

Marshall Govindan says, "Any damn fool can awaken the kundalini. The hard part's in the preparation!"[11]

Although ritual is most closely associated with karma yoga, the path ruled by Jupiter, there is a ritual aspect of all paths. One powerful ritual used by some kundalini yogis and tantrics is the worship of Shri Yantra, which symbolizes the microcosmic/macrocosmic union of male and female energies, and their transformation into spiritual power. Another Mars ritual with countless variations throughout the world is the fire sacrifice. The food and other gifts offered into the fire symbolize the ego we are burning in the fire of pure consciousness, freeing the spirit to rise to heaven.

Any technique that takes courage to confront problems directly also relates to Mars. Most of us live in denial on many levels. We shut out the memory of past trauma, especially emotional trauma of early childhood, when vulnerability and dependency are greatest. When a fragile ego or weak will is directly confronted with painful experience, whether through psychoanalysis, confrontational therapies, or accident, the trauma can be devastating. The same confrontation can be liberating to someone brave and strong enough to accept and rise above the pain. And what works for one person at one time may backfire for him at another time. So safety and success lie in knowing the appropriate technique for a given person, time, and place.

Where Mars addresses trauma with confrontation, other planets have other approaches. Venus, for example, dissolves it painlessly with sweetness and harmony, without ever confronting the problem directly.

Mars also governs conscious dying. He sees beyond the veil of death and transforms dying into rebirth. Many yogis are said to have mastered the art of conscious dying. One leaves the body on choice, not demand. One chooses to exit when the body has served its purpose in order to pursue new challenges outside the confines of the flesh.

Modern society tries to hide from death through a preoccupation with youth, sex, and staying busy. Contemplation of death is central to many Buddhist meditations. Although such practices strike many Westerners as morbid, they can liberate the seeker from deep-seated fears and help one live fully in the moment, without regret for the past or anxiety for the future.

Mars gives courage to face death. The awareness that death could strike at any time helps us see beyond the limitations of life in the body. Similarly, Mars looks beyond the veil of waking consciousness into dreaming and sleeping. Saturn actually rules deep sleep, and Venus the dream state, but Mars penetrates the boundaries between states of consciousness and has the courage to face the deep emotional issues released by dreams.

The greatest warriors and athletes integrate rest and activity. They maintain relaxation while fully engaged in action, and alternate easily between sleep and wakefulness. Napoleon was known to sleep on the battlefield, and John Kennedy and Winston Churchill took catnaps at unconventional times. Restful alertness is a trait common to enlightened persons on all paths, but it is most dramatic on the dynamic path of Mars. Watch the equanimity and poise of Joe Montana deftly throwing passes microseconds before brutally strong defenders smash him, and you will get an idea of the calm alertness needed by the kundalini yogi.

We have mentioned the risks of awakening the primal fire without adequate preparation. Another danger of the Mars path applies for people who should be on other paths. For them, excess emphasis on death can actually increase fatalism and passivity, rather than remove those traits.

Fatalism and passivity, so common in Buddhist and Hindu cultures, are the flip side of the imbalanced willfulness so common in the West. The Western conquest of nature through technology, an archetypical Mars syndrome, has precipitated environmental disaster. Fatalism and excess willfulness are just opposite faces of the same Mars disease: an egoic identification with the individual will, a result of nonsurrender to the Cosmic Will. Such surrender is neither a mood of acceptance, nor the torpid passivity so common in disempowered people everywhere. It is attunement to Natural Law, which requires a full awakening of awareness, not a dull acquiescence. The soldier who sleeps through his duties is no better than one who charges into his personal battles while ignoring his commander. Enlightened surrender has two sides which may seem contradictory: taking full responsibility for one's own actions, and innocently allowing Divine grace to flow through you.

6. Bhakti Yoga, the path of devotion, ruled by the Moon:

A mother thinks only of her children and forgets her personal needs for their welfare. The children easily win her favor by honoring their parents and helping their brothers and sisters. So it is on the path of the heart—honor God and serve your neighbor with selfless compassion.

The majority of modern Indians mistakenly consider themselves bhaktas (devotees on the path of divine love). Likewise in Christianity, the path of the heart is emphasized most, along with the path of action. Sufism also emphasizes the path of the heart. The sensuous poetry of Rumi and Omar Khayam strikes many as hedonistic, a quality of an unfulfilled Venus. The Sufis had to veil their devotions in the language of romance to protect their lives because they were often persecuted by orthodox Muslims. The yearning of lover for the beloved is a universal metaphor for the yearning for God, a simile that stirs hearts throughout the world in their quest for the Divine.

Whereas a karma yogi serves from love of duty, a bhakta (devotee) serves spontaneously from a heart overflowing with love. Saint Theresa of Avila and Saint Theresa of the Little Flower are two examples of western bhaktas. Anandamayi Ma and Mata

Amritanandamayi (Amacchi) are examples of modern Indian bhaktas.

Bhaktas gravitate toward prayerful meditation or daily conversations with God as one's most intimate friend and companion. Since the moon represents the mother principle, bhaktas tend to worship the Divine Mother more than the Divine Father.

Like karma yogis, bhaktas use ritual worship as an expression of their love, but their approach is less technical and more from the heart. Bhaktas become absorbed in simple recitation of the names of God. With extended conscious practice, that repetition becomes subconscious and instinctual. Their favorite prayers may become so automatic that they wake up in the morning feeling they have prayed all night, and go to bed at night feeling they have prayed all day. Their prayers and their actions are never selfish. They surrender all selfishness and delight in the joy of the beloved.

Bhaktas also love devotional song and dance, and are often less restrained than their friends from other paths. The ecstatic displays of devotion by St. John of the Cross, Ramakrishna, and countless other bhaktas have sometimes been a source of embarrassment to their more discrete and restrained friends.

Faith plays a larger role in the path of the heart than any of the other paths. For the cautious Saturn, faith grows slowly and must be based on concrete evidence and cold, dry logic. For the ever-harmonious Venus, it flowers with the experience of sweetness and bliss. For Jupiter it is most inspired by guru and scripture. For the observant and detached Mercury, faith is systematically developed through discrimination and observation of one's own inner experience. For Mars, faith can come in a flash, sometimes as an out-of-body or near-death experience.

Faith and love are natural for the Moon. "Love knows no reason," and the Moon is not afraid to love with abandon. She has no fear of love and needs no rationalization for caring and sharing. Feelings are primary, reasons and techniques, secondary. She may say, "God is Love. Why debate the obvious? Why hide the truth of God's love behind a veneer of words? What you feel is real."

Although most bhaktas worldwide believe in God, there are nontheistic bhaktas in Buddhism and Jainism. The object of devotion may be ancestors, masters, or even family members. There is a story of one elderly widow who had no interest in God, temples, meditation, or anything deemed spiritual. A sage asked her if there was anything she really enjoyed. She said, "Yes, my grandson." "Then worship him!" said the sage. She did, and she attained liberation by simply following her heart.

The moon rules the oceans and the oceanic consciousness, where the collective unconsciousness of humanity meets the collective consciousness of divinity. This is the simplest path because there is no prescription except to flow with the simplest, deepest, purest feeling of love.

The Mother is always compassionate and receptive, but in that compassion she may discipline. Watch a mother tigress alternate tender affection with a stiff slap to her cubs. Although devotion is a simple path, it is not always easy. It requires total surrender!

The bhakti path uses feeling to transcend feeling. The purest form of devotion transcends devotion. Feeling implies duality, a separation of lover and beloved. Devotion implies a subject and object of devotion. The devotee's intense pangs of separation must be seen as a transitional phase. Her goal is merger with the beloved, not perpetuating the agony of separation. This merger is at the deepest level of feeling, where differences dissolve in the unity of infinite love.

Dangers on the lunar path are contrived emotionality and denial of common sense. As with all paths, one who is naturally suited for the path will be much more intuitively attuned to right practice than someone who artificially attempts to follow another's path.

7. Surya Yoga, the path of integration, ruled by the Sun:

Just as the sun illumines all the other planets, the Solar yogi honors all the other paths, but is attached to none. His role is integration of heart, mind, and will.

These three fundamental modalities relate to the trinity of experience: Feeling (heart) relates to the knower. Thinking (mind and intellect) relates to the process of knowing. Acting (will) relates to the known. Seekers on other paths gain maximum results by staying within well-defined boundaries of spiritual practice. They generally lack the broad perspective required by true integral yoga. The Solar yogi basks in the glory of all paths, all philosophies, all techniques, all knowledge, and all of life.

The Sun is the king of the planetary court, and the true Solar yogi maintains a leadership role in upholding the integrity of all paths. He keeps the big picture and maintains balance in the inevitable turf battles among followers of other paths. His concern is unity; he does not get lost in the details of any one path or point of view. And he is ever concerned about the spiritual welfare of all humanity.

Followers of other paths need clearer boundaries and closer guidance. They lack the independence and integrative capacity required of the king. But the king exults in the freedom to define his own style. He loves his spiritual advisors and friends, but he is more independent of gurus than his fellow yogis of other paths. His spiritual practice is too free-form and internally guided to fit into the confines of externally received spiritual prescriptions. He enjoys enlightened persons more for their presence than their methods, and finds enrichment in everyone's spiritual aspirations, no matter what their beliefs or practices.

Just as wise kings uphold justice, a true solar yogi opposes spiritual malpractice and sectariansim. He is the ultimate father, disciplining his children, but quick to forgive and easily pleased. He blesses all with *shaktipat,* a direct transmission of love and light.

Integral yoga is often confused as an amalgam of other yogas, the eclecticism of those who cannot figure out what path they want. It is really much more than that, just as the proverbial house is far more than a collection of bricks. The Solar yogi knows what practice is appropriate at what time, just as the sun defines the time of day. He does not get stuck in techniques or limiting beliefs. Diversity is not possible without unity, and the solar yogi always sees the unity as primary.

The Sun has a tendency to steal the show. The biggest and brightest sounds like the best, but He is far too intense for most people to handle, just as looking straight at the sun is blinding. People who try to practice Integral Yoga without being naturally suited to it do not integrate anything. As they dabble in different paths, their hearts, minds, and wills are pulled in different directions, causing great inner strain. Only about one seeker in eight has the comprehensive solar inner nature to successfully tread this path.

A mid-twentieth century solar yogi was Shivananda who founded the Divine Life Society in Rishikesh, India. Another outstanding solar yogi is Swami Brahmananda Saraswati, Maharishi Mahesh Yogi's beloved "Guru Dev," who held the post of Shankaracharya of the North in India, the most prestigious religious position in Northern India. As a boy of nine he fiercely asserted his independence and ran away from home in search of God. For sixty years he lived in remote forests and mountains until he reluctantly accepted the post of Shankaracharya. This description of him by Maharishi elucidates his solar nature:

> "His policy of spiritual enlightenment was all-embracing. He inspired all alike and gave a lift to everyone in his religious, virtuous, moral, and spiritual life. He was never a leader of any one party. All parties found a common leader head in Him. All the various differences and dissensions of the various castes, creeds, and *sampradayas* dissolved in his presence and every

party felt to be a thread in the warp and woof of society, and that all the threads make the cloth, and that no thread can be taken out, with advantage, from it. Such was His Universality and all-embracing nature."[12]

The gyani finds himself through negation—stripping away all that he is not. The solar yogi is more likely to use affirmation. He accepts everything as himself—good and bad, absolute and relative, self and nonself. The solar yogi has the most direct relationship to the Infinite, without dependence on techniques. He may practice any spiritual technique, especially techniques of radiating the inner light. But his real practice transcends techniques and continues twenty-four hours a day. Any meditation practice which is not integrated into activity is not integral yoga. Integral yoga integrates waking, dreaming, and sleeping in an unbroken continuum of unbounded pure consciousness.

The danger of the solar path is pride—preoccupation with finite self and how one appears to others. Solar yogis with inadequate understanding of the ego's artifices and people not suited for this path may only inflate their egos by trying to follow it. For this reason, it is advisable for seekers on this path to combine negation and affirmation: negation of the small self, identified with the individual mind-body, and affirmation of the eternal, immortal Self of all beings.

8. Tantra—the path of desire, ruled by the Nodes of the Moon:

Tantra is as vast and varied as yoga. Tantra means "technique," and there are countless techniques in different tantric traditions. Tantra is flowing with desire without resisting, just accepting natural urges and becoming fully aware of every thought, every feeling, every moment. It is contrasted with yoga, which restrains and redirects desire. The yogi always keeps a firm hand on the floodgates of desire, permitting enough of a flow to maintain physical and emotional health, but never opening the gates wide. The tantric throws the floodgates wide open, unafraid of the rushing torrent of desire.

Tantra is ruled by the "shadow" planets, the North and South Nodes of the Moon (Rahu and Ketu). The nodes are rebels, outlaws, and iconoclasts. They reject any authority except their own experience. They always reflect the energy of one of the other planets in a very unique and unconventional way, so tantra is at least as vast and complex as all the yogas taken together.

Sensationalistic writers paint tantra as the path to enlightenment through sex, alcohol, drugs, and black magic, while ignoring the devastation that can ensue from abandoning caution and concern for others. Any path can be corrupted! Tantra involves a sense of play and freedom from spiritual convention, but requires absolute adherence to one rule—Be conscious, remain fully aware at all times. So the hedonist who dulls his mind through overindulgence is as far from true tantra as the celibate ascetic alone in his cave.

Real tantra takes as much time and practice as yoga. Tantra, like yoga, requires full awareness in the present every moment of the day. Although "pop" tantra is generally associated with sexuality, most tantric techniques do not involve sex. The classic textbook of tantra, the *Vigyana Bhairava Tantra* gives 112 different tantric techniques, of which only three deal with sexuality. Many of them are simple awareness tools for enjoying nature or becoming aware of your mind, body, and emotions. Unfortunately, without more guidance, most aspirants are befuddled by over-choice. If you are intimidated by the complexity of tantra, it suggests that you need a master, or should be practicing yoga, not tantra. The true tantric delights in experimentation, and trusts his own experience far more than any guru.

Since tantra plays directly with desire, it is dangerous for those whose inner nature is yogic (about seven people out of eight).

Tantra is for the one of eight who are natural spiritual rebels, not just those who abhor outer authority and convention.

Please note that we are using the word "tantra" in a very different sense than Tibetan Buddhist Tantra. Lord Buddha was North-nodian in his rejection of orthodox Hinduism and theism, but the term "Buddhist Tantra" is an oxymoron, as control of desire is central to all Buddhism. Tibetan Tantra is decidedly nontantric in its monastic discipline and veneration of authority.

Although India and Tibet are best know for tantra, techniques of using desire to go beyond desire have existed in some form in every culture. There is another worldwide category of pseudoreligious practices that are related to the "left-handed path" of tantra, but have nothing to do with genuine spiritual practices. These include black magic, Satanism, and esoteric power cults. The fact that all the paths have often been corrupted in no way detracts from the truth of their pure forms.

In astrological terms, the strength of the ruling planet governs the purity of its path for any given individual. Someone with a strong Moon governing his spirituality will lead a very compassionate life, while the same path ruled by a weak or afflicted moon may be cruel or obsessed by psychic power trips. The way to remedy the plane-tary affliction and advance spiritually is always to steer toward the positive qualities of the planet involved, such as unselfish love, harmony, or truth.

Mastery of desire is central to all forms of yoga, although most practices sublimate desire rather than confronting it directly. In the *Bhagavad Gita* Lord Krishna, the Lord of Yogis, tells Arjuna that it is desire, "all-consuming and most evil," which impels man to commit sin, even involuntarily, as if driven by force. "Know this to be the enemy here on earth."[13]

The secret to success in tantra is understanding desire as a friend, not an enemy. Desire is a friend we cannot live without. The only people who succeed in tantra are those who can appreciate the deeper levels of desire without getting lost in surface desire. Our deepest desire is for enlightenment—absolute freedom, bliss, and love. The danger is that surface desires often flow in the opposite direction of spiritual desires.

The tantric cultivates awareness of the flow of desire and, like the yogi, avoids attachment to the objects of desire. Desire for objects takes you out of the present. Awareness of the flow of desire keeps you in the present. Gradually, awareness of the flow grows into awareness of the silent source of desire. Then you become master of desire, not its slave.

To feel that you NEED something in order to be happy is to surrender your bliss and power to something outside of you, whether you are a yogi or a tantric.

The most articulate and enlightened modern tantric was Osho, previously known as Bhagavan Shree Rajneesh. He was a brilliant psychologist and outspoken critic of all that suppresses the human spirit, to the point that he encouraged his followers not to believe him, but to make up their own minds and not accept his authority on anything. He was surrounded by scandal, vilified by the press, and allegedly poisoned by U.S. Government officials prior to his expulsion from the U.S. for immigration fraud. His followers included both criminals and saints. A tantric to the core, he invited controversy and seemed to love being hated. Blasting orthodoxy and reveling in controversy is typical Rahu behavior, and no one surpassed Osho in this respect!

Desire

We have innumerable desires every day. Consciously or subconsciously, each desire confronts us with a primordial decision—what to do with it? We want to sleep, but have to work. We want to shop, but need to save. We want to be with someone, but that someone does not want to be with us. We want to rid the world of war, crime, disease, corruption, and pollution, but feel that we do not have the power. We want to live forever, but .... ad infinitum!

There are four possible responses to any desire:
1. Redirect its energy into something safer or more constructive
2. Satisfy it while recognizing that is small and fleeting
3. Suppress or deny it
4. Indulge it blindly without awareness

These four choices correspond to the four basic approaches to spirituality:
1. Yoga—restraint or moderation of desire and redirection/sublimation of destructive energies.
2. Tantra—Flowing with desire without getting drowned, by of values that transcend desire.
3. Surface control—trying to change outer behavior without refining inner awareness—the approach of conventional ethics, whether religious or not.
4. Hedonism and any form of blind self-gratification without concern for others or long-term consequences.

We can illustrate these primordial options with a diagram:

Refined Awareness

```
      ▲
      ┊         1. Redirect Desire:        2. Conscious Satisfaction
      ┊              Yoga                     of Desire: Tantra
      ┊
Spirituality
- - - - - - - - - - - - - - - - - - - - - - - - - - - - - - - - - - - - - -
Materialism
      ┊         3. Suppression of Desire:   4. Blind Indulgence of Desire:
      ┊              Surface Morality &        Hedonism & Nihilism
      ┊              Selfish Self-Control
      ▼
Dullness
              ◄---- Restraint     │    Indulgence   ----►
```

On the vertical axis we find whatever means the most to us—spiritual values or material ones. Higher is the direction of increasing awareness, harmony, love, and bliss; lower is the direction of increasing dullness, tension, separateness, and misery. On the horizontal axis is our approach—restraint or indulgence of desire.

Hedonism and nihilism are a vicious circle. Satiating the senses leaves one feeling empty and wasted (nihilism). This creates cravings to fill the void with more indulgence. And so the addiction cycle continues. Hollywood and Madison Avenue thrive on feeding this addiction. So if you are serious about spirituality in any form, cut back on the mass media and put your attention on more elevating recreations, such as meditation, spiritual gatherings, and communion with nature.

The reason the world is in a fix is that most people live in the bottom half of the diagram, in deep denial of their spiritual essence. Suppression of desire is a hot topic in modern psychology, but suppression of spiritual experience is far more damaging to the individual and society. Organized religions, at least in the West, have inadvertently collaborated in the growth of materialism by fostering blind faith, dogma, and dependence on external authority (the religious institution or leader). Spirituality and creativity can only blossom in an environment of freedom and respect for differences of experience and opinion.

The danger of tantra is that few people can really flow with desire without being drowned. Natural-born yogis, who are happiest in the first quadrant, get sucked into the fourth quadrant whirlpool if they try to practice tantra. We all have to follow some desires, but as a spiritual path, tantra is for the few, not the many. Excessive sensory indulgence is poison for most spiritual aspirants.

It is a great mistake to think that one can take the best of yoga and tantra as a spiritual practice, alternating periods of great restraint with periods of wanton excess. Just as it is hard on the physical body to alternate between fasting and gorging, it is hard on the spiritual body to alternate between restraint and indulgence of desire. After experiencing both asceticism and luxury, Lord Buddha taught the middle path, a balance between restraint and indulgence that can be maintained for a lifetime.

It is no wonder tantrics have been so despised by those who struggle to master desire! The human population is roughly equally distributed among the eight paths. About one-eighth are meant to practice each of these archetypal paths. Unfortunately, most are not really practicing any spiritual path beyond the first level, surface morality.

Summary

Here is a summary of the essence of each path:

Saturn: Absolute silence and simplicity
Venus: Infinite peace and bliss
Jupiter: Absolute adoration and gratitude
Mercury: Absolute detachment and truth
Mars: Infinite courage and power
Moon: Infinite personal love and compassion
Sun: Absolute unity and wholeness
Tantra: All of the above, flowing with desire rather than restraining it, and being very independent from outer authority

Whatever form of meditation a seeker is taught, he will tend to interpret it in accordance with his own spiritual nature, at least if his ruling planet is strong. If representatives from each of the eight great paths all try to practice the same meditation technique, no matter what it is, each will be most attuned to the essence given here for his own path. Thus the hatha yogi will be more aware of physical silence, the raj yogi will feel an idealistic attunement to peace and bliss through sensory refinement, etc. However, we must emphasize that the dangers are always greater and the progress less if you are not following your most natural path!

Each path is characterized by certain pairs of opposites—relative values which grow to absolute values with progress on the path. None of these pairs of opposites is exclusive to any one path. However, there is a predominant planet of influence for each pair:

Planet	Relative	Absolute
Saturn	physical	spiritual
	material	immaterial
	boundaries	boundless
	time	timelessness

Venus	sensory pleasure	transcendent bliss
	outer peace	inner peace
	selfish desire	selfless desire
	finite beauty	infinite beauty
Jupiter	obligatory duty	spontaneous right action
	morality by precept	morality from within
	limited giving	unlimited giving
	knowledge of scripture	inner intuition
	ritual sacrifice	habitual sacrifice, ceaseless prayer
	localized reverence	universal reverence
	outer guru	inner guru
Mercury	impermanence	permanence
	change	nonchange
	relative truth	absolute truth
	conditioned belief	unconditioned awareness
	finite knowledge	infinite knowingness
	speech and reason	silent pure consciousness
	active actor	silent observer in activity
Mars	mortality	immortality
	limited courage	unlimited courage
	individual will	cosmic will
	individual energy	cosmic energy
Moon	selfish love	selfless love
	love with attachment	love without attachment
	human love	divine love
	localized personal love	unbounded personal love
	yearning for the beloved	merger with beloved, infinite intimacy
Sun	diversity	unity
	separateness	integration
	individual	universal
	nonself	Self

The best indication of growth of consciousness is growth of the absolute values in the right-hand column. These are internal, subjective values, which are not readily visible to others. In the *Bhagavad Gita* Arjuna asks Krishna how the enlightened man looks and behaves. Krishna answers with a description of his inner state, not his outer appearance. Although unusually sensitive souls may be able to sense someone else's state of mind, it is generally dangerous and misleading to make judgments of inner conditions based on outer behavior.

Questions

Q: What is the role of faith?

A: It is a common denominator of all paths, but it is very different from the outward belief taught by many religions. True faith does not need to conquer or proselytize. Only an inwardly insecure person seeks the elimination of contrary opinions. A secure person is not threatened by opinions different than his own; he appreciates others, no matter what their political or religious persuasion.

When Christ said that faith the size of a mustard seed could move mountains, he was speaking of the inner knowingness that accompanies attunement to the infinite power that guides the growth and decay of everything in the universe. When the individual is consciously connected to the fundamental laws of creation, he experiences the infinite power of nature flowing through his mind-body vehicle, unimpeded by personal desires.

Real faith is inner knowingness, a deep intuitive sense of the deepest levels of reality that leaves no room for doubt. It is discovered in silence and tested in daily experience. It is an innocent experience characterized by infinite peace, bliss and silence. It comes from long-term spiritual practice in accord with one's natural path. It does not come from public proclamations of faith, any more than wealth comes from bragging about being rich.

Faith is misunderstood because so few people have the experience of real inner knowingness. It is fashionable to paint anyone who speaks of spiritual matters with absolute certainty as a fanatic. The fanatic and the saint are both certain of their views, but they are at opposite ends of the spectrum of personal development. The religious fanatic is rigidly attached to his beliefs, and unable to reason or feel deeply. He lacks spontaneity, flexibility, compassion, and all the other traits of growing consciousness. He is threatened by differing opinions. He is ruled by an ideal that has not been integrated into his daily life, so tension and conflict dominate his perception. He may even express his repressed frustrations in aggression toward persons of other beliefs.

The saint (the person of real faith) is just the opposite: There is no ego attachment to beliefs, no rigidity or fear of disapproval. He is spontaneous and may have a childlike innocence. He has no desire to impose his views on others; he only wants their happiness, not their belief. His ideals are lived naturally and without strain; conflicts are inevitable on the surface of life, but the silent depths of his awareness remain undisturbed.

Q: Why do enlightened masters often disagree?

A: In their descriptions of higher states of consciousness there is close agreement among the spiritual teachers mentioned in this book and countless other worthy masters not mentioned. It is natural, however, that while different seers may give similar descriptions of the goal, they offer very different paths to it. One's path to heaven may be another's road to hell, or at least boredom on earth. In addition to the different styles of knowing we have discussed here, from one master to the next there are wide differences in culture, language, style of expression, and degree of enlightenment. The old parable of the four blind men and the elephant also applies to wise men. Even when describing the same eternal Reality, they may use very different terms. Some speak of a personal God as a cosmic Grandfather, while others see no need for a divine person between abstract absolute and relative realm of ordinary human existence. Yet both aim at the permanence and nonchange underlying transitory existence, the supreme order underlying the apparent chaos of the world, and an unbounded love transforming the pettiness of selfishness into the grandness of communion with a higher power.

Western religions have historically been preoccupied with doctrine at the expense of inner experience. But spirituality is inner experience; no description of it can substitute for the experience, just as talking of water cannot satisfy one's thirst. If one master talks of a shady stream, another of a deep well, and a third an open lake, it behooves us to see that the common factor, water, is more important than the form it takes for any one person.

Q: Why is the history of religion a story of endless war, hypocrisy, and contradiction of every ill the religions purport to cure?

A: Ignorance of which path suits each person is a major cause. If you don't know what forms of meditation, prayer, and service are most natural to you, it becomes hard to live the loving, harmonious life all religions aspire to. With only a hazy and tenuous connection to the source of inner harmony, and the ever increasing pace and complexity of modern life, stress and strain have grown in society.

Q: Did Christ, Buddha, Muhammad, Krishna, and the founders of other religions teach these eight paths?

A: We do not pretend to know what they taught their close disciples in private. Elements of all the eight archetypal paths can be found in all the great religions of the world, but the knowledge of how to apply them to different individuals has been lost. Over time, religions founded on direct contact with inner truth lost their foundation, and focused on outer values of doctrine and ethics. It is infinitely harder to change thinking and behavior by outer means than by inner ones. It's as if we each have a powerful race car that we try to push up hill by hand because we don't know how to turn on the engine and drive it.

Misunderstandings follow every master like his shadow. The ultimate reality can never be expressed in words, so it is no wonder that people clash over the words to describe it! It is impossible to express spiritual truths uniformly for different ages, different cultural and language groups, different spiritual paths, and different levels of development.

No master has ever been done justice by his organization. The tragedy of knowledge is that the student's understanding rarely matches the teacher's, so each generation loses something of the founder's purity. Doctrine and dogma take the place of innocent inner vision, and condemnation of nonbelievers becomes a virtue sanctioned by religious authority. Occasionally a rare giant is born to re-cognize the timeless knowledge and express it in contemporary terms, only to begin again the gradual dilution of truth by true believers who insist their interpretation is the only valid one.

All of the major religious traditions encompass elements of all the seven yogas. The rebellious nature of tantra often puts it outside mainstream religious traditions, but tantra has ancient traditions, too. You can be a Buddhist, Jew, Hindu, Christian, Muslim, or whatever, and practice any of these paths in the context of your tradition. The Vedic tradition has kept the clearest understanding of the eight paths, but even in India they are usually muddled.

Actually, we have oversimplified the eight paths here. Each yoga has sixteen subyogas, so there are 112 yogic subpaths in total. Each one of these 112 subpaths is expressed differently in different times and cultures, so it is no surprise when the exponents of different paths disagree!

In summary, truth is multidimensional. No words can adequately express any one of the eight major approaches to the ultimate. Although the goal may be the same, it is imperative to honor the different approaches. Spirituality is awareness of the infinite source of life, not a matter of belief or behavior. As we blossom spiritually, the transcendent, unifying value unfolds in our awareness. Experience based faith replaces blind faith, and tolerance increases as we recognize that the ultimate truth always remains inexpressible.

Q: Is a master necessary?

A: It is very rare for a soul to be born with enough inner guidance to find the Supreme by himself. Everyone else needs a guide, someone qualified to guide one to one's inner guide in a manner appropriate to one's natural path. The master is especially important in hatha, bhakti, karma, and raj yoga. Integral yoga, laya yoga, gyan yoga and tantra tend to be more independent and experimental, but still require outer guidance until one is strongly inner-directed.

Q: How do I find a master?

A: There's an old saying, "When the student is ready, the teacher appears." Hone your desire for a master. Read and listen to different sources, paying special attention to your deepest feelings, not others' opinions. Be ready to invest many years with the right person, should you be fortunate enough to find him or her.

In ancient times, seekers spent years searching for a qualified guru, and did not become disciples until master and seeker had thoroughly tested each other. Now stores are full of books proffering easy nirvana, ashrams compete for seekers and dollars, and a whole subculture of shiftless seekers think they understand many paths, but have never gone beneath the surface of any.

Intelligent experimentation is a part of some paths, particularly integral yoga, kriya yoga, and tantra, but recklessness and dabbling are detrimental on any path. Serious spiritual renewal takes more patience and perseverance than becoming a doctor or professional athlete, so plan for the long-term, but also plan to relax and enjoy the journey.

The old guru model is dying. Seekers today tend to be impatient and resistant to authority, and qualified teachers are few. The twenty-first century needs teachers who abandon the aloof and autocratic methods of many of their predecessors. The new guru model will be a mentor and friend who honors the individual needs of each student and gives plenty of freedom to discover truth for oneself.

Unfortunately, most seekers are easily lost in the spiritual jungle, or too lethargic to care. I have tried to describe the major paths through the jungle, but this is no substitute for personalized guidance from someone who knows the jungle well. There are no super-highways, just narrow footpaths you have to travel alone. Even the greatest master cannot give you enlightenment. He can only be a guide. You have to make the journey yourself, and everybody's journey is unique in some way.

Establish your own criteria for a master before committing yourself to one's care. Once you commit, surrender your ego completely, but not your integrity or responsibility for your own decisions. Many spiritual seekers are devastated when their "perfect" master is exposed for a gross breach of ethics.

Lest we become attached to the idea of seeking, let us remember that in reality there is no journey! There is no one to seek and nothing to find: "How could there be a journey to absolute bliss consciousness, which is omnipresent and an essential constituent of all creation? The illusion of a journey is simply produced by the fact that in an unrealized man absolute bliss consciousness is hidden and smothered by the constant impressions upon the mind, the experience of gross objectivity. The only journey that is made is through the veil of objectivity, which has no thickness, and the purpose of the journey is to familiarize the mind with its own essential nature."14

Q: What can spiritual development do for all the material distress we hear about in the news every day—natural disasters, crime, war, pollution, etc?

A: In the long term, material progress depends on spiritual progress because materialism tends to self-destruct in war, anarchy, or environmental devastation. Spirituality is the central hub around which all other fields of living revolve. The environmental crisis is a perfect example of a physical/economic crisis precipitated by spiritual negligence and abuse. With the world's population growing by almost one hundred million people each year, the need for more effective approaches to spiritual development is accelerating. All attempts at political, educational, economic, and environmental reform are in vain until collective consciousness is elevated.

Most religious and spiritual teachers up to this point in history have promoted generic practices, like shoe stores that advertise "one size fits all." The current global cultural and environmental crises are vivid proof that the standardized spiritual recipes of the past are either obsolete or incomplete.

The only way to avoid a global environmental and cultural meltdown is to dramatically increase collective spirituality, which can only come when people follow their own unique spiritual yearnings. This is the opposite of trying to squeeze everyone into the same spiritual straightjacket, as most religious groups attempt to do.

Q: Rigid fundamentalism seems to be on the rise throughout the world, in both eastern and western spiritual groups. At the same time, we see the opposite tendency—increased lawlessness and social chaos. Why?

My coauthor, Edward Tarabilda, feels that both relate to the fact that our age is ruled by a weak Saturn operating through Rahu. The weak Saturn gives rigid boundaries and a dry, left brain logic that only recognizes tangible evidence. Therefore, the prevailing public authority today is a brand of materialistic science that either ignores or denies consciousness, feelings, and intuition. We are not debunking objective science and all its great gifts. We are just saying that it deals only with the physical, and it is wrong to overemphasize physicality at the expense of emotional and spiritual values.

Rahu is the ultimate rebel, outcaste, and outlaw. The good side of the worldwide social unravelling is that it is forcing deep-thinking people to look within for the values they cannot find in society at large, and to form small communities dedicated to higher values.

Underneath its many names, religious fundamentalism is the same everywhere—a materialistic approach to spirituality that interprets scriptures literally, preaches salvation through blind faith, shuns inner practices such as meditation, restricts personal freedom, and condemns nonbelievers.

Q: Affirmation is popular today. Where does it fit in this paradigm?

A: Affirmation is repetition of a statement of belief or purpose in order to embed it in the deeper areas of the psyche. Practiced intelligently, it is a benign and gentle way to deal with deep fears and conflicts.

Since Venus is the planet of maximum positivity and suggestibility, affirmation is a cousin of Raj Yoga. However, since it is based on meaning, it is very different than Raj Yoga techniques such as Transcendental Meditation which do not use meaning.

Although affirmation is Venusian archetypally, particular affirmations can take on the flavor of any planet. For example, a Mars affirmation to overcome the fear of flying might be "I am fearless in airplanes!" A Venusian version might be "I feel peace and bliss when flying!"

Many self-help books promote affirmation, often in ways that inadvertently promote egotism, attachment, and self-delusion. Suppose you constantly repeat, "I am flowing in abundance. Money comes to me easily. I experience vast wealth and power to buy whatever I want!" Such egocentric affirmations are likely to increase your laziness and greed more than your bank balance.

The more one repeats an affirmation, the greater the ego's investment and refusal to reason. The smallest shred of evidence becomes irrefutable proof of the power of the affirmation, and any deleterious effects are missed.

To avoid the ego trap of affirmation, turn it into prayer. Not petitionary prayer ("God, give me money!"), but innocent prayer for the welfare of others as much as one's own ("God, may all Thy children prosper in Thy service!"). As Amritanandamayi says, "Learn to derive your happiness from the happiness of others. Let their welfare be your desire and your prayer."

Prayer is only as powerful as our awareness. As Maharishi Mahesh Yogi says, to speak to God, we have to bring our awareness to the transcendent, where God abides. To merely voice a prayer in a distracted, unrefined state of mind is like throwing a letter out the window without an address, hoping it will somehow reach its destination.

So prayer is most effective if preceded by transcendence. For persons on the path of devotion, prayer can actually be a means of transcendence. With any program of higher awareness, a coherent group amplifies the effect exponentially.

In both material and spiritual matters, success is a combination of our own effects and the response of Nature. Hard work is in vain without good luck, and luck is in vain unless we accept it and use it wisely. Man rises toward heaven through his own efforts, and God descends to earth out of compassion. The active, masculine Western approach emphasizes human effort; the passive, feminine Eastern approach emphasizes Divine assistance. In reality, neither occurs without the other, and knowing the right combination for any time or place is one of the great keys to happiness.

Q: Is it possible to connect deeply with a master whose yoga is different from my own?

A: Yes, but it is generally not advisable. Maharishi Mahesh Yogi, who teaches Raj Yoga, and his Guru Dev, a solar yogi, are a perfect example of master and disciple with different approaches to spiritual teachings. However, their relationship was extremely rare in that it was above the need for yogas as we have discussed them.

Q: How can I know which path is for me?

A: As we said at the beginning, this may be the most important question we can ask. Here are a few guidelines:

1. Study the different paths.

Which of these eight paths are you most comfortable with? This a spiritual exercise itself. We are multidimensional beings. All eight planetary archetypes are found in everyone. The tricky part is knowing which archetypes apply to each field of living. (See The Eight Fields of Living, Part II, Chapter 3.) Most people confuse external aspects of their personality with their innermost spiritual nature. For example, you might have an aggressive Mars-dominated desire nature that obscures a gentle lunar or Venusian spiritual nature.

2. Trust your inner sense, but test your intuition with common sense.

The heart is really more important than the intellect in choosing a path. You must feel completely intimate and comfortable with your path, or you will inwardly resist it.

One thing all successful seekers have in common is a deep inner knowingness, a trust in their own ability to know the truth directly, rather than vicariously through another. All the great masters are guided from within from an early age. The hallmark of this inner guidance is a calm and quiet perseverance on the path, without external prodding or support, and without sudden changes in direction. They have faith, determination, and equanimity. Real seekers are totally unconcerned about others' criticisms, just as the proverbial elephant is unconcerned with yapping dogs at his feet.

Read the lives of great saints. They all responded to a deep inner call, often in the face of opposition by family and friends. Most had a master, and surrender to that master was spontaneous and complete from first sight. As we said, "When the student is ready, the master appears." The first prerequisite is honing your own ability to know the truth, so that when you meet the right master, you will be able to recognize him or her.

3. Follow your inner nature, not your strongest trait.

Some teachers say follow your strongest trait. That is, if you have a big heart, follow the path of the heart. If you have a strong will, exercise your willpower to find your Self. If you have a sharp intellect, use your intellect to cut the bonds of illusion. If your heart, mind, and will are weak, but your body is strong, use physical purification as a means to enlightenment.

The problem with this approach is that the strongest feature of your personality may have nothing to do with your spiritual nature. Your intellect might be razor sharp for mundane matters, but totally dull in philosophical pursuits. Wall Street and Silicon Valley are full of clever folks with no interest in spirituality. Your heart might be sensitive to other folks in the flesh, but numb to a God you have never seen. The great willpower that helps you climb lofty corporate ladders and mighty mountains might get altitude sickness before it begins to ascend spiritual heights.

The difference between aptitude and interest also applies to other fields of living. For example, career counselors are increasingly aware that doing what one loves is more important than matching one's skills to a job description.

4. Find a suitable guide.

I would dearly love to offer simple guidelines to determine your path, like so many books that promise you'll lose weight or find the perfect mate. But any such guidelines would be misleading, because no book can possibly give you sufficient understanding of the different paths or insight into your own innermost nature. Most of the hundreds of people we have discussed this with identify with more external aspects of their personality, which often are the opposite of their inner spiritual core.

If you are one of the rare individuals who have direct personal contact with a highly enlightened master, and if your master tailors his teachings to your personal needs, perhaps you need look no further. However, for most people I can think of no better guide than my coauthor, Edward Tarabilda. His clients invariably find that he describes their core personality with great precision and sensitivity. You may still need a spiritual master, but the choice will be much simpler because you will know which of the eight great paths he should teach.

Q: Is Edward Tarabilda a jyotishi (Indian astrologer)?

A: No. He uses astrological metaphors because they best express the universal archetypes as he sees them. He is not an astrologer because he completely rejects conventional astrology, both Eastern and Western. It is misleading to use a label like "astrologer" or "jyotishi" for someone who rejects everything done under such names. He feels that some astrologers may have spiritual or intuitive gifts, but none are capable of accurately reading any of the eight fields of living. Moreover, the countless modern books on both Eastern and Western astrology are all missing the key rules of chart interpretation.

As Part I of this book emphasizes, the planets, signs, and houses of astrology represent fundamental archetypes of energy and intelligence. Wherever sages have attuned themselves to the heavenly bodies, they seem to perceive the same energies. Mars is the warrior, Moon the mother, Venus the lover, etc. That is why these basic significations are common to both Eastern and Western astrological traditions. However, the application of these principles in chart interpretation has been completely lost in all these traditions. There is a stark contrast between the commonality of opinion on the major archetypes (planets, signs, and houses), and the vast differences of opinion in how to use them for practical purposes.

The first rule of all genuine spiritual and esoteric traditions is that the most fundamental rules are never put in writing. They must be discovered in consciousness, out of reach of those who would exploit the knowledge for personal power. The ancient masters of astrology only wrote down the outer rules. They intentionally omitted the key secrets for chart interpretation.

Many modern books and teachers profess to teach chart interpretation. In doing so, they only expose their ignorance of spiritual law. We strongly endorse an open, democratic approach to the kind of surface knowledge found in universities, but we must honor the iron law of all true spiritual and esoteric disciplines: the deepest knowledge has to be found within through intense inner work.

The danger of any presentation of higher knowledge is that charlatans will steal ideas and present them in a distorted form. Even a book such as this could be abused by pseudoastrologers claiming to know your spiritual path from your birth chart. The world has always had more false prophets than truthful ones. It is up to you to tell the difference!

2. Multidisciplinary Knowledge— The Twenty-Four Archetypal Disciplines

(Adapted from chapter 12 of Edward Tarabilda's book *The Spiritual Labyrinth: Alternative Roadmaps to Reality*)

Q: I've heard of something called "the trinity of experience," or "the triad of knowledge." What do these mean?

A: All knowledge can be seen from three perspectives:
   Knower (experiencer or subject)—corresponds to thinking
   Process (linking subject and object)—corresponds to feeling
   Object (of knowledge or experience)—corresponds to willing

These three can also be stated as the triad of mind, heart, and will.

All three components must be known for knowledge to be complete. The theoretical knowledge of the triad must be supported by the experience of higher consciousness, beginning with transcendental consciousness, a state beyond this trinity where subject and object merge in pure, unbounded awareness. Awareness continues with no object of experience. This completely silent and fully alert state of mind is also termed *samadhi, sartori,* or the state of least excitation of consciousness.

Education is in crisis because it focuses primarily on the object of knowledge, and at best, gives only lip service to the subject and process. Worse, it does not teach techniques for pure awareness.

Q: How does the threefold nature of experience relate to the twenty-four archetypal disciplines?

A: Each aspect of the triad has an eightfold nature and gives rise to a separate discipline of knowledge. Three times eight equals twenty-four archetypal disciplines. These twenty-four disciplines are the basis of multidisciplinary learning.

Q: *What are the eight aspects of the knower?*

A: There's a beautiful sevenfold model of the personality which different sages in the East and West have apparently cognized independently. :

Planet	Level or Faculty of Knower
Saturn	Body
Venus	Senses
Jupiter	Mind *(manas)*
Mercury	Intellect *(buddhi)*
Mars	Will
Moon	Heart
Sun	Integrative faculty or ego *(ahamkara)*

Saturn governs the physical body. This level of life is represented by the mineral kingdom.

Venus governs the senses and vital body, which connect the deeper aspects of the personality with the physical body and surroundings. This level of life is represented by the plant kingdom.

Jupiter governs the emotional or astral body, what Vedic teachers call *manas,* which is loosely translated as mind. It's just a part of what we ordinarily call mind—that part which forms simple concepts and has likes and dislikes. This level of life is represented by the animal kingdom. Animals exhibit strong emotions not evident in plants.

Mercury governs the intellectual or egoic body. The sense of self-consciousness and the use of language are the two capabilities that separate humans from animals, although the higher animals may have them to a very limited degree.

Mars governs the will and higher creative sense. The Moon governs the heart and higher emotional capacities, one's awareness of the collective subconscious and higher intuition. The Sun governs the integrative factor, or *ahamkara,* which is sometimes translated as "ego." In a sense it's just the opposite of the colloquial term "ego" as in "egotism." When the integrative factor is fully developed, one identifies with the totality of cosmic existence, not the puny little mind-body vehicle associated with egotism.

We could add an eighth aspect, governed by the Nodes of the Moon. They do not create an eighth level of the personality; rather, they can apply to any one of the seven levels, and thereby create an eighth archetypal discipline for knower, process of knowing, and object of knowledge. The Nodes bring a defiant independence and disdain for conventional or established ways. They contribute to uniqueness, innovation, and novelty in whatever field they affect.

Q: What are the eight disciplines related to process of knowing?

A: We already discussed them in the last chapter. They are the Eight Great Paths to God™, comprised of the seven yogas plus tantra.

Q: And the eight disciplines related to the will, or the object of experience?

A: The will relates to worldly action. It defines eight external disciplines of knowledge which maintain structure and harmony in society. Here is a brief view of these external disciplines and their ruling planets, and some of the Sanskrit terms:

1. Saturn
Medicine and all forms of health care, including ayurveda, the ancient Indian science of health and longevity. Includes diet, exercise, massage, and other bodywork.

Material science, especially the inorganic sciences, such as physics, chemistry, and geology, and the rigorous empirical logic of all the hard sciences.

Technical disciplines, such as construction, engineering, and computer science.

2. Venus

Sthapatya Veda, the art and science of ordering one's immediate environment so that energy flows harmoniously through it. Includes art, gardening, interior design, and city planning. Also includes the aesthetic side of architecture; the mechanical side is Saturnine.

Aesthetics—the fine arts, including music as commonly used for entertainment, but not music as primordial sound.

The observational aspect of material science is Venusian, because Venus governs the senses, and scientific observation depends on sensory perception, even when that perception is vastly extended through space probes, brain probes and electron microscopes. However, the rigorous attention to detail and cold, dry logic of science are purely Saturnine. Since Venus rules living systems, it also governs the subject matter of the organic sciences, such as biology, botany, zoology, and ecology.

3. Jupiter

Religion, sacred ritual (Kalpa), and sacred literature.

Celebrations, assemblies, including family reunions to church services, graduations, political inaugurations, and ceremonies at the beginning and end of sporting events.

The social sciences (psychology, sociology, anthropology, etc.)

Business and finance

4. Mercury

Jyotish, the science of the stars, which organizes all knowledge.

Mathematics

Language

Intellectual recreations like chess, crossword puzzles, scrabble, and most board games.

5. Mars

Primordial sound—the inner aspect of mantra and music

(Gandharva Veda), which subtly harm society or protect it from harm.

Military science (Dhanur Veda) and police science, which protect society physically.

Competitive sports

6. Moon

Myth and archetype, which nourish the heart and enhance attunement to the collective unconscious. The Sanskrit literature of *Puranas* (ancient histories of the gods) and *Itihasas* (ancient history of humans and gods in human form—the epics of the *Ramayana* and *Mahabharata*).

Epic literature and filmmaking.

Motherhood and child care.

7. Sun

The science of community, including political science, public administration, and jurisprudence.

Leadership and fatherhood.

8. Nodes of the Moon

Innovative and unconventional activities and lifestyles which depart from societal norms, exemplified by gypsies, beatniks, and hippies.

Rebellion against outmoded rules and conventions.

Q: Are all the academic disciplines related to the object of knowledge, not the knower or process of knowing?

A: Yes, as long as they exclude subjectivity. Educational psychologists have long known that we learn better from practice than through books and lectures, but grades are still based mainly on test scores, not a student's state of mind. An intellectual psychopath might outscore a simple, loving saint in all the standard tests of aptitude and achievement. But the saint is living a far higher state of knowledge, and of far greater benefit to humanity by his mere presence in the world.

Q: So an object-oriented educational system can produce freaks like the recent Unabomber, a brilliant mathematician with a deadly psychopathology. Would a holistic system soften the rough edges on such a personality?

A: Exactly. Now let's put all the archetypal disciplines together. This is how the seven planets and the nodes combine with the triad of experience to form a matrix of interdisciplinary studies:

Planet	Faculty of Knower	Process of Knowing	Known
Saturn	Body	Empirical logic	Physical science, medicine
Venus	Senses	Sensory experience	Fine arts, architecture, ...
Jupiter	Mind *(manas)*	Desire, visual symbols	Ritual, celebration, psych.
Mercury	Intellect *(buddhi)*	Verbal thought, discrimination	Math, astrology, language
Mars	Will	Creative impulse, adventure	Primordial sound, defense, ...
Moon	Heart	Compassion, mass subconscious	Myth, epic, archetype, ...
Sun	Integrative faculty	Wholeness, total awareness	Community, leadership
Nodes	All faculties	Innovative thinking, feeling, ...	Innovative living

We only have room to show a few of the many possible examples in the fourth column. This is the theoretical side of interdisciplinary studies in a nutshell. The experiential side has to be discovered in pure consciousness, but a careful consideration of these principles can facilitate that.

Q: Western education has been heavily biased toward the known, especially since the scientific revolution. We've been obsessed with the object of knowledge, almost to the exclusion of the knower and process of knowing. We're inundated with technological change, yet almost nobody is happy with education these days, or the direction of our culture as a whole. Is there a connection here?

A: Of course! Public education has become so dry, impersonal, and dehumanizing that even top scholars graduate with psychic scars, conditioned to undervalue their own emotions, intuitions, and spiritual inclinations. The subjective, or inner state of the learner is either ignored or left in the hands of psychologists who often have little or no spiritual training, which should be the basis of all mental health care. It is psychologically and spiritually damaging to treat all inner experience as irrelevant and outside the scope of education.

Q: Spiritual education has traditionally been handled by religions. Public education in the U.S. is founded on the separation of church and state. How can they be reconciled?

A: It is right to separate church and state, at least in public schools. Religious pluralism creates a real challenge to integrating the inner and outer aspects of education. Here are few of many possible approaches:

1. Encourage home schooling and private schooling where inner development can be encouraged.
2. Encourage nondenominational spiritual development classes as part of the curriculum in schools lacking religious affiliations.
3. Phase out government involvement in schools, except as a source of funds. Let schools be privately run, with parents and students choosing among options offered by competing not-for-profit spiritual and educational groups financed by private contributions, tax incentives, and tax monies currently spent on public schools.
4. Let teachers help select their students, so that good teachers are not driven from the field by uninterested or antisocial students.

Q: Our object-oriented cultural bias distrusts inner states as shifty, undependable and illogical, and therefore less real than the hard facts of objective science.

A: We're saying this view is backwards. The inner states are more real and relevant, and unless we have inner order in the individual, outer chaos in society is inevitable.

Q: How can this conceptual framework of twenty-four archetypal disciplines help?

A: It provides a checklist to see that education is balanced and holistic. No student can master all twenty-four disciplines in depth. However, it is easy to understand them in principle, and to experience their common basis (transcendence) in practice. Ideal education will guide each student to expertise, both theoretical and practical, in at least one inner (spiritual) discipline and one external discipline.

Modern education reflects the prevailing bias toward Saturnine, object-oriented thinking. We offer this matrix to give a framework for interdisciplinary studies, a map to guide students and teachers through the educational jungle.

Q: The social legacy of science and technology is material comfort with cultural chaos. Oddly enough, the general public is abandoning scientific thinking at the slightest excuse. Belief in channeling, psychics, and paranormal experience is booming, even among highly educated people. Why do westerners, educated in the use of reason, seem so quick to abandon it?

A: Because they only learn a narrow form of reason in school, a mechanical Saturnine type of reason based on material evidence. They don't learn how to use reason for inner development. Yet we all yearn for inner fulfillment, knowing innately that nothing material can ever fully satisfy us. We are taught to accept science as the great authority, but academic science doesn't awaken our innate capability for love, bliss and unbounded awareness. We're not saying that all paranormal exploration is bad. But there is a lot of commercial exploitation and sensationalism in these fields that would never take root if our educational system recognized the need for systematic inner development, including spiritual discrimination.

Q: Religions have been touting similar ideas for millennia. It was only the scientific revolution that broke the tyranny of the church and all its superstition.

A: That was centralized, authoritative religious structure corrupted by political power and wedded to a single worldview expressed in papal decree. We're proposing decentralized, free-choice education in an interdisciplinary, multidisciplinary, and transdisciplinary paradigm no religion has ever offered. It respects individual religious choices without the limitations of culture and belief system. In fact, it affirms the validity of different philosophies and ways of thinking which have always been thought to be diametrically opposed and irreconcilable.

Q: Can you put your message of multidisciplinary learning in a nutshell?

A: No one viewpoint of anything is complete by itself. It takes at least seven (you could say eight) different views to fully describe anything, whether subject, object, or process of knowing. Multidisciplinary learning develops the flexibility to take any of the twenty-four possible views, and the stability of seeing the entire arena of knowledge as one integrated whole. This multidisciplinary framework restores balance and wholeness to our fragmented educational system and enhances all aspects of life, physical, emotional and spiritual.

3. The Eight Fields of Living™

By Douglas Grimes

Astrology attempts to explain how the macrocosmic order of the heavenly bodies mirrors the microcosmic order of human life. By understanding the heavenly patterns, it is felt, we can understand our own lives and our roles in the universe.

The beauty and mystery of the starry heavens has inspired countless astrologers and astronomers since man first gazed upward in awe and wonder. Prior to the scientific revolution, when the objective science of astronomy divorced itself from the subjective art of prediction, astronomy served astrology, guiding priest-astronomers in counseling kings and timing sacred rituals. These roles applied in most, if not all, of the advanced ancient cultures—India, China, Sumeria, Babylonia, Egypt, Mesoamerica, and the British Isles, to name a few.

In the late seventies and early eighties, my coauthor, Edward Tarabilda, studied conventional astrology, both eastern (Indian) and western, trying to close the huge gap between theory and practice. The planetary personalities which the different schools of astrology have in common—the Sun as king and leader, Moon as mother and nourisher, Mars as warrior and adventure, etc.—spoke to him of primordial archetypes with deep significance in all areas of life. He saw that these archetypes describe different spiritual paths corresponding to the deepest level of our personalities. But in addition to its failure as a predictive tool, conventional astrology failed to address the question of spiritual paths. Nowhere in the literature, eastern or western, was there any mention of spiritual paths or core personalities. The so-called science did not even raise the most important issue in life—how to connect with our innermost nature, our spiritual essence, the only aspect of life capable of integrating and healing all the scattered pieces of our selves.

In the mid-1980s, after he had rejected the core assumptions of astrology, Edward began to have spontaneous inner cognitions in his meditations. The astrological archetypes took on more than symbolic meaning, appearing as intimate threads in the fabric of his own consciousness. A fundamental division of life into eight aspects also became apparent—another key revelation totally missing in conventional astrology.

In the 1950s Crick and Watson's discovery of the four-letter alphabet of DNA opened up a vast new science of molecular genetics. Similarly, Edward's discovery of how the fundamental archetypes apply to the eight fields of living has opened up a vast new holistic discipline, which we call the Art of Multidimensional Living. His discoveries made it possible to understand the ancient texts of jyotish (Indian astrology), which give only the outer rules of astrology, not the inner keys. He tested his theories on hundreds of charts, and he continues to refine them. The seminal cognitions not only remain valid, but receive ever-greater confirmation in application, just as thousands of geneticists continue to elaborate on the seminal discoveries of DNA by Crick and Watson. The Art of Multidimensional Living may never gain the widespread acceptance of genetics, because it requires deep inner work by each individual. Popular appeal is no barometer of truth.

Edward feels that the proper understanding of jyotish was lost three to five thousand years ago. Since that time, the different branches of Vedic science have evolved separately, without the multidisciplinary connections provided by a true science of the stars. All the Vedic disciplines, including jyotish, ayurveda (the science of health and longevity), stapathya (art and architecture), and kalpa (sacred ritual) have lost their potency. Even though India has been home to many great saints in the last few millennia, the disintegration of applied knowledge has led to a dramatic degeneration in the quality of life in India. Institutional corruptions such as the hereditary caste system and an authoritarian system of education have stifled creativity and impeded a rediscovery of the missing keys to holistic knowledge in that country.

A true science of the stars is far more than a guidebook for individual life. It provides a comprehensive paradigm for integrating different branches of knowledge, based on universal archetypes of creative intelligence. Through a common set of unifying principles, the Art of Multidimensional Living™ establishes a true basis for peaceful coexistence and freedom in all areas of life.

Here is a brief summary of the eight fields:

1. Spiritual Life—How to make maximum progress in spiritual life through one of The Eight Great Paths to God (Chapter 1).
2. Dharma—How we can best serve society.
3. Career—Professional aptitudes. How to be happy at work.
4. Creative Play—How to best relax and restore our creative energies.
5. Relationships—How to best use our own personal style of interacting with others.
6. Wealth—How to balance our worldly desires with our spiritual needs.
7. Mental Health—How to fulfill our emotional and energetic needs.
8. Physical Health—How to achieve optimum health and longevity.

A more complete explanation follows:

1. Spiritual Life

This is the most important field, the hub of the wheel of life; the other seven fields are its spokes. It is meant to guide and lead the other seven fields. As Christ said, "First seek the kingdom of God, and all else will be added unto you." Similarly, Lord Krishna said in the *Bhagavad Gita*, "Yogastah kuru karmani"—established in yoga (centered in your infinite Self), perform action.

How can the spiritual life lead the other fields if one does not know one's spiritual path? The greatest benefit of the Art of Multidimensional Living™ is to identify one's spiritual path with great precision.

2. Dharma

Dharma is action to uphold society—how to serve others in a way that brings maximum fulfillment to all. The great civilizations of antiquity had three or four major divisions of labor. These divisions were perhaps clearest in the four castes of ancient India:

Brahmins: priests, counselors, and teachers—serving society through higher knowledge and religion

Kshatriyas: rulers, administrators, warriors, and doctors—serving by protecting the physical welfare of society

Vaishyas: merchants and farmers—serving through trade and finance

Shudras: craftsmen and manual laborers—serving through crafts and physical labor

A fifth category is the outcastes, those whose service to society is to root out impurities.

The Vedic caste system was originally based on each individual's natural inclinations, not heredity. No one should be forced to follow a given caste or barred from a given caste against his or her will. The whole idea of caste, as revealed through the Art of Multidimensional Living™, is that we have different ways of serving with joy and love. People who receive consultations in the Art of Multidimensional Living™ invariably find this conception of caste and dharma confirms their natural inclinations in how to serve society.

The hereditary caste system that prevails in India today is a cultural abomination. For perhaps four or five thousand years caste has been based on parentage, not the natural inclinations of each individual. When people are barred from practicing a preferred profession they suffer enormous job stress, and the creativity and productivity of the whole nation suffers. The higher castes use the system as an excuse to exploit the lower castes, so that caste becomes a means of undermining society, rather than strengthening it. The hereditary caste system is the clearest indication that India lost the inner keys to astrology at least three to five thousand years ago, since the whole idea of hereditary caste contradicts the principle of determining caste from one's birth chart and personal inclinations.

In terms of responsibility to society, the servant has the least, the merchant the next least, the warriors and administrators more, and the Brahmins the most. In terms of their lifestyle, the Brahmin is expected to live simply, supported by his students and benefactors. The warrior is to be salaried and to live a life of strict discipline. The merchant can have as opulent a life style as he can afford. The servant can live as he or she pleases, as long as it is compatible with the spirit of service to the other castes. Those who want the privileges of Brahmins and kshatriyas must accept the concomitant responsibilities. If one's caste nature is clear, those responsibilities are a joy.

3. Career

Everyone has all eight planetary energies, each one ruling a different field of living. One of these governs how we best express ourselves in work. Dharma, creativity, and motivation all play a role in career success. But the most important factor is the intelligence available in our pursuit of a career. The field of creative gifts is more concerned with play—how we refresh ourselves when not obliged to be serious. The field of career governs work—how we best exert ourselves day after day, year after year, in the pursuit of a livelihood.

This field is intimate to our life mission, at least our outer mission. It is invaluable to know the ruling archetype of this field in order to choose a career we can succeed in.

Take Abraham Lincoln as an example. He will always be remembered as "honest Abe," a great-hearted and deep-thinking leader with a passion for justice and fair play. He had some unappealing traits, too, but due to a strong Jupiter ruling his career, he had the power to surmount personal trials and hold the nation together in its time of greatest stress.

When we are young, the planet governing our creative gifts may affect our career choice, especially if the planet governing career is weak. As we mature, the planet governing career becomes increasingly influential in our work habits.

Obviously, desires do not always lead to fulfillment. How fully we achieve our desires depends on all eight fields of living. A weakness in any field may sap energy from other fields. It is also possible for two fields to be in conflict. For example, one man who has a soft Venusian spiritual nature and an aggressive Mars desire nature frequently feels pulled between peace and war. Whenever such conflicts arise our advice is to let the spiritual nature lead, as it is the unifying factor in the personality.

Let us give a couple of examples regarding prosperity. A weak Mars governing wealth means a person tends to lose money through lack of energy to follow through. A weak Moon means a person swings in great waves of emotion from one desire to another, lacking the steadiness to achieve anything significant.

Understanding our desires is a wonderful aid for mastering them. The distinction between our spiritual nature and desire nature is particularly valuable. It helps us resolve inner conflict and recognize our *sattwic* (positive) attachments. For example, a Jupiterian desire nature may make us judgmental—we may pay more attention to others' morality than our own. If spirituality is our priority, it is easy to turn our attention to something naturally fulfilling in accord with our spiritual path.

4. Creative Gifts (Creative Play)

There are eight major styles of creative play, corresponding to the seven major planets plus the Nodes of the Moon. How we best express our creative aptitudes depends not only on the creative gift itself, but also on our dharma (caste nature) and career nature (success and influence).

Mercury governs speech, writing, and communication. If Mercury rules your creative gifts and your caste nature is Brahmin, then you probably enjoy teaching and dealing with higher knowledge, and you are likely to be very good as a teacher, priest, or counselor. However, if your creative gifts are ruled by Mercury and your dharma is the Vaishya (merchant) class, then you more likely enjoy negotiating and trading, making business a form of play.

The expression of our creative gifts is also affected by our career nature. For example, a publisher with Venusian creative gifts might deal in romance novels or idealistic books, while a publisher with Saturnine creative gifts would prefer detailed, technically oriented nonfiction.

Our creative gifts affect both our work and our play. What is your favorite recreation? Saturn likes solitude and quiet, Mars likes aggressive sports and competition, Venus likes idealistic romance, etc.

Children are a major expression of our creativity. If the planet ruling our creative gifts is weak or afflicted, we are unlikely to have children, or our children are likely to have difficulties. Joe and Rose Kennedy, pillars of the Kennedy clan, both had powerful but severely afflicted planets ruling their creativity. Three of their sons (John, Robert, and Ted) rose to very high positions of power, but two were assassinated, and the surviving children have suffered other tragedies.

5. Relationships

We have myriad relationships in family, school, work, and play. Throughout all of these, one planetary archetype governs our prevailing style. When the ruling planet is strong, we tend to relate well, and vice versa if the ruling planet is weak.

One special relationship for most people is the lover or spouse. The same planet that governs relationships in general also governs sexuality and intimacy. However, intimacy is only one aspect of marriage.

Marriage is actually governed by the interaction of all eight fields, especially dharma, spirituality, creative play, and relating style. Compatibility consultations in the Art of Multidimensional Living™ can prevent decades of frustration and wasted effort in such relationships. If two partners have severe incompatibilities, no amount of counseling will fix the problem. Consultations with Ed can identify the strengths and weaknesses of a relationship, and suggest ways to avoid conflict and enhance the harmony. Such consultations are valuable to all types of relationships, including business partnerships and parent-child interactions.

For example, if a strong Moon rules your relationships, you have deep compassion and sensitivity for the needs of others. People seek your company for the nourishment they feel in your presence. On the other hand, if a strong Sun rules your relationships, you have a confident, generous, extroverted style with others. One friend with such a Sun is a born salesman and spontaneous entertainer. When he walks into a party, his charisma lights up the room. If instead of an exalted Sun, his relating style were ruled by a debilitated or malefic Sun, he might come across as a domineering tyrant.

Ed recently consulted with a man whose relating style is governed by a debilitated Jupiter. He is never happy relating to others, especially if the interactions are long or intense. He is like a shallow well in dealing with others—a few words and he dries up.

A weakness in any field of life can often be overcome by strengths in other fields. For example, if one's relating style is weak, but career nature or mental health quotient is strong, it will ameliorate the lack of relating skills.

When we understand the different relating styles, we become more sensitive and tolerant. A Saturn relating style is often mistaken for aloofness or lack of concern. Saturn, of course, is by nature secretive and reclusive. He is silent and self-sufficient. Although independent, he is a pillar of strength in times of crisis. A friend has an exalted Saturn governing this field. He voluntarily lives thousands of miles from his wife and children. He loves them dearly, but a few months of family life every year or two provide enough intimacy for him. Conventional thinking would say he has a problem that needs fixing. We say he is following his natural instinct correctly, and is evidently happy with his family life. His wife and children may not be happy with his choices, but that's a compatibility issue requiring a deeper look at their lives, too. If they have similar Saturnine relating styles, they probably value all the privacy they can get.

6. Wealth (Primordial Desire)

Some people know exactly what they want in life. Others spend a lifetime trying to figure out what they want. The first type has clear desires; the second type suffers from a lack of will. The planet ruling wealth governs the strength and nature of our deepest desires. Although it is by no means limited to material desires, it affects our prosperity by shaping our confidence and motivation for material wealth.

Saturn, for example, is the simplest and most reclusive planet. If he governs your wealth nature, you value privacy and simplicity, longevity, and a good physique. However, if Jupiter rules your wealth, then you value family, proper conduct, and a more opulent lifestyle. If the Sun rules your wealth, then you love to shine in public, and dream of being a famous celebrity or politician.

7. Mental Health

In the last century or so in the West, the term "mental health" has taken on connotations of mental disease. The mere term is enough to make many people fear, "What's wrong with me?" Mental health is associated with the dark, murky depths of a twisted subconscious mind that sometimes erupts blindly to overpower our puny little conscious minds and wreak havoc in our lives.

We use the term very differently. All the eight fields have a role in unconscious motivations. Mental health is how we project ourselves, the energy behind our actions in the world. It has a direct effect on our fame and public image. Ronald Reagan, for example, was hardly the most intelligent person to hold the presidency, but he is remembered as a well-intentioned president because of a strong planet ruling his mental health. His Alzheimer's disease is another matter, entirely predictable by a weak Saturn governing physical health.

Even in the prevailing Western model, mental health is largely a matter of how others perceive us. One lady who has spent over a quarter century in mental hospitals has a debilitated Mercury ruling this field. As a teenager, she was bright, charming, a good student, and talented in music and drama. But the weak Mercury left her devoid of common sense, preoccupied with others' opinion of her, and powerless to express herself verbally. Now she is so frozen with guilt and fear that she hardly has the courage to speak to her own family, who have patiently born her decades of torment. It is a tragedy that her expensive doctors and hospitals have been unable to help her, except to restrain her from suicide and drug her to suppress symptoms.

The ayurvedic model of ancient India offers a less morbid view of the mind than the Western psychotherapeutic model. Ayurveda teaches that the universe is the interplay of three opposing forces, or *gunas*, and that each individual can find a point of balance between the opposing forces. There are three basic types of mental constitution corresponding to the three :

> *Sattwic:* Calm, pure, harmonizing, and inclined toward upright behavior and the pursuit of truth
>
> *Rajasic:* Driven by material desires, such as wealth, power, sensuality, or anything exciting
>
> *Tamasic:* Lazy, indolent, careless, and dull-minded

Within each of these broad types there are many gradations and subtype. Different areas of the mind also display different tendencies. One may have a very *sattwic* attitude toward reading scriptures every day, a *rajasic* attitude toward competition in a cutthroat business, and an indolent, *tamasic* attitude toward preparing one's tax returns. Nevertheless, one of the three tendencies tends to dominate one's mental activity.

A *sattwic* disposition is conducive to meditation and spiritual pursuits. It also promotes mental and physical health and heals disease tendencies developed from *rajasic* or *tamasic* habits.

A strong spiritual nature often compensates for a weak mental nature, so that one is able to function adequately in society in spite of a lack in confidence. However, if both the mental and spiritual natures are weak, the result is usually mental illness, criminal behavior, or at least a tendency for poor decisions which seriously undermine the quality of life.

The best antidote for any weakness in this field is a spiritual regimen in accord with one's natural path of spirituality. The various yogas and tantra, properly practiced, have a profound effect on all aspects of our life. Hundreds of studies have shown the benefits of Transcendental Meditation (TM) in relieving stress. More research is needed on other techniques, and the different effects of various meditation practices. We believe that the results are greatest when one practices in accord with one's own spiritual nature.

How we play and how we care for our bodies also affect our mental health. The ancient masters of ayurveda saw that mental illness is often just a symptom of physical imbalance, and vice versa. By treating the physical cause, such as a blood-sugar imbalance, the behavior frequently corrects itself.

8. Physical Health

Western medicine can rightly claim many remarkable achievements. It has doubled our life expectancy in this century alone. It has almost eliminated many dread diseases. It can reconstruct broken bodies and exchange body parts almost like a mechanic swapping used-car parts.

However, it has many noteworthy failures. It is outrageously expensive, and getting more costly at twice the average inflation rate. It is cold and impersonal in its growing tendency to treat the body as a biomechanical device with no feelings or soul. It is increasingly dependent on powerful drugs with horrendous side effects. It is incompetent to heal psychosomatic and psychological disorders (although it is adept at masking them with drugs), and is becoming more reliant on brutal electroshock therapy . Even the germ theory of disease, a cornerstone of modern medicine, has a gaping hole: Every new generation of antibiotics is met by a new generation of drug-resistant germs. Hospitals are the breeding grounds for the most virulent germs known—nature's clever adaptations to man's attempt to heal the part without the whole. In spite of huge sums spent on pharmacological research, society as a whole is suffering from an increased incidence of cancer, AIDS, and other degenerative and immunodeficiency syndromes.

Dr. Herbert Benson, the late cardiologist at Harvard Medical School and author of *The Relaxation Response* and *Beyond the Relaxation Response*, said that three out of four patients cannot be helped by modern medicine. If you have a cold, a sore back, or the flu, all the doctor can do is give you a pain killer and tell you to get some rest. He cannot speed the healing process.

Hundreds of natural healing practices are rushing in to fill the void left by the failures of mainstream Western medicine. Herbology, acupuncture, ayurveda, massage, and a multitude of other mind-body modalities are in vogue. Many health-seekers are bewildered by the sudden plethora of choices in the alternative medicine marketplace.

Edward Tarabilda's Eightfold Ayurveda™ is a branch of the Art of

Multidimensional Living™. It integrates the various alternative and conventional approaches to health care, and gives each individual basic guidelines that apply to all healing modalities.

Ancient physicians of East and West saw a direct connection between health care and the stars. Hippocrates, the father of Western medicine said that the physician who does not know the science of the stars is not worthy of being called a physician. Renaissance doctors likewise saw a close symbolic connection between one's health and one's star configurations, although it is doubtful they knew how to read the stars correctly.

In recent centuries the schisms between individual and cosmos and between matter and mind have grown wider. Astrology is ridiculed in scientific circles. Unfortunately, without a true understanding of the science of the stars, those who condemn astrology as a superstitious pseudoscience are mostly right, although for reasons they do not understand.

In India, too, the connection between health care and astrology was apparently lost at least three or four thousand years ago. Since the advent of written records, the various branches of Vedic science have evolved separately. In particular, the connection between astrology and the major disease types was lost. By about 500 to 1,000 B.C.E, when authors like Charaka, Shushruta, and Bhagvat founded conventional ayurveda, the eightfold paradigm of disease and its connection to astrology had been completely lost.

The Art of Multidimensional Living™ restores the natural connection between health care and astrology as part of the mutual mirroring of microcosm and macrocosm. The eight fundamental disease types correspond to the seven major planets plus the nodes of the moon. Students invariably find that their archetypal disease type corresponds to their own health history.

Fortunately, there are many safe, simple, and inexpensive therapies for each disease type. Diet, exercise, hatha yoga postures, music, mantra, and herbs are recommended. Homeopathic therapies to stimulate the body's natural defenses complement allopathic approaches to provide missing nutrients. Each person receives homeopathic recommendations for one of the seven great metals and one of the twelve cell salts. The allopathic aspect employs one or more of the seven basic therapies: heating, cooling, nourishing, lightening, oiling, drying, and a mixed type. The eighth type, related to the nodes of the moon, involves treatment through one of the other seven therapies, plus propitiation for karmic influences.

Conventional ayurveda is based on analysis of the three doshas: vata (light, airy, cold, quick, and dry); pitta (hot, fiery, and oily); kapha (cold, heavy, slow, and phlegmatic). It distinguishes *prakriti* from *vikriti*. *Prakriti* is the basic balance of the three doshas you are born with. *Vikriti* is the balance, or lack of balance, at a given time. Conventional ayurveda teaches that *vikriti* tends to follow *prakriti.* If you were born kapha, then your whole life you will be fighting excess kapha.

The Eightfold Ayurveda sees this conventional understanding as a distortion, based on an inability to differentiate between prakriti and vikriti. They can be very different. We feel that the underlying disease type is an essential third factor which gives a prevailing tone to the doshic balance at any given time. For example, one may have a kapha prakriti, evidenced by a slow, heavy physique, along with a vata disease tendency, with light, dry, airy symptoms like Alzheimer's or Parkinson's disease, dry constipation, stuttering, tuberculosis, or just low body temperature and aversion to cold weather. Although conventional ayurveda might accept such an analysis in theory, most practitioners we know seem unable to apply these distinctions in their diagnosis.

A forthcoming book by Edward Tarabilda, *Ayurveda Revolutionized: Integrating Ancient and Modern Ayurveda,*[15] will contain many case histories of people who respond well to the multifaceted therapeutics of the Eightfold Ayurveda often after years of frustration with other approaches. Here are three typical cases:

1. A lady who was a teacher of ayurveda was surprised when Ed suggested she take more oil if she wanted to lose weight. The advice ran contrary to both conventional scientific thought (oil has too many calories) and conventional ayurveda (oil would aggravate her pitta-kapha constitution). But it worked. She took more oil, lost weight, and felt better.

2. A middle-aged fitness fan had chronic insomnia, indigestion, and recurrent pain in his knees and shoulders. Ed's analysis confirmed a tendency for coldness and a drying of the synovial joints. The prescription was to avoid milk and cold or raw food, and to favor warm environments and spicy well-cooked foods. His sleep and digestion are much improved and he has almost no pain in the knees and shoulders.

3. A chronically thin, exhausted lady had been taking lots of oil for more than ten years because oil is the key in standard ayurvedic treatment for vata. Ed diagnosed her as having the disease type of oiliness, ruled by a weak Venus, which also governs the reproductive organs. In other words, the oil was aggravating her health, especially her kidneys and ovaries. Unfortunately, she did not receive his diagnosis until the day she had her ovaries removed. However, once she reduced her oil intake and began his other simple recommendations, her health stabilized.

In an age of increasing dependence on health care professionals, the Eightfold Ayurveda seeks to educate people to take control of their own health, thereby saving money while improving their quality of life. The New U, a not-for-profit educational organization, offers audio tape courses in this new health care paradigm.

Three personal consultations with Edward Tarabilda cover all eight fields of living:

1. Spiritual initiation: Which of the eight archetypal spiritual paths is

ideal for me? This field is the foundation of the other seven. (Includes "How do my primordial desires affect my spiritual development?")

2. What is my life mission? (Includes dharma, career, creative play, and relationships)

3. How can I maintain optimum physical and mental health? (Includes how to avoid the diseases one is most prone to develop.)

Edward travels frequently. Please contact him through
  Sunstar Publishing
  116 N. Court St.
  Fairfield, IA 52556
  800-532-4734

Appendices

Appendix A:
The Lunar Mansions (Nakshatras)

We offer here a listing of the nakshatras from standard astrological texts. Just as the 360 degrees of the zodiac can be divided into 12 signs of 30 degrees each, it can be divided into 27 nakshatras of 13 degrees 20 minutes each. Each nakshatra is subdivided into four quarters or padas of 3 degrees 20 minutes each. Since each sign takes 30 degrees, there are nine padas or two and one-quarter nakshatras for each sign.

There are two standard beginning points for listing the nakshatras. The more common listing, shown on the next page, begins with the nakshatra Ashwini, because it starts at the beginning of Aries, the first sign. The less common starting point, the nakshatra Krittika, is also found in some ancient texts. Our discussion of the nakshatras in Part 1 begins with Krittika, the twenty-third principle. "D.M" means Degrees & Minutes:

| | From | | To | |
Nakshatra	Sign	(D.M.)	Sign	(D.M.)
1. Ashwini	Aries	0 0	Aries	13 20
2. Bharani	Aries	13 20	Aries	26 40
3. Krittika	Aries	26 40	Taurus	10 0
4. Rohini	Taurus	10 0	Taurus	23 20
5. Mrigashira	Taurus	23 20	Gemini	6 40
6. Ardra	Gemini	6 40	Gemini	20 0
7. Punarvasu	Gemini	20 0	Cancer	3 20
8. Pushya	Cancer	3 20	Cancer	16 40
9. Ashlesha	Cancer	16 40	Leo	0 0
10. Makha	Leo	0 0	Leo	13 20
11. Purva Phalguni	Leo	13 20	Leo	26 40
12. Uttara Phalguni	Leo	26 40	Virgo	10 0
13. Hasta	Virgo	10 10	Virgo	23 20
14. Chitra	Virgo	23 20	Libra	6 40
15. Swati	Libra	6 40	Libra	20 0
16. Vishakha	Libra	20 0	Scorpio	3 20
17. Anuradha	Scorpio	3 20	Scorpio	16 40
18. Jyestha	Scorpio	16 40	Sagittarius	0 0
19. Moola	Sagittarius	0 0	Sagittarius	13 20
20. Purva Shadha	Sagittarius	13 20	Sagittarius	26 40
21. Uttara Shadha	Sagittarius	26 40	Capricorn	10 0
22. Shravana	Capricorn	10 0	Capricorn	23 20
23. Dhanishta	Capricorn	23 20	Aquarius	6 40
24. Shatabhisha	Aquarius	6 40	Aquarius	20 0
25. Purva Bhadrapada	Aquarius	20 0	Pisces	3 20
26. Uttara Bhadrapada	Pisces	3 20	Pisces	16 40
27. Revati	Pisces	16 40	Aries	0 0

Appendix B:
How to Use this Book as an Oracle

To communicate with the deeper levels of existence we must be silent, receptive, and respectful of the perfect intelligence found in every atom of creation. We recommend avoiding petty questions and hurried responses. If you don't have time for a meditative approach, we suggest postponing your consultation until you can approach the Supreme Intelligence with genuine respect. Blind faith is not required. Skepticism is fine, as long as you are open to surprising new insights. A mechanical approach will bring random, mechanical answers. A deeply meditative approach will allow deeper inspiration.

As Part I shows, all the major oracles share a common numerical sequence. Any method of thoughtfully generating a number in that sequence can be used—picking a card from a deck of sixty-four, spinning a "Wheel of Fortune" with sixty-four divisions, tossing sticks or coins, etc. The simplest way for most of us is to toss a coin six times. Use this table to translate to a number from one to sixty-four ("H" = head, "T" = tail):

Coin						Archetype
1	2	3	4	5	6	
T	T	T	T	T	T	1
T	T	T	T	T	H	2
T	T	T	T	H	T	3
T	T	T	T	H	H	4
T	T	T	H	T	T	5
T	T	T	H	T	H	6
T	T	T	H	H	T	7
T	T	T	H	H	H	8
T	T	H	T	T	T	9
T	T	H	T	T	H	10
T	T	H	T	H	T	11

```
T  T  H  T  H  H            12
T  T  H  H  T  T            13
T  T  H  H  T  H            14
T  T  H  H  H  T            15
T  T  H  H  H  H            16
T  H  T  T  T  T            17
T  H  T  T  T  H            18
T  H  T  T  H  T            19
T  H  T  T  H  H            20
T  H  T  H  T  T            21
T  H  T  H  T  H            22
T  H  T  H  H  T            23
T  H  T  H  H  H            24
T  H  H  T  T  T            25
T  H  H  T  T  H            26
T  H  H  T  H  T            27
T  H  H  T  H  H            28
T  H  H  H  T  T            29
T  H  H  H  T  H            30
T  H  H  H  H  T            31
T  H  H  H  H  H            32
H  T  T  T  T  T            33
H  T  T  T  T  H            34
H  T  T  T  H  T            35
H  T  T  T  H  H            36
H  T  T  H  T  T            37
H  T  T  H  T  H            38
H  T  T  H  H  T            39
H  T  T  H  H  H            40
H  T  H  T  T  T            41
H  T  H  T  T  H            42
H  T  H  T  H  T            43
H  T  H  T  H  H            44
H  T  H  H  T  T            45
```

H	T	H	H	T	H		46
H	T	H	H	H	T		47
H	T	H	H	H	H		48
H	H	T	T	T	T		49
H	H	T	T	T	H		50
H	H	T	T	H	T		51
H	H	T	T	H	H		52
H	H	T	H	T	T		53
H	H	T	H	T	H		54
H	H	T	H	H	T		55
H	H	T	H	H	H		56
H	H	H	T	T	T		57
H	H	H	T	T	H		58
H	H	H	T	H	T		59
H	H	H	T	H	H		60
H	H	H	H	T	T		61
H	H	H	H	T	H		62
H	H	H	H	H	T		63
H	H	H	H	H	H		64

We recommend that you prepare with at least two minutes of silent meditation and a reverent petition for guidance. Pray to the Divine in whatever form is dearest to you. If you are a Buddhist or for some other reason you are not comfortable praying to God, then address whatever power commands your greatest love and respect. If you just want to play, not pray, that is fine, too, but at least keep focused and undistracted.

Let your whole attention dwell on the question, and surrender it totally to the Supreme. Then use whatever method you have chosen for selecting a number, keeping your prayer for guidance gently in your awareness. Look up the corresponding principle in this book, study the picture, and contemplate the meaning.

Ask yourself how the archetype applies to your question. It may suggest how nature will react to some contemplated action, or it may be guidance to the best choice among several alternatives. If there is a secondary question, select a second principle in the same manner. In rare cases a third may be appropriate.

Never ask the same question twice. Ask only those questions you feel a deep need to answer. Asking trivial questions undermines the sense of meditation needed for the oracle to serve its purpose.

Guidance in daily decisions is secondary. The primary purpose is to see how these universal principles apply to your life. Every situation we face is a gift from Divine Intelligence to help us learn whatever we most need to know at that time. Outer challenges are understood and mastered through inner change. This book is only an outer tool. The inner tool is the consciousness you put into the learning process. Your thoughtfulness and sincerity are essential prerequisites for this growth.

This book does not make decisions for you. Rather, each principle suggests a path for you to follow to reach your own decision. No principle is any better or worse than any other. Whichever one you choose applies to your question at the time of the question. The explanations are guidelines for directing your attention toward the highest values in life and seeing the perfect order in every situation you encounter.

No oracle can give you intelligent guidance without your intelligent input. One introduction to the I-Ching makes this clear:

"Divination was also used not simply as a mechanical prognostication device but as a framework for contemplative practices of self-analysis and analysis of situations; ... (prognostications) require active participation with concentrated attention, and the danger of trivialization was seen by some thinkers as a product of reliance on the I-Ching as an oracle independent of the efforts of the individual."

Every principle offers both opportunity and danger. Each one also indicates either the source of your problem or the solution. So exercise your creativity in the interpretation!

Appendix C: Preliminary Thoughts on Subjective Science

By Douglas Grimes

This appendix is for those interested in the philosophy of science and creating a subjective science of archetypes

Q: What does "science" really mean, in the broad sense of the term?

A: The word "science" has evolved over time. Prior to the scientific revolution, the term included theology, astrology, alchemy and other disciplines that are generally considered unscientific today. Common usage today is limited to the physical sciences, and to some extent, the social sciences. This understanding, however, is not exclusive. Webster's Ninth New Collegiate Dictionary has five definitions for "science". We use the term in a broad sense to mean any systematic approach to knowledge which develops logical, verifiable laws to explain and explore the vast diversity of creation, both subjective and objective.

Any science has two aspects—theory and practice. Thus, sciences are best taught by supplementing abstract theory with experimentation and/or application in the field.

Popular thinking holds that the physical sciences and technologies (physics, chemistry, biology, engineering, electronics, etc.) are the real sciences; because they have been so remarkably successful in predicting and controlling nature they should be held as models which the social sciences and other disciplines must emulate to be worthy of the name "science". The term "subjective science" therefore strikes many as an oxymoron. In our view it is completely valid, although it does not lend itself easily to objective demonstration. We feel the term is merited, because subjective exploration can be at least as systematic and reliable as objective exploration.

Q: Why do we need a subjective science?

A: To complement objective science and heal the spiritual, emotional, physical, and environmental problems that elude the fragmented, materialistic approach of a strictly objective approach. (More on this later.)

Q: How is subjective science different from objective science?

A: In at least three ways. First, there is a big difference in how the knowledge is taught. Public propagation of objective science is appropriate to the impersonal nature of that knowledge, but inappropriate for the intimately personal nature of inner development. Key teachings in the spiritual and esoteric disciplines of different cultures have always required strictest confidentiality and rigorous tests of character. They are released to the student only when he demonstrates a readiness for them; otherwise they would be misunderstood or misused. Hitler is only one of many malefactors who tried to use the esoteric arts for evil ends. We can only be thankful he failed.

The bona fide teachers of inner development do not advertise the ancient mysteries like used cars or fast foods. They may give preliminary instruction to millions, but wait for qualified students for advanced work, and patiently guide them toward self-discovery.

Second, since the methodologies of material science deal only with measurable physical phenomena, they are inadequate for subjective research. At best, they crudely monitor physiological correlates of inner states, not the inner states themselves. In the early 1950s physiologists learned to distinguish waking, dreaming, and sleeping states by the corresponding physical activity, such as brain waves, respiratory patterns, biochemical changes, and rapid eye movements. However, even the most sophisticated labs are incapable of appreciating the myriad subtleties of human experience. Physiological correlates of brain activity are like views of New York or Tokyo from an airplane, incapable of following the private lives of the inhabitants.

The exclusion of subjectivity has been necessary for the development of material science, but holistic knowledge must unveil both subject and object and their intimate connection. If subjective exploration is to be a science, not a new form of mysticism, we must not suspend reason, skepticism, or experimentation. We need a disciplined fusion of intellect and intuition to discriminate between inner reality and self-delusion. Here eastern psychology, with roots in Hindu, Buddhist, and Taoist cultures, is of greater help than western psychology, which has been overly influenced by a disease-based medical model and the absurd Freudian notion that spiritual experience is a form of regression to the womb.

Third, inner development requires classic virtues admired throughout the world—a warm heart, calm mind, healthy body, and absolute integrity.

Q: Why bother with subjective science when objective science has advanced much faster?

A: The physical sciences have succeeded by excluding the vagueness and variability of ordinary subjectivity. That success has had a staggering cost. Objective science has given us power without wisdom or compassion. The money-driven monster of technology solves problems in a piecemeal fashion, often blind to side effects which surface only years later. We are only beginning to realize the damage created by early experiments with radiation half a century ago. We teeter at the brink of ecological collapse because external science and technology have dramatically reduced mortality rates while raising our per capita use and abuse of natural resources. The sad consequence has hardly been the techno-utopia widely envisioned a hundred years ago. On the contrary, population explosion and pollution threaten the very biosphere that support us.

The quantity of human life, measured in average longevity, has certainly increased. Whether the quality of life has improved is much less clear. The average American life span has risen sixty percent in the twentieth century alone. Degenerative diseases, however, have increased in all age groups, while mental and social maladies have mushroomed. If consumption of tranquilizers, pain killers and all manner of other legal and illegal substances is any indication, the quality of human life is near an all-time low. The U.S. may be the greatest military and scientific power in history, but 88,000,000 Americans are either suffering from a chemical addiction, or closely related to someone who is.[16] How happy is our technology-rich society when at least one in ten adults has a serious addiction or substance abuse problem and we have more people behind bars than any nation in history?

Objective science is adept at destroying life but inept at creating it. In addition to the terrifying array of new killing machines we have deliberately created, our technological offspring include thousands of inadvertently created poisons contaminating our air, food, and water. However mighty science may be, it cannot create life, not a single blade of grass, not even a single living cell. We say this not to disparage objective science, but to point out the inadequacy of the current scientific paradigm that dissects better than it reconnects and analyzes better than it synthesizes. In truth, we are grateful for the fruits of science, but suspicious of any discipline that tries to confine the unbounded realms of spirit and mind within the narrow boundaries of matter.

The need for holistic knowledge is acute. Even in the most intellectually gifted members of the human race, the sequential nature of object oriented learning is far too slow and error-prone to keep up with the pace of change. The deeper intuitive skills latent in all of us must be tapped to harness cosmic intelligence in our individual lives.

It has become a cliché to say that science knows more and more about less and less. The blinders on each branch of science become narrower as the need for communication becomes greater. Scientists have become so specialized that they strain to communicate with colleagues in neighboring disciplines. Each subspeciality has its own language and its own gurus. Biochemists, biologists, and biophysicists have difficulty understanding each other, even when discussing the same liver, kidneys, or brain. Similar rifts divide every branch of science.

Training in the physical sciences develops the capacity for rational thinking and careful observation, but an over emphasis on fragmented, linear, object-oriented reasoning is an impediment in understanding the human soul and spirit. Here a holistic approach to truth is needed, one which encompasses the physical sciences, but recognizes their great limitations.

The shortcomings of conventional science are most evident in the discipline of psychology, which tries to bridge the abyss between mind and matter. Stuck in a rational, objective medical model, mainstream western psychology is highly skilled at masking deep-seated emotional disorders with drugs, but usually inept at healing the underlying psychic disease.

Popular psychology is unaware of the vast difference between enlightenment and psychic disorders, both of which can manifest outwardly as absolute certainty. On one extreme are religious fanatics and psychotics who strain to maintain their faith. They tend to be anxious, rigid, and dogmatic. On the other extreme are the rare saints who spontaneously live in perfect harmony. They are flexible, contented, and unperturbed amidst the greatest turmoil.

The systematic development of consciousness has been practiced by a relatively small number of serious seekers and adepts in diverse cultures throughout the world. It is not to be confused with popular religion, the outer garment of spirituality oriented to the mass of humanity. The Art of Multidimensional Living offers a new perspective on spiritual traditions, but in no way replaces them.

Countless masters, many of them mentioned in Part II, have described the states of consciousness and the validation procedures appropriate to each spiritual path.

The scientific revolution has given us physical influence and affluence while it has robbed us of romance and reverence. It has reduced love, peace, and happiness to the chemistry of hormones. It has blessed us with undreamed of power over nature while threatening the survival of life on earth. It has pumped our egos with the illusion that we can conquer nature while it teaches that we are no more than hairless apes and biology-driven robots. Science cannot answer the ancient riddles of philosophy; it is mute as to the purpose and meaning of life; it cannot strengthen character or bring solace to the tormented soul; yet we have made it our highest authority for knowledge. Our schools, courts, media, and elected leaders rightly defer judgment to science whenever possible, and wrongly expect it to solve broader emotional, social, and spiritual problems beyond its scope.

Even in the most educated countries ninety-nine percent of the population is scientifically illiterate. The remaining few, the scientific elite, are mostly ignorant of the broader practical and philosophical implications of a paradigm that subordinates mind to matter, ignores spirit, and shatters the wholeness of life into myriad disjointed pieces.

Q: Is the need for inner development any greater today than in the past?

A: Definitely. The ever-increasing pace of outer change demands ever-greater inner equanimity and adaptability. The disintegration of family and community places greater demands on ethical and emotional integration from within each individual. The rise of reason and decline of second-hand faith demand a rational return to belief through first-hand experience. One of the most pragmatic benefits of inner development is to relieve the stresses of modern life and balance outer dynamism with inner silence. When you find equanimity within, inner values blossom spontaneously.

Q: Art is also subjective. What is the connection between art and archetypes?

A: Two modern pioneers in understanding archetypes, Carl Jung and Joseph Campbell, approached the subject more as an art than a science. Art is traditionally more subjective, guided by aesthetics and intuition, rather than reason and objective verification.

Q: Why is the Art of Multidimensional Living both an art and a science?

A: It is an art in that it began as subjective intuitions in the founder's consciousness and is capable of being cognized by others in the same way. It is a science in that it is systematic, disciplined, rational, and verifiable. It is holistic in that it offers a unified framework integrating subject and object, art and science, part and whole.

Q: Can the methods of objective science be used for subjective science?

A: It is clear that the methods of objective science are inadequate for subjective science. In objective science, verification is objective, quantitative, and impersonal. In subjective science, it is subjective, qualitative, and personal. The physical world has tangible attributes that reasonable people agree on, and intangible ones like the laws of gravity and thermodynamics, which are inferred through reason and verified through experimentation. Inner experience is less tangible, but the common elements of inner experience can be inferred from a cross-cultural study of spiritual adepts throughout the world. The modern ecumenical movement seeks to unite different religions through the recognition of their common ground. We commend this holistic intention, but see it as too vague and generalized to meet the pressing problems of the world.

Q: What is missing from the ecumenical and new age movements?

A: An understanding of the spiritual blueprint of life and how it manifests in all the eight fields of living. Without an understanding of the primordial order at their common basis, none of the eight fields can be fulfilled in itself or integrated with the others. All the lofty ideals of these movements are commendable, but until they can systematically apply archetypal understanding to all fields of living, their ratio of talk to achievement will remain very high.

Q: How is this subjective science systematic?

A: Because the archetypes are systematically ordered and can be systematically interpreted. Furthermore, they make possible a systematic development of spiritual, emotional, and physical health. Please see the "Further Research" page at the end of this book for other materials on the Art of Multidimensional Living^{TM}

Q: How can a subjective science be verified?

A: There are different means of subjective verification for each of the eight archetypal spiritual paths we discussed in Part II, Chapter 1. Let us mention here just two—reason and intuition. Most of us already try to use these skills every day, so we obviously have to learn to use them in a new way if we are to accelerate our progress. Part I of this book lets you verify the archetypes through reason, in conjunction with your own inner ability to resonate with them intuitively. Taken individually, the archetypes may appear to lack the mathematical rigor of the physical sciences. Taken collectively, their innate rigor becomes more evident. Any change in the order of any oracle would upset its simple sequential correlation with the others and its application in the different fields of living.

Other examples of reason are certainly possible and desirable. We encourage you to look for the archetypes in your own work and play. This requires clear, unbiased thinking and the ability to penetrate surface values to uncover inner essence. You may find them in other people, in nature, in science, history, math, business, or your favorite hobby.

These are examples of an outer use of reason. Inner reason is useful to avoid mistakes. It helps us recognize useless thoughts and wishful thinking, leaving the mind clear for higher inspiration. Inner reason is most useful on the spiritual path of gyan yoga, the path of discrimination. The intellect is honed like a sword to cut through the ego's binding knots and thoughts to unveil the limitless horizon of self-awareness or the archetypal patterns of the sunrise.

Whatever your spiritual path, if you are patient and fortunate you may ultimately find the archetypes within. Experiential verification of pure consciousness is far more common than direct cognition of the archetypes. Both require spiritual development. Outer reason tells you the different oracles express the same archetypal order, but only if you have heard about them from someone else. Inner experience, however, can stand on its own, provided that spirituality is sufficiently developed.

The ability to experience the archetypes intuitively begins with a sense of resonance when you hear archetypal truths, whether in the dramatic forms of mythology, literature, or music, or an expository form like this book. As your intuition develops, you spontaneously recognize more of the primordial order in daily life. Eventually, your inner growth may culminate in the spontaneous re-cognition of the archetypes in your own awareness, without dependence on anything external. Although valid intuitions of a lower order are common, direct cognition of the higher archetypes is extremely rare. In fact, many saints appear to enjoy a permanent state of unbounded peace and bliss without clear cognition of the archetypes. Those few who do are best qualified to integrate the absolute and relative phases of life for both inner and outer fulfillment.

Q: Is there more that can be said about verifying inner experience?

A: Of course. Many great saints have written about it at length, and much more cannot be put in books, as it is only appropriate in the intimate communion between master and disciple. However, we need not make it sound so esoteric. Skilled teachers lead their students step by step from wherever they may be at the time, recognizing their limitations and individual needs.

Perhaps the most important way of verifying your inner development is through its fruits. If your equanimity, patience, clarity of mind, and warmth of heart are growing, you are doing something right. A flowering of such universally desirable character traits is more important than flashy experiences in meditation. If you do have ecstatic visions, don't talk about them except with a teacher who can understand them and keep you from getting over excited about your new-found peace of mind.

Q: Objective science has institutions for peer-group review to filter out the wild-eyed schemes that outnumber every true discovery. Is this possible in subjective science?

A: Yes, but we have to be cautious of would-be spiritual authorities, as their history is often less than sterling. Different spiritual traditions have different means of avoiding spiritual fantasy, illusion, and deliberate deception. Sometimes it is review committees, like the inner circle of high Tibetan monks who identify young children for special spiritual training, or the Vatican committee that reviews candidates for sainthood. Sometimes it is a single master who is recognized for his own attainment. Indeed, in many traditions an accomplished master is deemed an absolute prerequisite for serious spiritual practice. The spiritual literature of the East abounds with stories of masters who steered their disciples through the rocky, storm-tossed waters of the soul.

Ultimately, inner experience is self-validating because it is knowledge by identity, free of the limitations of time, space and ego characteristic of outer experience. Outer experience is through duality, separation of subject and object. You see a flower or hear a song, and you are not fully aware of either yourself or the flower or song. Inner experience is through unity, being unbounded, undivided, fulfilled from within. In pure consciousness you are fully aware of your Self, where subject and object are one. In archetypal awareness, within that oneness is an awareness of difference, a not yet manifest diversity within unity, an unchanging structure beyond change.

Q: Every country has legends of saints who were recognized by their miracles or selfless service. There must be some rules of thumb for recognizing inner development in others.

A: The preoccupation with judging others is usually misplaced. Our own consciousness should be our primary concern, not others'. And we need not give ourselves labels, grades, or merit badges, because spiritual growth depends more on surrender to the gentle touch of grace than conquest through personal effort. Furthermore, as we said in the chapter on the Eight Great Paths to God, there are no outer signs of enlightenment. The enlightened person may look and behave in a completely unexceptional way, unnoticed by others and often unconcerned about being noticed. Those who crave public recognition may assume others want the same. Enlightenment, however, is its own reward and has no more need of public approval than the Sun has for the light of a few flickering candles.

Q: Why do spiritual seekers often seem lost in a dreamy world of make-believe?

A: It could be due to a weakness in any field of living, not necessarily their spiritual aspirations. It may also be that their spiritual practice is too generalized and not tailored to their individual needs. They intuitively sense the goal, but cannot connect it to their daily lives. Individually-tailored development of body, mind, and spirit integrates idealism with pragmatism.

Q: Subjective and objective approaches to science both require freedom from bias. Can inner development contribute to outer science?

A: Most definitely. Tolerance, patience and equanimity, hallmarks of inner development, are also prerequisite to good objective science. Any scientist, subjective or objective, does better work when free of impatience, egotism, and cultural bias. A calm, flexible, happy physicist is more effective than an anxious, neurotic one.

Q: There is an odd contradiction in the post-industrial world today. Science has replaced religion as the dominant belief system. Our commerce-driven culture is increasingly addicted to gratification of the senses, yet science tells us the information of the senses is very limited and misleading.

A: The dominant belief system today is not science, but scientism— the belief that objective science is the only source of reliable knowledge. It devalues subjectivity and the importance of feeling, intuition, scriptures, and inner guidance. It is insidious because it is so pervasive, yet hardly recognized. It is the dominant paradigm in politics, commerce, schools, and the media. The myth and dogma of religion have been replaced by the myth and dogma of scientism.

Scientism, like other forms of materialism, assumes that only the physical universe is real; mind and spirit are, at best, an accidental by-product of matter. Paradoxically, a tremendous body of scientific evidence contradicts this assumption. Modern medicine is discovering that mental phenomena have far greater influence on the body than biological science can explain, especially with alternative medical practices that treat mind and emotions as primary. Anyone familiar with hypnosis has direct evidence of the mind's power to override bodily functions.

Physics, the most profound and successful of the sciences, underscores the importance of the subject. Einstein's theories of relativity and Heisenberg's uncertainty principle show that neither subject nor object can be considered without the other. Indeed, the closer physicists approach the invisible basis of the universe, the more they sound like eastern philosophers. Space, time, and causation become increasingly interdependent and distorted. Energy levels increase beyond imagination. The apparent solidity of matter vanishes in the near-vacuum of atomic space, which vanishes in the vacuum state and nonphysical fluctuations of the quantum field. As Fritzof Capra and other physicist-philosophers have pointed out, the correlations between modern physics and ancient descriptions of higher consciousness are far too striking to be accidental.[17]

Q: Two of the greatest Western philosophers, Plato and Rudolf Steiner, said that mathematics is the best training for philosophy, which for them included spiritual experience. Many of the greatest mathematicians in the West have also been great philosophers—Newton, Leibnitz, Kant, and Bertrand Russell, to name a few. Physical science is based on mathematics. What is the role of math in spiritual science?

A: It cultivates abstract, unbiased reasoning, but it is valuable training, but not a prerequisite on any of the eight great paths. Mathematics, at least as taught in schools today, is an intellectual discipline, not a spiritual one. Western academic philosophy is also heavily oriented toward analysis and the implicit separation of subject and object. It functions solely in the waking state, and hardly recognizes other states of consciousness.

We would love to see an archetypal approach to mathematics. The Pythagoreans may have had one. Possibly the ancient Hebrews, Egyptians, and Vedic rishis, too, as all considered number and geometry sacred.[18]

Q: Some spiritual teachers emphasize an attributeless absolute, others speak of subtle realms more vast than anything on earth. Is this an important distinction?

A: The difference is significant, yet they are intimately linked. Without taking the time needed for a thorough discussion of states of consciousness, let us consider two broad categories of inner experience—transcendental awareness and archetypal awareness. The non-dual state of transcendental awareness is beyond space-time dimensions. All doubts dissolve in the oneness of unbounded awareness, which is the only reality in that state. Whether you call it samadhi, pure consciousness, or the state of least excitation of consciousness, the term is not important; the experience is. Unbounded awareness, infinite peace, universal love—these are known to seers all over the world to different degrees.

A second type of inner experience, archetypal awareness, is awareness of the fundamental meta-order that underlies all change. Where undifferentiated, formless, transcendent awareness is the unseen foundation of spirituality, archetypal cognitions are the hidden pillars that give it form. The transcendent Absolute is silent and attributeless. The primordial archetypes have attributes and dynamism in that silent, attributeless vastness. Just as different architectural styles flower in different times and climes, archetypal experiences are expressed in myriad ways. In the Vedas, they are the devas. In shamanic and Native American lore, they are akin to the animal guides. In mythologies throughout the world, they are the progenitors, gods, and higher spirits who create the world and intervene on our behalf when we honor them. We cannot say that all mythology represents pure archetypal awareness, for it is frequently mixed with confused, collective dream consciousness. But the common themes of religion, art, literature, and mythology throughout the world speak powerfully of underlying realities transcending time and culture. Pure archetypal awareness is characterized by the coexistence of opposites—infinite dynamism within infinite silence, attributes within the unmanifest, relative within the Absolute. Any boundary in time-space, any shade of fear, limitation, or sorrow, any sense of agitation, anticipation, or separation is a symptom that the experience is not yet complete. Likewise, idle drifting in an undifferentiated soup of consciousness, however pleasant and relaxed, is incomplete if the delicate inner structure of life is not crystal clear, vibrant, and radiant with all the colors of the rainbow and all the harmonies of heaven and earth.

The archetypal powers operate in the frictionless, infinitely interconnected realm at the basis of space, time, and causation. This home of all the laws of nature is the fulcrum of creation, where maximum is accomplished with least effort. Activity from this level is analogous to superfluid and superconductive behavior in physics—it is effortless, blissful, and superefficient.

Eastern religions, especially in India, have emphasized transcendence at the expense of the archetypes. The external side of life has deteriorated because it was thought to be an impediment to spiritual development. On the contrary, the archetypal metastructure of relativity holds the secrets of health and happiness in the world, while also illuminating the different paths to the infinite. The applied disciplines of the Vedas—ayurveda (health care), stapathya veda (art and architecture), dhanur veda (military science), etc.— lost their efficacy when they lost contact with the archetypal order that originally interconnected all fields of knowledge. That break may have occurred before the invention of writing, in a distant age when human intuition was far more developed than it is today. Our challenge now is to reawaken our ancient intuitions and integrate them with our modern intellectual and physical gifts.

Q: Spirituality has often been associated with denial of worldy challenges. How can inner knowledge, completely personal, subjective, and unrelated to the objective world we share in common, give reliable and practical solutions to all the problems we face in that world?

A: Unlike theoretical abstractions, real inner knowledge is always completely appropriate to the time, place, and circumstances. Thus it is not surprising that different seers express it differently, even when their experiences share a great deal in common. They are like ardent ice cream lovers, each extolling the wonders of his favorite flavor. To someone who does not know ice cream from hot tamales, they may sound like their tastes are fundamentally opposed. Yet they all love the cold, sweet, creamy essence that is the same to all flavors.

How is enjoyment of life's sweet inner essence related to solving mundane problems? The more we are attuned to our unique archetypal blueprint, the more support we gain from the higher powers of nature (you may prefer to say "God" or "cosmic intelligence"), because we are swimming with the current, not against it. And we are more relaxed and energetic. We don't waste energy in either spiritual denial or sensual excess. We are not confused by others' values; we know our own, and we live in spontaneous joy and gratitude.

Q: How is the Art of Multidimensional Knowledge different from other spiritual knowledge?

A: First, it is not limited to spirituality. It encompasses all eight fields of living, of which spirituality is the central core. Second, it is systematic. Third, it is cross-cultural and can be applied in the context of diverse lifestyles, religions, and belief systems. Fourth and most important, because it is based on the fundamental principles of creation, the universal archetypes underlying all change. This makes it is highly specific to individual needs and highly effective in resolving problems at their source.

Q: It sounds like the ideal is neither subjective nor objective knowledge in isolation, but an integral synthesis of the two.

A: Absolutely.

Notes

1. Two contemporary pioneers of archetypal psychology, James Hillman and Thomas Moore, have advanced the idea of archetypes at play in society and the world at large. We take the concept much further, adding an understanding of their essential order, and practical applications in all fields of living.

2. Unless otherwise noted, our quotes on the other oracles are from these editions:

> The *I-Ching,* or *Book of Changes,* Richard Wilhelm, translator/commentator, rendered into English by Cary F. Baynes, Princeton University Press, Princeton, N.J., 1977.
>
> *A Dictionary of the Tarot,* by Bill Butler, Shocken Books, N.Y., 1977.
>
> *The Secret Dakini Oracle,* by Nik Douglas and Penny Slinger, Destiny Books, Rochester, VT, 1979.

3. We have been able to find only one book in print on the Secret Dakini Oracle, which appears to be a modern formulation by Nik Douglas and Penny Slinger, with roots in both the Tarot and the tantric tradition of Eastern India. We make reference to it because it creatively expresses the same archetypes in the same order as the major oracles.

4. Our mention of astrology in no way endorses current astrological practice, either eastern or western. The ancient keys of the art have long been lost!

5. "The Religious and Psychological Problems of Alchemy," quoted in *The Basic Writings of C. G. Jung,* p. 441, The Modern Library, N.Y.

6. For further discussion of this subject, see *Meditations on the Tarot,* by Valentin Tomberg under the guise of "an unknown author."

7. *Knowledge of the Higher Worlds and Its Attainment*, by Rudolph Steiner, p. 8.

8. *The Osho Neo-Tarot*, by Osho (Bhagavan Shree Rajneesh).

9. To reach Edward Tarabilda for a spiritual consultation, please request his current location from Sunstar Publishing at 800-532-4734.

10. *The Twelve Stages of Healing*, by Donald M. Epstein, with Nathaniel Altman, p. 120.

11. Private conversation.

12. *Love and God*, MIU Press, p.10.

13. *Bhagavad Gita*, III.37.

14. *Meditation*, by Maharishi Mahesh Yogi, publisher unknown, limited distribution, p. 27.

15. *Ayurveda Revolutionized: Integrating Ancient and Modern Ayurveda*, by Edward F. Tarabilda.

16. This statistic is from the Hazelden Foundation, which distributes hundreds of books and other aids for recovery from substance abuse from its offices in Center City, MN.

17. Capra's classic is *The Tao of Physics: Parallels Between Modern Physics and Easter Mysticism*.

18. Ancient Indian mathematicians discovered zero and infinity. Both numbers came to western civilization via the Arabs in the early Renaissance. Neither can be directly observed in the external world, but both can be experienced internally. You can see one apple or a hundred, but you cannot see zero apples. Nor can you count to infinity in a finite time. But you can experience zero thought, zero desire, zero anxiety. You can experience infinite bliss, infinite peace, infinite awareness. It is curious that both zero and infinity are central to scientific understanding of the physical world.

Zero, one, and infinity are the three most important numbers. All rational numbers can be generated from these three. Many animals can perceive the difference between one and more than one. The concept of one is central to every language and culture. But zero and infinity are not, at least as we routinely use them today. The concept of zero as nothing is commonplace in primitive cultures, but not as a place holder as in 10, 100, or 1000. Zero and infinity are the inverse of each other—infinity is one divided by zero, and vice versa. You may have been taught that division by zero or infinity is undefined. That is a necessary restraint for finite mathematics, which has great utility in everyday application. But the mathematics of infinity does not wriggle out of the problem so quickly.

The parallel with inner experience is striking—in transcendental consciousness, mental activity subsides to zero, while awareness opens to infinity. The ancient Pythagoreans explored mathematics as a tool for inner experience. However, since they prescribed death as the penalty for divulging initiatory secrets to non-initiates, we have no written record of their knowledge of archetypes from the perspective of mathematics. What we can say is that any symbol or concept that pervades diverse disciplines suggests an underlying archetypal truth with potentially infinite applications.

The Global Oracle:
A Spiritual Blueprint
Selected Bibliography

Aurobindo, Sri. *The Life Divine.* Sri Aurobindo Ashram Press, Pondicherry, India.

Bhagavad Gita—dozens of English translations.

Butler, Bill. *A Dictionary of the Tarot.* Shocken Books, N.Y. 1977.

Capra, Fritzof. *The Tao of Physics: An Exploration of the Parallels Between Modern Physics and Eastern Mysticism.* Bantam Books, N.Y., 1984 (2nd ed.).

Douglas, Nik, and Slinger, Penny. *The Secret Dakini Oracle.* Destiny Books, Rochester, VT 1979.

Mahesh Yogi, Maharishi. *Love and God.* MIU Press, Fairfield, IA.

Pawels, Louis, and Bergier, Jacques; Myers, Rollo, tr. *Morning of the Magician.* Stein and Day, 1983.

Osho (Bhagavan Shree Rajneesh). *Neo-Tarot* (card deck with small booklet).

Rama, Swami. *Choosing a Path.* Himalayan Press.

Satprem. *Sri Aurobindo, or the Adventures of Consciousness.* Institute for Evolutionary Research, Mt. Vernon, WA.

Steiner, Rudolf. *Christianity as Mystical Fact,* and any other books by Rudolf Steiner.

Vigyana Bhairava *Tantra.* An ancient Kashmiri text with commentary by Osho (Bhagavan Shri Rajneesh).

Wilhem, Richard, translator and commentator; rendered into English by Cary F. Baynes. *The I-Ching, or Book of Changes.* Princeton University Press, Princeton, N.Y. 1977.

Further Resources

The New U is a non-profit tax-exempt organization dedicated to promoting the Art of Multidimensional Living™. The New U offers books, audio tapes, correspondence courses in the Art of Multidimensional Living. The following publications and courses are available through the New U:

1. *The Spiritual Labyrinth: Alternative Roadmaps to Reality*—A detailed examination of the Eight Fields of Living with insightful application to your life. Presented as a stimulating dialog among representatives of different spiritual groups. To order call 303-730-7960.

2. *Ayurveda Revolutionized: Integrating Ancient and Modern Ayurveda*—A truly revolutionary approach to the practice of Ayurveda. A detailed guide for self health care. Available through Lotus Light Publications at 800-643-4211 or through your local bookstore.

3. *Home-Study Course in Spiritual Science*—A comprehensive understanding of the theory and practice of spiritual science and the 224 principles and processes which make up this science. Intended primarily for independently minded spiritual seekers. $375.00

4. Personal consultations with Edward Tarabilda. Please contact:
   The New U
   P.O. Box 751
   Fairfield, IA. 52556
   515-472-3809
   Web page: http://www.dimensional.com/~risaacs

Additional Titles by Sunstar Publishing Ltd.

• *The Name Book* by Pierre Le Rouzic
ISBN 0-9638502-1-0 $15.95
Numerology/Philosophy. International bestseller. Over 9000 names with stunningly accurate descriptions of character and personality. How the sound of your name effects who you grow up to be.

• *Every Day A Miracle Happens* by Rodney Charles
ISBN 0-9638502-0-2 $17.95
Religious bestseller. 365 stories of miracles, both modern and historic, each associated with a day of the year. Universal calendar. Western religion.

• *Of War & Weddings* by Jerry Yellin
ISBN 0-9638502-5-3 $17.95
History/Religion. A moving and compelling autobiography of bitter wartime enemies who found peace through their children's marriage. Japanese history and religion.

• *Your Star Child* by Mary Mayhew
ISBN 0-9638502-2-9 $16.95
East/West philosophy. Combines Eastern philosophy with the birthing techniques of modern medicine, from preconception to parenting young adults.

• *Lighter Than Air* by Rodney Charles and Anna Jordan
ISBN 0-9638502-7-X $14.95
East/West philosophy. Historic accounts of saints, sages and holy people who possessed the ability of unaided human flight.

• *Bringing Home the Sushi* by Mark Meers
ISBN 1-887472-05-3 $21.95
Japanese philosophy and culture. Adventurous account of of an American businessman and his family living in '90s Japan.

• *Miracle of Names* by Clayne Conings
ISBN 1-887472-03-7 $13.95
Numerology and Eastern philosophy. Educational and enlightening—discover the hidden meanings and potential of names through numerology.

• *Voice for the Planet* by Anna Maria Gallo
ISBN 1-887472-00-2 $10.95
Religion/Ecology. This book explores the ecological practicality of native American practices.

• *Making $$$ At Home* by Darla Sims
ISBN 1-887472-02-9 $25.00
Reference. Labor-saving directory that guides you through the process of making contacts to create a business at home.

• *Gabriel & the Remarkable Pebbles* by Carol Hovin
ISBN 1-887472-06-1 $12.95
Children/Ecology. A lighthearted, easy-to-read fable that educates children in understanding ecological balances.

• *Searching for Camelot* by Edith Thomas
ISBN 1-887472-08-8 $12.95

East/West philosophy. Short easy-to-read, autobiographical adventure full of inspirational life lessons.

- *The Revelations of Ho* by Dr. James Weldon
ISBN 1-887472-09-6 $17.95
Eastern philosophy. A vivid and detailed account of the path of a modern-day seeker of enlightenment.

- *The Formula* by Dr. Vernon Sylvest
ISBN 1-887472-10-X $21.95
Eastern philosophy/Medical research. This book demystifies the gap between medicine and mysticism, offering a ground breaking perspective on health as seen through the eyes of an eminent pathologist.

- *Jewel of the Lotus* by Bodhi Avinasha
ISBN 1-887472-11-8 $15.95
Eastern philosophy. Tantric Path to higher consciousness. Learn to increase your energy level, heal and rejuvenate yourself through devotional relationships.

- *Elementary, My Dear* by Tree Stevens
ISBN 1-887472-12-6 $17.95
Cooking/Health. Step-by-step, health-conscious cookbook for the beginner. Includes hundreds of time-saving menus.

- *Directory of New Age & Alternative Publications* by Darla Sims
ISBN 1-887472-18-5 $23.95
Reference. Comprehensive listing of publications, events, organizations arranged alphabetically, by category and by location.

- *Educating Your Star Child* by Ed & Mary Mayhew
ISBN 1-887472-17-7 $16.95
East/West philosophy. How to parent children to be smarter, wiser and happier, using internationally acclaimed mind-body intelligence techniques.

- *How to be Totally Unhappy in a Peaceful World* by Gil Friedman
ISBN 1-887472-13-4 $11.95
Humor/Self-help. Everything you ever wanted to know about being unhappy: A complete manual with rules, exercises, a midterm and final exam. Paper.

- *No Justice* by Chris Raymondo
ISBN 1-887472-14-2 $23.95
Adventure. Based on a true story, this adventure novel provides behind the scenes insight into CIA and drug cartel operations. One of the best suspense novels of the '90s. Cloth.

- *The Symbolic Message of Illness* by Dr. Calin Pop
ISBN 1-887472-16-9 $21.95
East/West Medicine. Dr. Pop illuminates an astonishingly accurate diagnosis of our ailments and physical disorders based solely on the observation of daily habits.

- *On Wings of Light* by Ronna Herman
ISBN 1-887472-19-3 $19.95
New Age. Ronna Herman documents the profoundly moving and inspirational messages for her beloved Archangel Michael.

- *Destiny* by Sylvia Clute
ISBN 1-887472-21-5 $21.95
East/West philosophy. A brilliant metaphysical mystery novel (with the ghost of George Washington) based on *A Course In Miracles.*

- *The Husband's Manual* by A. & T. Murphy
ISBN 0-9632336-4-5 $9.00
Self-help/Men's Issues. At last! Instructions for men on what to do and when to do it. The Husband's Manual can help a man create a satisfying, successful marriage — one he can take pride in, not just be resigned to.

- *Cosmic Perspective* by Harold W.G. Allen
ISBN 1-887472-23-1 $21.95
Science/Eastern philosophy. Allen, an eminent cosmologist, disproves the "Big Bang" theory and opens new horizons with his dynamic principle of cosmic reincarnation, plus his revolutionary insight into Christian origins, bibilical symbolism and the Dead Sea scrolls.

- *Twin Galaxies Pinball Book of World Records* by Walter Day
ISBN 1-887472-25-8 $12.95
Reference. The official reference book for all Video Game and Pinball Players—this book coordinates an international schedule of tournaments that players can compete in to gain entrance into this record book.

- *How to Have a Meaningful Relationship with Your Computer* by Sandy Berger
ISBN 1-887472-36-3 $18.95
Computer/Self-help. A simple yet amusing guide to buying and using a computer, for beginners as well as those who need a little more encouragment.

- *The Face on Mars* by Harold W.G. Allen
ISBN 1-887472-27-4 $12.95
Science/Fiction. A metaphysical/scientific novel based on man's first expedition to investicate the mysterious "Face" revealed by NASA probes.

- *The Spiritual Warrior* by Shakura Rei
ISBN 1-887472-28-2 $17.95
Eastern philosophy. An exposition of the spiritual techniques and practices of Eastern Philosophy.

- *The Pillar of Celestial Fire* by Robert Cox
ISBN 1-887472-30-4 $18.95
Eastern philosophy. The ancient cycles of time, the sacred alchemical science and the new golden age.

- *The Tenth Man* by Wei Wu Wei
ISBN 1-887472-31-2 $15.95
Eastern philosophy. Discourses on Vedanta—the final stroke of enlightenment.

- *Open Secret* by Wei Wu Wei
ISBN 1-887472-32-0 $14.95
Eastern philosophy. Discourses on Vedanta—the final stroke of enlightenment.

- *All Else is Bondage* by Wei Wu Wei
ISBN 1-887472-34-7 $16.95